Metadiversity

The Grand Challenge for Biodiversity Information Management

through Metadata

THE CALL FOR COMMUNITY

Proceedings of the Symposium

Sponsored by the U.S. Geological Survey

Biological Resources Division

&

The National Federation of Abstracting & Information Services

November 1998

Edited by Richard T. Kaser

& Victoria Cox Kaser

NFAIS gratefully acknowledges the support and collaboration of the Department of the Interior, U.S. Geological Survey Biological Resources Division under Cooperative Agreement #1434-HQ-98-AG-01922.

Original transcription by Lana Germaine Thomas

Cover design by Anthony Tripido

TABLE OF CONTENTS

SESSION 6: The Metadata Challenge for Museums

SESSION 7: Working Groups

Preface

Background on "Metadiversity"

RICHARD T. KASER, NFAIS Executive Director, Principal Investigator Metadiversity

"Metadiversity" was an interdisciplinary symposium jointly organized and held by the National Federation of Abstracting & Information Services and the Biological Resources Division of the U.S. Geological Survey, November 9-12, 1998, at Natural Bridge, Virginia.

Statement of Purpose

The purpose of this symposium was: "To respond to the national and international grand challenges in the area of biodiversity information management, to help define, contribute, support, and enhance the biodiversity research mission and metadata agenda and build an information infrastructure to support scientific advances."

Participants

The three-day symposium was attended by 82 representatives from government agencies, academic institutions, not-for-profit non-governmental organizations, associations, national laboratories, funding agencies, and commercial firms from the U.S. and abroad.

Agencies, organizations, and institutions represented at the symposium included:

U.S. Government	Universities
EPA	University of Kansas
NOAA	University of Reading (UK)
Defense Technical Information Center	University of Illinois (Urbana
NASA	Champaign)
Office of Scientific & Technical Information	Stanford University
National Agricultural Library	University of California (Berkeley)
National Marine Fisheries Service	University of New Orleans
Department of the Interior	Texas A&M University
USGS-BRD	Harvard University

Library of Congress
Federal Geographic Data Committee

University of Amsterdam (NL)
Cornell University
Columbia University
Stanford University
University of Georgia
University of Virginia

Centers & Labs

Oak Ridge National Labs
National Plant Data Center
California Academy of Sciences
European Bioinformatics Institute
Base de Dados Tropical (Brazil)
National Center for Ecological Analysis &
  Synthesis

Abstracting & Indexing Services

BIOSIS
CABI
Chemical Abstracts Service
OCLC

Associations

Association for Biodiversity Information
Canadian Biodiversity Information
  Initiative
Convention on Biological Diversity
  (Canada/UN)
Digital Library Federation
American Meteorological Society
Association of Systematics Collections
Coalition for Networked Information
American Association of Botanical
  Gardens & Arboreta

Data Centers

UKOLN
EROS Data Center
European Topic Center (Germany)

Private Enterprises

Datafusion
Elsevier Science
Island Press
Gene Logic
Bell Labs

Funding Agencies

National Science Foundation
Nature Conservancy

Museums & Other Institutions

Smithsonian Museum of Natural
  History
Natural History Museum (London, UK)
California Academy of Sciences

Program

The Metadiversity program consisted of six formal sessions, each followed by interactive question-and-answer periods. The six sessions were designed to provide all attendees with exposure to the wide range of work being conducted in the area of metadata for biodiversity information management:

1. **The Nation's Call to Action**, which featured speakers from the international Convention on Biological Diversity, the President's Committee of Advisors on Science & Technology's Committee on Biodiversity and Ecosystems, and the National Biological Information Infrastructure. The session reviewed the PCAST Report *Teaming with Life*, the Convention on Biological Diversity's Clearing-House Mechanism, and the NBII Framework Plan. Participants also received an overview of metadata initiatives from OCLC.

2. **The Challenge in Species Discovery & Taxonomic Information**, which featured representatives from organizations sponsoring initiatives in the area, including the Species 2000 project, the All-Taxa Biodiversity Inventory, the Integrated Taxonomic Information System, and the American Society of Plant Taxonomists.

3. **The Challenge in Earth Observation, Ecosystem Monitoring, and Environmental Information**, which featured speakers from CIESIN, NASA, USGS, EPA, and European Environmental Agency.

4. **Building the Infrastructure**, which featured presentations by representatives of the National Biological Information Infrastructure, the Federal Geographic Data Committee, and the National Science Foundation's Digital Libraries Initiative.

5. **The Metadata Challenge for Libraries**, which featured presentations by the Coalition for Networked Information, UKOLN, the Alexandria Digital Library, and Cornell University.

6. **The Metadata Challenge for Museums**, which featured presentations by the University of Kansas, the University of New Orleans, and the Natural History Museum of London.

These six sessions were designed to highlight the wide range of fields involved in biodiversity information management and the great number of metadata initiatives taking place throughout the world.

Session 7: Facilitated Discussions

On the final day of the symposium, participants were broken out into working groups to consider the implications of what they had heard in the formal program and to develop recommendations in the form of a call to action.

The topics the participants chose to discuss in these groups were:

1.   **Leadership & Consensus Building**, including national vs. global issues, organizational framework (infrastructural issues), interconnection of efforts (across domains, disciplines, and organization types), and how to achieve support from individual organizations (including one's own organization) and related communities.

2.   **Technology**, including how to establish priorities, how to assure distributed but interoperable systems, how to handle data archiving and assure long-term data access, and data security.

3.   **Standards for Biodiversity Data**, including taxonomy (controlled vocabulary), thesauri, models, and tools. This group also touched on the larger issues of how to involve professional communities in developing interoperable systems.

4.   **Funding & Economics**, including funding strategies, developing incentives and rewards, business models, test beds, and business plans.

5.   **Users**, including identification of user groups, their requirements, standards, privacy issues, etc.

Each group presented its recommendations before the meeting was adjourned.

Conclusions

"Metadiversity" was conceived as an event that would draw together members of a large and diverse community to discuss matters of mutual importance.

At this point, I can do no better in summarizing what took place at Natural Bridge than to repeat the words of my opening and closing comments.

1.   It was not the intent of NFAIS, as conference organizer, to dictate the decisions of this group, but merely to create a forum and bring the group together.

2. However, it was difficult to bring this group together. We identified and invited representatives from 200 different organizations, involved in many different, but related, efforts—and these 200 are only the tip of the iceberg. It was difficult to convince some sectors that they should participate, and as a result, some sectors ended up not being represented at all. Those who attended, however, are the ones who saw the need. They came to participate, and participate they did—not only during the formal and interactive sessions, but also on the side during dinners, receptions, and nature outings.

3. I observe that due to the extent and breadth of the subject matter related to biodiversity, the "biodiversity community" is a community that is not fully aware that it *is* a community. As a result, there are a lot of different organizations working on the same problem. One conclusion would seem to be that the answer lies in distributed systems that are yet interoperable. But this cannot happen without community-building and cooperation.

4. At least one of the working groups called for NFAIS to sponsor a follow-on event to continue the discussion.

5. I continue to observe a vast gulf between and among mission-oriented organizations. Biodiversity information management needs to draw in organizations that have, as their primary mission, charters that do not specifically include biodiversity. Yet, of all subjects, biodiversity would seem to have the potential to be a great integrator—a field that could draw together many different interests and result in a common, interoperable information system. However, I also observe, among those participating in this group, a lack of incentive to do so.

6. If I could be so bold as to conclude one thing from this symposium, it would have to be that Metadiversity's "call for action" was, in fact, a call for community . . . and for community-building. Before the National Biological Information Infrastructure can be built, there must be a consensus that it *needs* to be built. The various communities that need to be a part, must buy off on this fact. Another way of saying this is that as a first step, the community must recognize itself.

    ❧ One of the participants at Metadiversity, Linda Hill from the Alexandria Digital Library Project, observed:

        "During and after the meeting, I kept trying to think about how to characterize the "biodiversity community," like identifying the significant professional associations, journals, conferences, etc., that are associated with the group. But I finally decided that "biodiversity" is like "global climate change" in that it is an umbrella concept that links various communities together toward a particular focus. So, for what it is worth, I think BRD might think in terms of establishing a program like that for global climate change. . . ."

7.   I closed the symposium with the following remarks, which I still believe constitute the bottom line:

Three things happened at Natural Bridge:
1.   We put on a program to inform you.
2.   We have produced a tangible result—these proceedings.
3.   But, most importantly, I sense, hope, and feel that what actually happened at Natural Bridge is that a dialogue began.

It is the dialogue that at this point needs to continue.

Dick Kaser

Introduction

Metadiversity:
Welcome and Charge to the Participants

DENNIS FENN, Chief Biologist, U.S. Geological Survey (USGS)

I'm very happy to be here. I hope all of you enjoyed your trip out to Natural Bridge today, through the last hurrah of our beautiful Virginia autumn. I think it's fitting that we're meeting here in these surroundings, at this time of year, because it reminds us of the important task we have as stewards of our environment and its biodiversity. We've come together for a few days to address biological information management issues, but it will serve us well to remember that the objectives of this meeting are only a means to an end: improving and protecting our natural heritage for generations to come.

However, we do have a specific task before us, so I'd like to take a few minutes to outline what we hope to accomplish over the next two and a half days. Plans for this symposium were initiated in response to a general concern—sharing the metadata expertise of the library and abstracting and indexing community with the biological information management community—and a specific opportunity—responding to the recommendations of the report of the President's Committee of Advisors on Science and Technology (PCAST).

Today's rapidly evolving information technology supports increasing accessibility of a variety of information resources, which can contribute to the quality of biodiversity and ecosystem science and decision-making. In addition to traditional journal literature and associated abstracting and indexing services, these information resources include— among others—primary data, maps and other visual representations of data, museum specimens, multimedia objects including digital audio and video segments, and software for analysis and modeling. While this wealth of information awaits us, we currently don't have the tools to locate, explore, and exploit these resources effectively. Various agencies, universities, and communities are pursuing ways of making these resources available, but too often they are going their separate ways toward the same end.

The federal government is no exception to this "separate way" approach. According to a recent report by the Carnegie Commission on Science, Technology and Government:

> "The government's environmental R&D system is excessively fragmented among numerous agencies and jurisdictions, and ... this fragmentation is a severe obstacle to developing the scientific information base necessary for effective protection of the nation's environment."

Clearly, an integrated approach to information management is warranted.

The indexing, classification, and cataloging generally implied by the relatively new term "metadata" are not new ideas; rather, they represent techniques that bibliographic database producers have developed and deployed over the past 25 to 30 years, and they're founded in traditions for cataloging printed materials that date back even earlier. The National Federation of Abstracting and Information Services (NFAIS) and USGS, then, began planning this symposium to bring the cataloging, indexing, and abstracting communities together with the various sectors of the biological sciences community currently wrestling with the problems of describing information resources in order to increase accessibility. The science community, we envisioned, would benefit from the "been there, done that" experiences of the cataloging community, and in turn the cataloging community would benefit from a better understanding of the needs of a community whose information resources are not primarily bibliographic.

During the planning for this symposium, however, an opportunity arose with the release of the PCAST report to leverage the deliberations of this august gathering to address not only the concerns of our own communities but those of the greater community addressed in the report. The report of the PCAST Panel on Biodiversity and Ecosystems recommends to the Administration that leading-edge information science and technologies be applied to electronically organize, interlink, and deliver biological information for use by all sectors of society. While our general concern with sharing metadata expertise among our various communities provided an incentive to meet and collaborate, the PCAST report provided the Grand Challenge that has become a specific focus for this meeting.

The report states:

> "It is becoming more and more important that we actively conserve biodiversity and protect natural ecosystems in order to preserve the quality of human life. We propose that this can be done by enhancing understanding of the interdependence of the economy and the environment."

The report goes on to state that to achieve this understanding, the United States must utilize its scientific knowledge in its conservation strategies, and incorporate new knowledge into these strategies as that knowledge is generated. In addition, because the strength of our own economy is linked inextricably to that of the world economy, the reports states the United States should participate fully in the management and conservation of global biodiversity resources by sharing information and expertise and assisting in building scientific infrastructure in developing nations.

How shall we do that? How shall we respond to this challenge to gather, use and share biodiversity information, both domestically and internationally? How shall we collaborate to draw together existing, planned, and developing information systems and databases into an integrated, interoperable whole that is capable of providing the tools of discovery, and techniques of analysis necessary for 21st century environmental and economic policy planning?

You, the participants in this symposium, represent the database, library, museum and data communities. You bring—from your different communities—different perspectives, different knowledge and different experiences that can be brought together collaboratively to address these questions.

Over the next few days, we'll discuss these questions in both plenary and break-outs sessions. We'll have time, as well, for informal and small group discussions. We'll talk about biodiversity information, the role of metadata in organizing and managing biodiversity information, the National Biological Information Infrastructure—the NBII—as it is currently developed, and the requirements for a next-generation NBII. And, we'll discuss how we can share our experiences and expertise beyond our own national borders. At the conclusion of these few days, we'll consider all of these deliberations and develop a collaborative Call to Action—a tangible, concrete set of recommendations. This Call to Action is not only for ourselves and our colleagues, but for those responsible for considering—and, more to the point, for funding—the recommendations outlined in the PCAST report.

And somewhere in the middle of all of this, we'll enjoy the results of the stewardship of earlier generations of the environmentally-minded, with a picnic lunch and expedition to Natural Bridge!

So to conclude, thank you all for agreeing to be a part of this effort and for contributing to what we expect will be an important document—our Call to Action—as well as an important step forward in a collaborative process to meet our Grand Challenge to understand America's "Living Capital."

Session 1

The Nation's Call to Action

Teaming with Life: The PCAST Report on Biodiversity and Its Implications for Biodiversity Informatics

GEOFFREY C. BOWKER Graduate School of Library and Information Sciences, University of Illinois at Urbana-Champaign

JOHN L. SCHNASE The Missouri Botanical Garden Center for Botanical Informatics, LLC

MEREDITH A. LANE Division of Botany, Natural History Museum, Department of Botany, Division of Biological Sciences, University of Kansas

SUSAN LEIGH STAR Graduate School of Library and Information Sciences, University of Illinois at Urbana-Champaign

ABRAHAM SILBERSCHATZ Information Sciences Research Center, Bell Laboratories, Lucent Technology

(This talk was adapted from a paper by the authors above; it was presented by Shubha Nagarkar at the Metadiversity Conference).

ABSTRACT

In 1998 the President's Committee of Advisers on Science and Technology (PCAST) presented a report to the President entitled *Teaming with Life: Investing in Science to Understand and Use America's Living Capital.* I report on the work of that committee and, in particular, on the findings of the biodiversity informatics subcommittee. The report argued that we must elevate the global biological information infrastructure to a new level of capability that will allow people to share on a world-wide basis the knowledge created by biodiversity and ecosystems research. It also proposed a strategic framework for achieving this goal.

The grand challenge for the 21st century is to harness the accumulating knowledge of Earth's biodiversity and the ecosystems that support it. To accomplish this, we must mobilize biological information—assemble it, organize it, and deliver it with dramatically increased capacity. We must elevate the global biological information infrastructure to a new level of capability—a "next generation"—that will allow people to share on a world-wide basis the knowledge created by biodiversity and ecosystems research.

Realizing the urgency of this task, the President's Committee of Advisors on Science and Technology, through its Panel on Biodiversity and Ecosystems, recently coordinated a review of the United States' National Biological Information Infrastructure. Over a six-month period in 1997, people from a broad cross section of the public and private sectors contributed their insights, experiences, concerns, and hopes.

What emerged was a renewed understanding of the importance of biological information to all aspects of human society. It also became clear that much remains to be done to assure that this information is complete and usable. While the purpose of the review was to develop recommendations to build capacity in the United States, many of the Panel's findings address global concerns of relevance to biodiversity research wherever it occurs. In this paper, I provide a summary of the Panel's report, a view of what a "next generation" biological information infrastructure might encompass—with an emphasis on issues of metadata—and suggestions about how it might be achieved.

Background

In the United States, the National Biological Information Infrastructure (NBII) is the primary mechanism whereby biodiversity and ecosystems information is made available to all sectors of society. It is the biological component of the National Information Infrastructure and, as such, is the framework that connects US activities to the global biodiversity and ecosystems research enterprise. Its meaning is expansive and intended to convey the idea that an information infrastructure is comprised of more than just computers, networks, and the like, but also the information, policies, standards, and people who use it. Initiation of the NBII was one of the primary recommendations made by the National Academy of Sciences National Research Council in their 1993 report, *A Biological Survey for the Nation*. Since our fate and economic prosperity are so completely linked to the natural world, information about biodiversity and ecosystems—as well as the infrastructure that surrounds it—is vital to a wide range of scientific, educational, commercial, and governmental uses. Unfortunately, most of this information now exists in forms that are not easily accessed or used. From traditional, paper-based libraries to scattered databases and physical specimens preserved in natural history collections throughout the world, our record of biodiversity and ecosystem resources is uncoordinated, and large parts of it are isolated from general usage. It is not being used effectively by scientists, resource managers, policymakers, or other potential client communities.

Fortunately, research activities are being conducted around the world that, if leveraged, could improve our ability to manage biological information. In the United States, the Human Genome Project is producing new medical therapies as well as developments in computer and information science. Geographic Information Systems (GIS) are expanding the ability of federal agencies to conduct data-gathering and synthesis activities more responsibly while creating opportunities for commercial partnerships that can lead to new software tools. The National Spatial Data Infrastructure is improving the management of geographic, geological, and satellite data sets; the Digital Libraries projects are beginning to produce useful results for some information domains; and the High-Performance Computing and Communications initiative has enhanced certain computation-intensive engineering and science areas.

Unfortunately, little attention has been paid to computer and information science and technology research in the biodiversity and ecosystems domain. We must produce mechanisms that can efficiently search through terabytes of Mission to Planet Earth satellite data and other biodiversity and ecosystems data sets, make correlations among data from disparate sources, compile those data in new ways, analyze and synthesize them, and present the results in an understandable and usable manner. Despite encouraging advances in computation and communications performance in recent years, we are able to perform these activities on only a very small scale. We can, however, make rapid progress in these areas if the computer and information science and technology research community becomes focused on the needs of the biodiversity and ecosystems research community.

Managing Complexity

Knowledge about biodiversity and ecosystems is a vast and complex information domain. The complexity arises from two sources. The first of these is the underlying biological complexity of the organisms themselves. There are millions of species, each of which is highly variable across individual organisms, populations, and time. These species have complex chemistries, physiologies, developmental cycles and behaviors, resulting from more than three billion years of evolution. There are hundreds if not thousands of ecosystems, each comprising complex interactions among large numbers of species, and between those species and multiple abiotic factors. The second source of complexity in biodiversity and ecosystems information is sociologically generated.

The sociological complexity includes problems of communication and coordination—among agencies, among divergent interests, and across groups of people from different regions, from different backgrounds (academia, industry, and government), and with different views and requirements. The kinds of data humans have collected about organisms and their relationships vary in precision, accuracy, and in numerous other ways. Biodiversity data types include text and numerical measurements as well as images, sound, and video. The range of other databases with which biodiversity data sets must interact is also broad, including geographical, meteorological, geological, chemical, and physical databases. The mechanisms used to collect and store biological data are almost as varied as the natural world they document. Additionally, biological data may be politically and commercially sensitive, and entail conflicts of interest. User skill levels are highly variable, and training in this area is not yet well developed. Because of these complexities, humans will always play a crucial role in the processing of biological data. Biological data is not as amenable to automatic correlation, analysis, synthesis, and presentation as many other types of information, such as in the field of radioastronomy where there is more coherent global organization, and the problems being studied are frequently conducive to automatic analysis. In biodiversity research, people act as sophisticated filters and query processors—locating resources on the Internet, downloading data sets, reformatting and organizing data for input to analysis tools, then reformatting again to visualize results. This process of extracting higher-order understanding from dispersed data sets is a fundamental intellectual process, yet it breaks down quickly as the volume and dimensionality of the data increase. Who could be expected to "understand" millions of cases, each having hundreds of attributes? Yet problems of this scale are commonplace in biodiversity and ecosystems research.

In order for a biological information infrastructure to be effective, it must provide the means to manage complexity. It must allow scientists to extract new knowledge from the aggregate mass of information generated by the data gathering and synthesis activities of other scientists. It must use the power of computers to facilitate the queries, correlations, and processing activities that are impossible for humans to perform alone. And it must deliver this functionality within a physically and intellectually accessible framework. This means developing ways of delivering the information to a wide range of users, with differing skills, ages, and investment in the material.

We are only beginning to develop a vocabulary to describe these large-scale, synthetic, information-processing activities. Some sociologists use the term "distributed cognitive system" to emphasize the role of humans within a synergistic, information-processing network. "Data mining" is a term that is often used by the database community. Whatever the name, these activities form only a part of a larger process of knowledge discovery that includes the large-scale, interactive storage of information (known by the unintentionally uninspiring term "data warehousing"), cataloging, cleaning, preprocessing, transformation, verification, and reduction of data, as well as the generation and use of models, evaluation and interpretation, interpersonal communications, the evolution of sophisticated user interfaces, and finally consolidation and use of the newly extracted knowledge.

These processes will become increasingly important if we are to use what we know and expand our knowledge in useful directions. At present, there is little support for these activities. At best, the NBII can be used to access information in databases held by federal agencies and other institutions around the country. Once accessed, however, the task of organizing, integrating, and interpreting the information remains, for the most part, a laborious, manual process. The development of computational tools for the biodiversity and ecosystems enterprise lags behind other sciences. Important classes of information are missing (fewer than 1% of the specimens in our natural history collections have been databased!), and existing databases are uneven in the types of information that they hold. The development and implementation of metadata standards is of central importance. It is difficult for individual scientists to publish their data electronically in meaningful ways. Standards for information exchange have not been widely adopted. We have no mechanism for archiving data over generations of use and generations of technologies—and in the field of biodiversity we frequently have need of data sets of great temporal length and heterogeneous forms. Further, the power of communication networks to build communities remains largely untapped. In summary, the NBII is currently neither a system nor an infrastructure: it is a cumbersome and brittle patchwork—presenting as many obstacles to scientific work as it does opportunities. It is clearly time to transform it into a coherent and empowering capability.

The Next Generation

In the PCAST report, we envisioned a "next generation" National Biological Information Infrastructure (NBII-2) that would address many of the concerns described above. Its overarching goal would be to become a fully accessible, distributed, interactive digital library. It would provide an organizing framework from which scientists could extract useful information—new knowledge—from the aggregate mass of information generated by various data gathering activities. This would be accomplished by using the power of computers and communications networks to augment the processing activities that now require a human mind. It would make analysis and synthesis of vast amounts of data from multiple data sets easier and more accessible to a variety of users. It would also serve management and policy decision-making, education, recreation, and the needs of industry by presenting data to each user in a manner tailored to that user's needs and skill level.

We envisioned NBII-2 as a distributed facility that would be considerably different than a "data center," considerably more functional than a traditional library, considerably more encompassing than a typical research institute. Unlike a data center, NBII-2's objective would be the automatic discovery, indexing, and linking of data sets rather than the collection of all data sets on a given topic into one facility. Following the best practice of traditional libraries, this special library would update the form of storage and upgrade information content as technologies evolve. Unlike a typical research institute, this facility would provide services to research going on elsewhere, while its own staff would conduct biodiversity and ecosystems research and research in biological informatics. The facility would offer "library" storage and access to diverse constituencies.

The core of our proposal was a "research library system" that would comprise at least five regional nodes, sited at appropriate institutions (national laboratories, universities, museums, etc.) and connected to each other and to the nearest telecommunications providers by the highest bandwidth network available. In addition, NBII-2 would seamlessly integrate all computers—laptops, workstations, fileservers, and supercomputers—capable of storing and serving biodiversity and ecosystems data via the Internet. The providers of information would have complete control over their own data, but at the same time have the opportunity to benefit from (and the right to refuse) the data indexing, cleansing, and long-term storage services of the system as a whole.

NBII-2 would be:

- the framework to support knowledge discovery for the nation's biodiversity and ecosystems enterprise and would involve many client and potential-client groups;
- a common focus for independent research efforts, and a global, context for sharing information among those efforts;
- an accrete-only, no-delete facility from which all information would be available online—twenty-four hours a day, seven days a week—in a variety of formats;
- a facility that would serve the needs of (and eventually be supported by partnership among) government, the private sector, education, and individuals;
- an organized framework for collaboration among federal, regional, state, and local organizations in the public and private sectors that would provide improved programmatic efficiencies and economies of scale through better coordination of efforts;
- a commodity-based infrastructure that utilizes readily available, off-the-shelf hardware and software and the products of digital libraries research wherever possible;
- an electronic facility where scientists and others could "publish" biodiversity and ecosystem information for cataloging, automatic indexing, access, analysis, and dissemination;
- a place where intensive work on how people use large information systems would be conducted, including studies of human-computer interaction, the sociology of

scientific practice, computer-supported cooperative work, and user interface design;

- a place for developing the organizational and educational infrastructure that will support sharing, use, and coordination of massive data sets;
- a facility that would provide content storage resources, registration of data sets, and "curation" of data sets (including migration, cleansing, indexing, etc.);
- an applied biodiversity and ecosystems informatics research facility that would develop new technologies and offer training in informatics;
- a facility that would provide high-end computation and communications to researchers and institutions throughout the country. This facility would not be a purely technical and technological construct, but rather would also encompass sociological, legal, and economic issues within its research purview. These would include intellectual property rights management, public access to the scholarly record, and the characteristics of evolving systems in the networked information environment. The human dimensions of the interaction with computers, networks, and information will be particularly important areas of research as systems are designed for the greatest flexibility and usefulness to people.

The needs that the research nodes of NBII-2 must address are many. A small subset of those needs includes:

- new statistical pattern recognition and modeling techniques that can work with high dimensional, large-volume data;
- workable data cleaning methods that automatically correct input and other types of errors in databases;
- strategies for sampling and selecting data;
- algorithms for classification, clustering, dependency analysis, and change and deviation detection that scale to large databases;
- visualization techniques that scale to large and multiple databases;
- metadata encoding routines that will make data mining meaningful when multiple, distributed sources are searched;
- methods for improving connectivity of databases, integrating data mining tools, and developing better synthetic technologies;
- methods for improving large-scale project coordination and scientific collaborations;
- ongoing, formative evaluation, detailed user studies, and quick feedback between domain experts, users, developers and researchers;
- methods for facilitating data entry and the digitization of large amounts of irregularly structured information;
- ways of engaging society in the pursuit of global information sharing.

None of these problems is unique to biodiversity research. However, there is an urgent need to address these questions within the biodiversity domain, since research has demonstrated that there can be no domain-independent solutions. We cannot "borrow" discoveries wholesale from other disciplines; we must work through these problems ourselves. In order to comprehend and utilize our biodiversity and ecosystem resources, we must learn how to exploit massive data sets, learn how to store and access them for analytic purposes, and develop methods to cope with growth and change in data. The NBII-2 envisioned here can be the enabling framework that unlocks the knowledge and economic power lying dormant in the masses of biodiversity and ecosystems data that we have on hand now and will accumulate in the future.

Infrastructure Requirements

The total volume of biodiversity and ecosystems information is almost impossible to measure. We do know that whatever the total, only a fraction has been captured in digital form. Our natural history museums, for example, contain at least 750 million specimens, the vast majority of which have not been databased. The same holds for the published record, where most biodiversity and ecosystems information still resides in paper-based journals, books, field notes, and the like. Clearly, one of the most important infrastructure issues is to move the biodiversity and ecosystems enterprise into a digital world by digitizing on a large-scale the existing corpus of scholarly work.

A fully digital, interactive library system such as NBII-2 will require substantial computational resources, although little is known now about the precise scope of the necessary resources. In many areas that are critical to digital libraries, such as knowledge representation and resource description, or summarization and navigation, even the basic algorithms and approaches are not yet well defined, making it difficult to project computational requirements. We do know that many existing information retrieval techniques are intensive in their computational and input-output demands as they evaluate, structure, and compare large databases in a distributed environment. Distributed database searching, resource discovery, automatic classification and summarization, visualization, and presentation are also computationally intensive activities that are likely to be commonplace in the NBII-2 digital library.

Finally, NBII-2 will need massive storage. Even though the library system we are proposing would not set out to accrue data sets in order to become the repository for all biodiversity data—after all, many other federal agencies have their own storage facilities, and various data providers will want to retain control over their own data—large amounts of storage on disc, tape, optical, and an array of other future storage technologies will still be required. As research is conducted to produce new ways to manipulate large data sets, these will have to be sought out, copied from their original source, and stored for use in the research. And, in serving its long-term curation function, NBII-2 will accumulate substantial amounts of data for which it will be responsible, including redundant data sets that will have to be maintained in order to insure against loss.

Research Agenda

New approaches to managing information must be developed in the context of NBII-2. Faced with massive data sets, traditional approaches in database management, statistics, pattern recognition, personal information management, and visualization collapse. For example, a statistical analysis package assumes that all the data to be analyzed can be loaded into memory and then manipulated. What happens when the data set does not fit into main memory? What happens if the database is on a remote server and will never permit a naive scan of the data? What happens if queries for stratified samples are impossible because data fields in the database being accessed are not indexed so the appropriate data can be located? What if the database is structured with only sparse relations among tables, or if the data set can only be accessed through a hierarchical set of fields? Furthermore, challenges often are not restricted to issues of scalability of storage or access. For example, what if a user of a large data repository does not know how to specify the desired query? It is not clear that a Structured Query Language (SQL) statement—or even a program—can be written to retrieve the information needed to answer a query such as "show me the list of gene sequences for which voucher specimens exist in natural history collections and for which we also know the physiology and ecological associates of those species." Many of the interesting questions that users of biodiversity and ecosystems information would like to ask are of this type: they are "fuzzy," the data needed to answer them must come from multiple sources that will be inherently different in structure and conceptually incompatible, and the answers may be approximate.

Major advances are needed in methods for knowledge representation and interchange, database management and federation, navigation, modeling, and data-driven simulation; in approaches to describing large complex networked information resources; and in techniques to support networked information discovery and retrieval in extremely large scale distributed systems. In addition to near term operational solutions, new approaches are also needed to longer-term issues such as the preservation of digital information across generations of storage, processing, and representation technology. Traditional information science skills such as thesaurus construction and indexing must be elaborated upon and scaled to accommodate large information sources. We need to preserve and support the knowledge of library and information science researchers, and help scale up the skills of knowledge organization and information retrieval.

Also much needed are software applications that provide more natural interfaces between humans and databases than are now available. For example, a valuable data cleansing activity might be to "show the data relating to all specimens in our natural history collections whose likelihood of being mislabeled exceeds 0.75." Assuming that certain cases in the database can be identified as "labeled correctly" and others "known to be mislabeled," then a training sample for a data-mining algorithm could be constructed. The algorithm would build a predictive model and retrieve records matching that model rather than a structured query that a person might write. This is an example of a much needed and much more natural interface between humans and databases than is currently available. In this case, it eliminates the requirement that the user adapt to the machine's needs rather than the other way around. We must refine and augment the interactions between people and machines, expand the role of agentry in information systems, and discover more powerful and natural ways of navigating the scientific record.

In return, computer and information science and technology research in the biodiversity and ecosystems domain is likely to yield discoveries of value to other areas. Certainly, nowhere do we find the problems of heterogeneous database federation more challenging than in the life sciences. A fully implemented digital library for biology would include everything from ideas to physical objects, and enormous amounts of information in every media type imaginable. Research on global climate change, habitat destruction, and the discovery of species are among the most distributed of our scientific activities, creating extraordinary opportunities to learn about computer-mediated project coordination and communication. At almost every turn, scale, complexity, and urgency conspire to create a particularly wicked set of problems. Working on these problems will undoubtedly advance our understanding and use of information technologies, perhaps more than in any other circumstance.

Call to Action

In the 21st century, work will be increasingly dependent on rapid, coordinated access to shared information. Through the shared digital library of NBII-2, scientists and policy makers will be able to collaborate with colleagues across geographic and temporal distances. They will use the library to catalog and organize information, perform analyses, test hypotheses, make decisions, and discover new ideas. Educators will use its systems to read, write, teach, and learn. In traditional fashion, intellectual work will be shared with others through the medium of the library—but these contributions and interactions will be elements of a global and universally accessible library that can be used by many different people and many different communities. By increasing the effectiveness of information, NBII-2 is likely to lead to scientific discoveries, advance existing areas of study, promote disciplinary fusions, and enable new research traditions. And most important, it could help us protect and manage our natural capital so as to provide a stable and prosperous future.

The National Biological Information Infrastructure (NBII) Framework Plan—A Roadmap for Interoperable Sharing of Biodiversity Information

JAMES L. EDWARDS, Deputy Assistant Director, Directorate for Biological Sciences, National Science Foundation

ABSTRACT

The NBII is a growing network of collaborating organizations that make available a wide range of biodiversity and other biological data. The PCAST report envisions the next generation network (NBII-2) in which both technological innovation and institutional cooperation take a quantum leap. An essential step in developing the NBII-2 is a framework, similar to the *Strategy for the National Spatial Data Infrastructure*, published by the Federal Geographic Data Committee, that lays out strategic goals and sets a process for fully involving the wider biodiversity community. The Biodiversity and Ecosystems Informatics Working Group (BioEco), a subgroup of the National Science and Technology Council's (NSTC's) Committee on Environment and Natural Resources (CENR), has developed a draft framework for NBII-2 that includes five major goals: 1) getting the broadest possible participation of both public and private sectors; 2) encouraging greater coordination of and support for research and development on advanced systems and technologies; 3) promoting the use of collaboratively developed standards; 4) increasing federal R&D to support biodiversity and ecosystems informatics; and 5) cooperatively developing the long-range implementation plan for the next generation National Biological Information Infrastructure. These goals will be presented in the context of where the NBII is today; the vision for the future; and how the NBII-2 intends to work synergistically with other biodiversity data-sharing efforts at the national, regional, and global levels.

As noted in the previous paper, the President's Committee of Advisors on Science and Technology (PCAST) has an extremely ambitious vision for what our next generation of the National Biological Information Infrastructure should be. It is going to be a magical place that will let us do everything we want to do in the area of biological information. What I will present is where are we in realizing that goal and what our road map is for trying to make it happen.

One of our problems in implementing the National Biological Information Infrastructure is dealing with biologists. When we went to graduate school or undergraduate school, biologists didn't really get that much training in quantitative methods. Also, as Bill Brown pointed out in his opening remarks last night, when he was in graduate school, computers did not exist—students had to utilize mechanical calculators. A few years ago at a conference on computing and biology, Michael Levitt made what I think was a very prescient quote: "Computers have changed biology forever even if most biologist don't yet realize it." I think most of you in this room have realized it—and this is what this conference is all about. But one of the things we are going to have to do as a group is to find out how to get biologists to utilize computers. Most importantly, we will have to figure out how to get the information that we need to use in our daily lives—as biologists, as computer scientists, as whatever—digitized and utilized. Part of the way we get there is through the National Biological Information Infrastructure (NBII).

The Purpose of the NBII

The NBII was first conceived in the 1993 report put out by the National Academy of Sciences—a report not coincidentally chaired by Peter Raven, the individual who was also the chair of the PCAST subgroup that produced *Teaming with Life*. So, it is not surprising that many of the recommendations in the *Biological Survey for the Nation* report and in *Teaming with Life* are quite congruent with each other. As has been pointed out, the NBII is a federated activity, in which the databases, the control of the data, and the feeding and care of the data reside out in the sites that collect and own those data. The NBII acts as a pointer, as a metadata source for information about these databases. It is managed by the Biological Resources Division of the United States Geological Survey (USGS/BRD).

The USGS does not do this work alone. It works in cooperation with a growing number of partners. Many collaborators—including museums, universities, other federal agencies, libraries, commercial organizations, and nongovernmental organizations—are involved in the partnership that leads to the NBII. Currently there are about 300 active data sets. The Integrated Taxonomic Information System (ITIS), a system that provides access to accredited names of organisms in North America, is being used to pull together the taxonomic coordination of these various data sets.

The NBII is working on vocabulary and metathesaraus development. In addition, one of the most important aspects of the current NBII is the Metadata Clearing-House Gateway. The metadata descriptions in the NBII are developed using a biological profile from the Federal Geographic Data Committee's (FGDC's) Content Standard for Geospatial Metadata. The Clearing House also is a participating node in the National Spatial Data Clearing House. The NBII must, and is, working with other relevant organizations and other relevant standard setters in order to develop its activities.

Where do we go from these 300 data sets that currently exist within the NBII? How do we implement the grand vision that the President's Committee of Advisers on Science and Technology has laid out for us? The answer lies with the next generation—the NBII-2.

Challenges Facing the NBII-2

The NBII-2 will not simply be a data center, a traditional library, or a research institute. Rather it will partake of attributes of all of these kinds of things. It will be a distributed facility with the capability to interoperably access these various data sets to simultaneously query them; to synthesize, correlate, and analyze the information; and to be able to produce and present the information in a way that is visually appealing and useful to a wide variety of users.

Obviously this is going to take a lot of research relating to the kinds of data that we are talking about—the difficult data, the complicated data that individuals dealing in biodiversity are developing. This leads to the first challenge facing NBII-2: to find a way to get the research done that would allow the NBII-2 dream to become reality.

The second challenge is to develop an infrastructure and an organization that would allow us to pull this information together and make the NBII-2 happen. As mentioned in the previous paper, PCAST suggests that this should happen through a series of nodes—at least five nodes regionally distributed around the United States. These nodes would act as sites where the appropriate software and the appropriate computing power would allow users to interoperably dial into the node to get information to do the kind of searches they want to do. These centers will also be able to act as archiving sites. The NBII does not want to take over data—instead, it wants to leave data out in the sites that developed those data, so that the data are locally owned. We all know that there are many situations occurring where data sets are being orphaned, where information is being lost. We need some way, when a researcher retires or when an institution goes out of existence, to archive the information that would otherwise be lost and to make that data available to future users. The NBII-2, through its national nodes, will be able to act as a place where that kind of archiving and central data storage can occur.

The third challenge in making NBII-2 happen is semantic or social interoperability. How do we get the various people, the various organizations, the various institutions necessary to this project to work together? To help start us on that path, the Biological and Ecological Informatics Working Group has prepared a draft framework for NBII-2, with five goals. The framework is attached (see Appendix B).

The Goals of the NBII-2

The first goal of the framework is to obtain the broadest possible participation of both public and private sectors in developing the NBII-2. We cannot do it alone. Even though we appear "all-powerful" in Washington, we still need to have interactions with and help from the rest of society (unless you want to give us all your tax dollars!). We need to develop a common vision and understanding of the mutual benefits and activity the NBII-2 can bring to define what the fundamental data and information components of the NBII-2 should be; to develop a long-term plan; to encourage broad participation; to coordinate with other national and international initiatives like the Clearing-House Mechanism; and to promote policies and programs to fulfill this vision. These are the broad kind of goals that any organization has, but we really need to do this by interacting and pulling together as many different kinds of public and private organizations and individuals as we possibly can.

Second, we need to encourage better coordination and support for research and development on advanced systems and technologies. This is in response to a challenge I have already mentioned: to do the right kinds of research to develop the tools, technologies, and architectures that will allow us to implement the vision of PCAST; to find ways to define the respective interests and the complementary roles that will be necessary to do this research and development; and to identify and overcome the barriers that exist to developing software, hardware, and other interoperable tools.

Third, and very germane to this particular meeting, we need to promote the use of highly collaboratively developed standards. We all know that there are hundreds—thousands—of different biodiversity databases out there. How do we develop the means for them to interoperably talk to each other? Subsequent papers will refer to these problems and present suggestions about how we can get around them. In this framework, we suggest that we need to work in public and private partnerships to identify and prioritize the kinds of standards that we need through activities like this particular conference, to promote standards development, and to encourage linkages with other groups doing similar kinds of things—groups like the Geospatial Data Committee and like the national and international standards organizations.

The fourth goal in the framework is to increase federal support for R&D on biodiversity and ecosystems information. Federal support will be used both for funding within the government and for funding outside of the government—in universities, in museums, and in other research venues. We need to identify existing research and development activities like the digital libraries, like the Knowledge and Distributed Intelligence thrust at the National Science Foundation. We need to work through things like the National Science and Technology Council's high performance computing thrust, where part of the goal is to promote biological and ecological information as an important application area within the National Biological Information Infrastructure.

Finally, the fifth goal is to cooperatively develop the long-range implementation plan for the next generation of the NBII. How do we propose to do that? First we propose to put together an interagency and public/private task force that will work to construct this framework, work to develop the next generation, and work to implement the vision of PCAST. It will identify funding and other means for bringing information systems R&D to the next generation, will help develop an out-year budget for implementing this within the federal sector, and will figure out how to develop partnerships of the industrial sector, the private sector, and the Non-Government Organizations (NGOs).

When we are able to fulfill the grand dream for the next generation of the NBII, it will truly be a gateway to a wide diversity of different kinds of biological data, not just biodiversity data. We need to be able to link biodiversity data to genetic data. For example, we need to find ways to link the large sequence databases and the Protein Data Bank (PDB) to biodiversity data, in order to answer lots of different kinds of questions that we all have.

We see the NBII-2, then, as being a "one-stop shopping" node, a place where you can go to get access to not only biodiversity data, but also other kinds of data, and where competent technologies make the information available to everybody.

Connecting to Other Entry Points

Now, I said we wanted it to be this one-stop shopping node, this place where you can go to get access to other kinds of information and data developed at other places. We see it as providing access to information from local-level sites—county parks, the nature conservatories, state heritage sites, museum collections, etc. The NBII would also be the U.S. entry point that would work with common or similar kinds of entry points in other countries. The Canadian Biodiversity Information Infrastructure, CONABIO in Mexico, ERIN in Australia, INBio in Costa Rica—these are examples of the kind of national-level node that the NBII-2 intends to become. We see it then as also providing information to allow integration with activities at the regional and global level—to the North American Biodiversity Information Network, the InterAmerican Biodiversity Information Network, the Clearing-House Mechanism, and the Global Biodiversity Information Facility. I will say just a couple of words about a few of some of these regional- and international-level activities.

The North American Biodiversity Information Network. The North American Biodiversity Information Network (NABIN), as the name implies, focuses on North America. It is sponsored by the Council for Environmental Cooperation under the North American Free Trade Agreement (NAFTA). NABIN intends to develop standards and protocols for the exchange of biodiversity information—focusing, of course, on the North American perspective—to develop Internet-based query systems. NABIN has a pilot project up and running. The pilot project is looking at the birds of North America, building on the quite successful activity begun in Mexico to determine which birds of Mexico are catalogued in data sets and museums in the rest of the world.

The InterAmerican Biodiversity Information Network. The InterAmerican Biodiversity Information Network (INABIN) covers North America, South America, and the Caribbean. As with all these activities that are Internet-based, it is intended to be a site that will be especially useful for decision-making and education activities. It builds on other initiatives—the Clearing-House Mechanism, the Man and the Biosphere, MABNET, and the Biodiversity Conservation Information System. Its implementation support is through the Organization of American States (OAS), and Brazil is going to host an InterAmerican INABIN meeting in the Spring of 1999.

Global Biodiversity Information Facility. Finally I would like to say a couple words about the Global Biodiversity Information Facility (GBIF). Not least of the reasons for doing this is that I chair the group that is making this recommendation. The Organization for Economic Cooperation and Development (OECD) has something called the Megascience Forum. The Megascience Forum is intended to focus on big-scale science. Up until now, big-scale science has meant big, fixed physics facilities, primarily telescopes and synchrotrons. A few years ago, we in the U.S. made the argument that if you look at information, information is not—in and of itself—something that requires one big, fixed facility. But if you look at the need for information, the need for developing databases, and the need for pulling those databases together, then information is indeed a megascience—one that is a distributed megascience, but nevertheless requires thinking about and development of the same kinds of things needed for big, fixed physics facilities. We were able to convince the other Megascience Forum members of the OECD that this was an important and appropriate area of consideration.

OECD thus formed a Biological Informatics Working Group that has focused on two major kinds of biological information—neuroinformatics (how do we develop databases and tools?) and biodiversity informatics. The Biodiversity Informatics subgroup is recommending the formation of a Global Biodiversity Information Facility—GBIF, as we like to refer to it. GBIF, like all the other things we talked about today, is going to be a distributed activity—one that will focus on biodiversity information and one that will pull together the large amount of biodiversity information that resides in OECD countries and, we hope, elsewhere.

Part of the rationale for making this recommendation is to note that information about the world's biodiversity—not the biodiversity itself, but information *about* that biodiversity—largely resides in OECD countries. Mobilizing that information, digitizing it, and making it available to the world at large is something that the OECD countries can do on behalf of the world at large. So, we see providing that information as a component, as something that the OECD can do to aid the Clearing-House Mechanism of the Convention on Biological Diversity, even though all OECD countries are not signatories of that convention. In order to make that happen, we recognize that one needs to have, in essence, an authority file of the names of the species of the world—something that currently does not exist. So, one of the major activities of GBIF will be to help pull together a list of the names of the world's species. Of course, there are other international activities that are already ongoing to make that happen—most especially, Species 2000. We are working with Species 2000 in order to help develop this worldwide authority file of the names of existing species in the world. This is another big idea of PCAST for NBII-2.

When and how is GBIF going to happen? We have made the recommendation that GBIF will start when five countries have agreed to form a secretariat to pull together the activities within those countries that will be the nucleus of the formation of GBIF. That is likely to happen sometime in the middle of 2000. There will be a ministerial meeting of the OECD countries held in June, 1999, and I am quite hopeful that we will have five countries at about that time that will agree to form GBIF. If that happens, we will then put out a request for proposals from countries to host the secretariat.

I want to stress that although the idea for and planning of the GBIF has happened within the OECD, it is not simply intended to an OECD activity. Rather it is one where we want any country to be able to join in. Certainly the data, once they are up and available, will be open to anybody to retrieve, but we would also like to try to get everybody to help provide data that they have available.

Conclusion

Finally, I would like to go back to why we need something like the NBII-2 —what is it going to accomplish and what do we want to do with it. Here are some lofty words that come from the NBII framework. They say that "The basis for all efforts to effectively conserve biodiversity and natural ecosystems, while at the same time supporting economic development, lies in our ability to get at the widest possible access to the existing body of knowledge on biodiversity and ecosystem resources and processes." Another quote I really like is by someone who does not work in biodiversity—Alan Bleasby. In *The Biochemist,* he said, "Two months in the lab can easily save an afternoon on the computer." This is a situation that already pertains for people working in many parts of biochemistry. The databases exist for people doing genomics, for people who want to look at sequence activities, for people who want to look at protein structure. The data already exist for them to be able to *not* have to spend two months in the lab. But we don't yet have that situation for people working in the area of biodiversity informatics. However, I am quite hopeful that as a result of this conference and others like it, we will at least be on the road to having that capability be developed.

The Clearing-House Mechanism of the Convention on Biological Diversity:
Biodiversity Metadata and Information

BEATRIZ TORRES, Secretariat of the Convention on Biological Diversity, 393 St. Jacques St. Suite 300, Montreal H2Y 1N9, Canada. Phone: (514) 287 7018, Fax: (514) 288 6588, beatriz.torres@blodiv.org, <http://www.biodiv.org/chm>

ABSTRACT

The Convention on Biological Diversity (CBD), which was one of the successful outcomes of the Rio Earth Summit of 1992, is one of the most powerful and important international treaties regarding biodiversity and the environment. To date it has been ratified by 175 countries. The CBD established a Clearing-House Mechanism (CHM), which promotes and facilitates scientific and technical cooperation. The governing body of the Convention (Conference of the Parties) decided that a transparent and decentralized approach would be the most suitable way to establish a mechanism to exchange and disseminate information while promoting and facilitating technical and scientific cooperation. This decentralized approach is also intended to avoid new and costly databases, as the CHM is foreseen to function at a metadata level. The CHM Focal Points and partners are the key driving forces of the CHM. Their functions include responsibility for their own data and information. The characteristics, perspectives, new developments, as well as the potentials and opportunities under the CHM, will be discussed. Visit the CHM site at <http://www.biodiv.org/chm>.

One of the successful outcomes of the United Nations Conference on the Environment and Development (UNCED) held in Rio, Brazil in 1992, was the adoption of the Convention on Biological Diversity (CBD). The Convention entered into force in December 1993, and to date it has been ratified by 175 Contracting Parties (countries).

To date the CBD constitutes one of the most powerful and important international treaties regarding biodiversity and the environment. Because of its legally binding nature, it has opened a new set of concrete opportunities for the conservation and sustainable use of species, habitats and ecosystems in our planet. In addition, the Convention provides for a financial mechanism—the Global Environment Facility (GEF)—to support the compliance and implementation processes of country-driven initiatives in developing countries and countries with economies in transition.

In order to achieve the 3 objectives of the Convention, namely,

- the conservation of biological diversity,
- the sustainable use of biological resources, and
- the equitable sharing of benefits arising out of the utilization of genetic resources,

the CBD Parties need to fulfill several obligations, including the preparation of national inventories, strategies, and action plans. They must also integrate the conservation and sustainable use of biological diversity into relevant sectoral and cross-sectoral plans, programs, and policies. In this context, the exchange and dissemination of information is seen as a key tool for the implementation of the Convention. Such exchange of information shall include the exchange of results of technical, scientific, and socio-economic research, as well as information on training and surveying programs, specialized knowledge, indigenous and traditional knowledge, and technologies including biotechnology. It shall also, where feasible, include repatriation of information.

Purpose of the Clearing-House Mechanism (CHM)

The Clearing-House Mechanism (CHM) promotes and facilitates technical and scientific cooperation at all levels among Parties to the Convention (Art. 18(3) of the Convention).

Through the CHM, global access to and exchange of information on biodiversity and its sustainable use will be facilitated. COP[1] identified the CHM as a key tool, which contributes to and actively assists in fulfilling the three objectives of the convention.

The CHM constitutes a new and innovative shift away from the central data-source concept. It is an innovative process in that it is transparent, interactive, open and accessible. In addition, it calls for a decentralized system with shared responsibilities under a globally owned mechanism. In fact, the CHM is different than the already existing information systems, since it is much more than a pure information retrieval system. It is, rather, a tool to facilitate and enhance scientific and technical cooperation and development. It relies on the interaction of participating partners and users involved.

A crucial component of the Clearing-House Mechanism's operational framework is that it is needs driven and service-oriented. The CHM is geared towards linking its meta-information to respond to queries on topics relevant to the implementation of the Convention, pointing the users to the location of relevant information.

CHM Characteristics and Attributes

Among others, COP assigned the following characteristics to the CHM:

- The CHM should develop in a neutral, transparent, cost-effective, efficient and accessible manner.

---

[1] The Conference of the Parties (COP) is the supreme decision-making body of the Convention on Biological Diversity.

- It should also be developed through specific and focused areas of activities related to the promotion of international technical and scientific cooperation.
- It should be compatible with national capacities, needs driven and decentralized in nature. It also has to provide access to metadata, support the decision-making process, and should to the extent possible involve the private sector.
- The CHM should include information exchange modalities additional to the Internet to ensure the participation of Parties without Internet access and must integrate and link global and regional information structures.
- The CHM will enhance networking between existing national, regional, sub-regional and international centers of relevant expertise, as well as with governmental and non-governmental institutions and the private sector.
- The CHM must work in close cooperation with relevant international organizations and entities as partners, in order to maximize the existing experience and expertise.
- The Clearing-House Mechanism needs to be clearly focused on the implementation of the Convention.

The decisions made by the COP have broadened the scope of the CHM. *In-situ* conservation, taxonomy, access to genetic resources, technology transfer, biosafety, indigenous knowledge, incentive measures and capacity building in general, were identified as fields in which the CHM has an important role to play.

Information about Biodiversity through the CHM

Information about biodiversity is gathered and maintained by a large number of public, private, governmental, inter-governmental and non-governmental institutions and agencies.

Scientists, managers of both public and private agencies, decision-makers and the public in general should be able to have easy access to this information, and to the tools that help us to locate, analyze and combine such information. The overall aim is to improve the levels of informed decision-making processes and ultimately the quality of life on our planet.

The reliance upon those who collect or maintain information about biological diversity as stewards of those information resources is fundamental. These individuals and institutions know best the biological resources, as well as the nature, quality and conditions of the resulting information, and are thus most likely to maintain the data appropriately.

Furthermore, the Clearing House operates in a transactional rather than in a custodial manner. It facilitates transactions through the provision of means to cover both the demand and the offer needs. A Clearing House implements operational procedures that ensure effectiveness and transparency. Finally, it has been established that the ownership of all information made available through the Clearing-House Mechanism shall remain with the provider of the information.

Effective sharing of information is greatly enhanced by a common understanding of terms, nomenclature and operating standards. Achieving some level of consistency with respect to common terminology and operating approaches will greatly increase the degree to which these systems can communicate with each other, users can find the information they need, and data can be combined and aggregated where appropriate. Issues include technical standards by which information is described, formatted and transmitted, as well as issues involving pricing, protection, and use of data.

The contribution of each partner will be included in the information system of the Clearing-House Mechanism and will be made available to all users. In this way, updating the information in the system will not be the responsibility of any one institution, or of a program officer in the Secretariat. Rather, it will be a decentralized activity, to be undertaken by the CHM partners.

The concept of the CBD's Clearing House is straightforward. The CHM central node is not a centralized database, which may duplicate the efforts of its national nodes and thematic centers. The CHM makes available only that information that is common to all members and Partners and is a reference center and switchboard to the information providers and seekers. In order to achieve this, the system has to know where the specific information is hosted in order to open a channel from the information seeker to the information holder.

Levels of Operation

The CHM functions at both national and international levels. At the national level, the CHM is envisaged to serve the information needs of those national organizations involved in implementing the provisions of the Convention. The nature of their needs is often complex and multi-faceted. Numerous sources of relevant information are likely to be identified in local and national government agencies, universities, research centers, UN organizations, agencies, indigenous and local communities, Non-Government Organizations (NGOs), and the private sector. In fact, the potential volume of information is such that the National Focal Points of the CHM could invest significant amounts of time conducting searches through a massive wealth of information. Moreover, such searches would most likely reveal the need to distinguish relevant information amidst the overall wealth of information held by institutions, while ensuring its availability in an appropriate format.

The CHM framework provides the means by which access to, and the interactive nature of an information exchange system could be maximized during the present period. Such an approach takes into consideration the complexity of the many Convention-related topics and is especially relevant when considering the demands for inputting and updating the different types of information to be submitted by a growing number of partners and participants.

Focal Point Concept

The contributors to the Clearing-House system are broad and diverse. Supported by the Secretariat of the Convention, the National Focal Points are the load-bearing columns of this process. They provide and use the information contents, as well as, actively furnish national experiences. The underlying understanding is that the 175 Contracting Parties to the Convention are both the target group and the main actors at implementing the Convention and its Clearing-House Mechanism.

In addition to the National Focal Points, Thematic Focal Points (TFPs) have been envisaged. TFPs are visualized as resources or centers that posses solid and specialized experience in a given field of biological diversity.

Regional approaches or supra-regional initiatives are also important contributors to the system. In that regard, for the Americas, the Inter-American Biodiversity Information Network (IABIN) and the North American Biodiversity Information Network (NABIN) are substantial and far-reaching initiatives. Furthermore, supra-regional initiatives such as the Biodiversity Information Network (BIN 21), the OECD Megascience Subgroup on Bioinformatics and the G-8 ENRM Subgroup on Biodiversity Data, constitute key and important associates to the system. Since many other initiatives are under way, it appears necessary to the Secretariat that at least some levels of harmonization of efforts are needed to avoid duplication of work and resources.

Role of the Secretariat

The Secretariat focal point should encourage the development of a network of active partners for the CHM. Moreover, it should also support the partners in developing specific training for the effective participation of users in the clearing-house network.

The role of the Secretariat should be that of a facilitator, ensuring:
* the dissemination of experience and knowledge amongst all partners;
* that the system as a whole is learning from shared experience; and
* that different solutions to similar problems are being recorded and exchanged.

This leads to a conceptual network model where we find the Secretariat node to the CHM acting as a coordinating switching-center with facilitating linkages to the associated nodes.

Regional and National Focal Points, Thematic Focal Points or other partners might take over a specific theme or issue of the Convention in order to structure the information and provide a single pointer on the CHM. This could avoid duplication of effort, promote synergy within the CBD process, maximize effectiveness, help to structure information in a decentralized manner and make the international CHM a globally distributed information source with clearly shared responsibilities.

CHM Partners

The development of the CHM has to be supported by a large number of different partners enabling the mechanism to fulfill its tasks and the expectations of its users. This is only possible when all the contracting Parties and focal points and other users and providers conceive the development of the CHM as a joint responsibility from which they can gain profit while ensuring the national implementation of the Convention. Consequently, adding value to biodiversity through information is one of the utmost tasks of the CHM. There is a wealth of human and institutional resources around the world. The providers of these resources should be natural partners to the CHM process and our challenge is to duly incorporate them.

Cooperation with Other Processes and Organizations

Synergies and close cooperation are needed and sought with other conventions, agreements and processes. The Secretariat has to identify those activities and organizations that could support the Clearing-House Mechanism. They could also provide timely and appropriate advice to the Subsidiary Body on Scientific, Technical and Technological Advice (SBSTTA). Concrete efforts with the Framework Convention on Climate Change, Convention to Combat Desertification, CITES, Ramsar, World Heritage, and Convention on Migratory Species on the harmonization of information management are currently under way.

Informal Advisory Committee

The Clearing-House Mechanism is assisted in its functioning by an Informal Advisory Committee (IAC), as stipulated by the Parties to the Convention. The advisory committee guides and integrates the development of the CHM pilot phase[1] activities and endeavors to ensure that all Parties can participate in the Clearing-House Mechanism.

Call to Action: CHM 21

As agreed by the Conference of the Parties the CHM, during the period 1996-98, is developing its pilot phase, encouraging and developing methods of cooperation for the development and use of technologies, including indigenous and traditional technologies in pursuance of the objectives of the convention.

In order to achieve the goal of promoting and facilitating technical and scientific cooperation, the CHM must also promote the access to and transfer of environmental technology in the field of biodiversity.

The CHM node at the CBD Secretariat is currently developing a strategy to further develop the area of technology transfer. In order to be an incentive for other national focal points and networks to start working on technology transfer issues the facilitation and promotion of the transfer of environmental technology in biodiversity needs to promptly be addressed by the CHM. In the field of technology transfer the CHM is focusing on country driven efforts to promote the access to and transfer of technology.

At the end of its three-year pilot phase in which the CHM has successfully implemented the information infrastructure, it is now engaging in its overriding priority, namely, to facilitate and promote scientific and technical cooperation.

The results of the pilot phase achieved thus far can be used as a platform to launch the challenging approach of the Clearing-House Mechanism. The CHM has to be developed into something more than a referral system. As a first approximation, this referral system is important and necessary to explore the scientific and technical realm of biodiversity in its inter-linked complexity in a cross-sectoral manner. However, interactive and cross-sectoral components have to be added to meet the needs of future generations.

Some tools may be flagged to indicate the nature of such a system:

• development of national reports into central information sources;
• visualization of metadata for the evaluation and monitoring of trends as well as the development of indicators to measure changes in biological diversity;

---

[1] The Pilot Phase of the Clearing-House Mechanism lasts until the end of 1998.

- integration and linkage of global and regional information structures through the utilization of a few key words (attribute lists) which in turn can open new information spaces;
- development of a "CHM-tool kit" to support the CHM partners in the establishment, integration, and exchange of their existing data sources within commonly agreed information structures of the CHM; and
- development of novel and user friendly search mechanisms to help explore the biodiversity information space in step-by-step manner.

The Clearing-House 21 becomes a globally managed information source under common and shared responsibilities to contribute to sustainable development, conservation of biodiversity and the equitable sharing of benefits.

It is apparent that big and important challenges are in front of us. In addition to the effective promotion and facilitation of technical and scientific cooperation, the biggest challenge by far is the one related to matters of national implementation, where capacity-building issues are of paramount importance, in particular for developing countries. The ultimate success of the CHM will be tested on the ground and at the national level.

The Metadata Landscape: Conventions for Semantics, Syntax, and Structure in the Internet Commons

STUART L. WEIBEL, Senior Research Scientist, OCLC

ABSTRACT

The Internet has brought previously distinct communities into closer contact in the Internet Commons. Effective resource discovery in this global information environment requires international, cross-disciplinary conventions for the creation management and exchange of resource description information. The Dublin Core and the Resource Description Framework provide two of the foundation building blocks necessary to support a resource description infrastructure of sufficient power and extensibility to meet the needs of the digital information age.

What I would like to talk to you about today are three aspects of metadata and why metadata might be relevant to you in your community. First I will discuss the motivation for developing new conventions for resource description and, in particular, resource descriptions about electronic resources. Secondly, I would like to tell you a little bit about the Dublin Core metadata initiative, which is the development of semantics for resource description on the Net. And finally I would like to tell you why you really don't need to care about the Dublin Core, because—whether you like it or not—there are in fact some other things that can help you, irrespective of your particular choice of a metadata standard.

What Is Metadata?

I bet that everybody in this room already knows the definition of metadata, or you all probably would not be here now. It is such a popular topic in so many venues that it is really hard to avoid the definition, but the standard definition is "data about data." I would like to modify that definition and say that, in fact, metadata is "structured data about data." Now, before I get off this topic, I want to point out that there is a strong temptation for people to say, we might need metadata about other metadata—does that make it "metametadata"? In fact, I think that if you use the term "metametadata," you are barking up the wrong tree. It is a failure to understand what metadata is really all about. Metadata is about relationships.

Resource Description Communities

One of the phrases important to discussions of this kind is the phrase "resource description community." I would like to suggest that a resource description community is any group of institutions and people that is characterized by a common understanding of three things: semantics, structure, and syntax. The community I come from—the library community—has had these common understandings for 30 or more years now. We call them MARC and AACR2—our names for the rules in populating element sets. That is really all they are—rules for helping us pass records around. So, if all libraries want to do is talk to themselves, we know how to do that, and we have known how for a long time. We use MARC cataloging. And the rules that we use to fill those MARC'd cataloging fields are the Anglo-American cataloging rules.

Living in the Internet Commons

But we live now in what I like to refer to as the Internet Commons. This is one of the important metaphors I will bring to you today. The notion of the Internet Commons means that we, in fact, all live in that little box that is now sitting on top of our desks. If we do not live there, then our users live there, and they want to get to us and to our information through the screens on their desks. Period. They don't want to walk to your library. They don't want to walk to your data repository. They don't want to go to the nearest store. They want it to be available on their desks. That is what I mean by the Internet Commons.

So now geospatial repositories and museums and libraries are all forced into this common box that I call the Internet Commons. And now our own little communities have to learn how to speak with one another, because we do not have those shared conventions about syntax, structure, and semantics—we have to develop them all anew.

In addition to that, there are lots of scientific databases that you have in your laboratories and that you might want to make available and visible to other communities. There also are 14-year-old boys and girls doing work on the Internet. And you know, some of those 14-year-olds are going to eventually win Nobel prizes, and we would like to be able to find metadata about what they did back when they were 14 years old. This kind of information also is going to be important.

Also, people are doing commerce on the Internet, so we want to be able to find information about commerce as well. You name it and there will be people who will want to provide metadata for it. I am, in fact, suggesting to you that it will be useful to be able to have these common conventions so that you can find even those kinds of information.

Even when you are doing scientific data searches, there is often heard this complaint about our community: We don't talk to each other. I had a lunch conversation yesterday at which someone remarked that the ornithologists don't talk to the ichthyologists and the ichthyologists don't talk to the herpetologists. Well, we need to be able to talk to one another more effectively. We need to be able to share information. So, developing those conventions is important for a lot of us.

Three Levels of Interoperability

Semantic Interoperability. Semantic interoperability is achieved through agreements about content description standards. The Dublin Core is an example of one of those. It is a new one. AACR2 is an old one. TEI, very popular in the humanities, is a relatively new one. The Federal Geographic Data Committee (FGDC) is one that is popular among many of the communities represented here. In other words, you name it and there is somebody who has a content description standard for it. There are zillions of these things.

Structural Interoperability. Structural interoperability is another level of interoperability that we need to be able to define. I am going to be talking about mechanisms for supporting structural interoperability later. But basically my remarks are going to be about the Resource Description Framework (RDF), which is a data model for specifying semantic schemas in a way that they can be shared.

Syntactic Interoperability. Finally, we need syntactic interoperability. This is the easiest interoperability to understand. It just means that we want to be able to mark up our data in a similar fashion so we can share the data and so that our machines can understand and take the data apart in sensible ways. The kind of syntactic interoperability that I will be talking about later on is supported by something called eXtensible Markup Language (XML)—a markup idiom for structured data on the web. If you are unsure as to whether this is going to be an important standard in the future because it is relatively new, I will tell you just one salient fact: Microsoft has publicly announced that its future versions of Word are going to marked up in XML. And if the future versions of Word and also the future versions of Excel and Access and all of these other Microsoft products are marked up in XML, it is because they need to be able to exchange data. I think that is enough said about whether XML is going to be important to us in the future. Whether you like it or not, Microsoft makes a lot of the decisions for us.

The Dublin Core Metadata Workshop Series

I would like to talk a little bit about the metadata workshop series that I have been involved in for the last several years. It is called the Dublin Core because it began at a workshop in Dublin, Ohio, where I worked three and a half years ago. These workshops were initially called simply to answer the question of how we could improve resource discovery on the Web. We were looking for simple resource description semantics. (Remember, at the time when we originated the series there were all of 500,000 individually addressable items on the web, compared to today's 500 million and growing.) The goal then was to set up an interdisciplinary consensus about a core element set for resource discovery. It was very important that it be interdisciplinary—not just librarians, not just archivists, not just museum people, but a broad range of content experts and disciplines for resource discovery for electronic information. This was our starting point, so we wanted it to be simple and intuitive. We wanted it to be cross-disciplinary. We certainly wanted it to be international—after all, we were not talking about the Ohio Wide Web or the U.S. Wide Web, but the *World* Wide Web. We also wanted it to be flexible enough that it could be applied to a broad diversity of problems and a broad diversity of complexity as well.

Characteristics of the Dublin Core Metadata Element Set. The central characteristics of what was developed at that workshop have been elaborated since.

- There are 15 elements. They are descriptive metadata for resource discovery. Half of these elements are the kinds of things you would expect to see in a catalog card, so this is the kind of simple metaphor for the Dublin Core. It is a catalog card for resource description. But just as the catalog card does not hold all of the information that libraries keep about resources, there are additional elements that provide you with the ability to add richness. The 15 elements in the Dublin Core Metadata Element Set are:

1. Title	6. Contributor	11. Source
2. Creator	7. Date	12. Language
3. Keywords	8. Type	13. Relation
4. Description	9. Format	14. Coverage
5. Publisher	10. Identifier	15. Rights

- All elements are optional. You see something you don't like, don't use it.
- All elements are repeatable.
- The element set should be extensible, a starting place for richer description. Fifteen elements will not provide all the richness that all of us want in ultimate metadata element sets. So we want to be able to extend it, to enrich it through a variety of ways
- The element set should be interdisciplinary.
- The element set should be international. We now have translations in the Dublin Core in 20 different languages and there are new ones appearing on a regular basis.

Let's talk about extensibility for a moment. How can you take this catalogue card and, in fact, provide within it enough flexibility to build in the richness that you need to support much more sophisticated metadata applications? There are a couple of kinds of extensibility that I would like to talk about. Let me describe them in terms of metaphors.

The first metaphor that I will offer you is the Ukrainian doll model. You take the top off one doll and there is another doll inside, and another doll inside that one, and so on. In other words, there is a substructure. Without a substructure, interoperability is not supported very well. The idea here is that if you take a basic element called Creator, you could just plop some stuff in there. For example, you could plop in an unstructured name. But that is not going to support interoperability very well. So, you want to add some additional substructure to that element—perhaps a given name and a surname. You might also want to have some information about affiliation there because one of the ways you find people and resources is to know with what organizations they are connected. In addition, you might want a telephone number or e-mail address or something like that. So, you are basically unpacking this structure and finding that within it there are some well-defined additional structures that support the needs that you have in your particular database. That is one kind of extensibility.

The second, and I think perhaps the more important, kind of extensibility is what I refer to as the Lego™ metaphor—modular extensibility. Let's say you want additional elements to support local or disciplinary specific requirements. In addition, you want them to be complementary—that is to say, you want them to be able to fit together. So, you might have a block of metadata that we call description metadata, such as the Dublin Core, but you also want species distribution metadata. This morning, it was stated that there are something like 750 million specimens in natural history museums around the world. Wouldn't it be great to have unified databases that would allow those sorts of things to snap together, Lego™-like, with description metadata? I like the Lego™ metaphor, because it really has a lot of richness to it. Legos™ are child's play—except that they are not child's play at all. It's true our kids play with them, but there are some interesting things about them. One is that there are lots of different kinds of Legos™. There are the Jacques Cousteau Undersea Legos™. And there are the Astronaut Legos™. And there are the Medieval Knight Legos™. The amazing thing is that they all snap together and work together—they *interoperate*.

Now I don't exactly know the semantics of mixing Jacques Cousteau and medieval castles, but my 12-year-old does. And one of the things we want about the metadata environment is not to have to anticipate what the semantics are gong to be in the future. We want people to be able to invent new semantics, the things that we don't think about or haven't thought of or maybe don't even think are even a good idea, but that might be important in the environments and for the tasks and problems in the future. That is one point about Legos™. Another is that your kids' Legos™ can interoperate with the Legos™ that you played with 30 years ago. That is a very impressive degree of interoperability, and it comes at the cost of very highly engineered products. Legos™ are manufactured to tolerances that approach the internal combustion engine. So yes, they are child's play. But they are child's play only because they are easy to snap together from simple components into much more elaborate components. They *interoperate* because somebody has put a lot of thought into engineering those things so that they fit together right (and will continue to fit together right). This is the kind of interoperable metadata architecture we are trying to develop for the future.

What does this sort of extensibility mean to you, to the scientific data communities? You can think of the Dublin Core as a semantic framework—a set of top-level descriptors. These high-level descriptors can be used to describe data sets in ways that allow you to find things in a relatively straightforward manner. In addition to that you can use domains, specific schemes for further precision, so that a collection of four billion objects might be aggregated according to a particular set of standards and specifications regarding how they are encoded. You can have your own schemes that refine the semantics of subjects, of formats, of relations, and of coverage. You can use controlled vocabularies and thesauri, name spaces, and coding rules to make your metadata very specific.

Someone was also telling me yesterday about a database that was developed in Europe that has the same set of descriptors in 10 different languages. That is a very important and valuable thing to have in an international community. And you can apply such a database in something like the Dublin Core and Resource Description Framework (RDF).

The Resource Description Framework (RDF)

Let me talk to you a little bit about the Resource Description Framework (RDF), because RDF can provide you with the kind of architecture that allows you to snap different components together in a modular way. RDF is a World Wide Web Consortium (W3C) initiative. The RDF group is a formal working group under the W3C, and it is intended to develop conventions to support interoperability among applications that exchange metadata, not only among people, but among machines as

The RDF Data Model

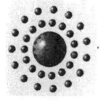

Nodes are **resources** connected by **named properties**

The degenerate case is an arc terminating in a fixed value

An **RDF description** consists of a directed graph of **arbitrary complexity**

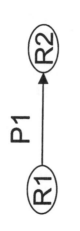

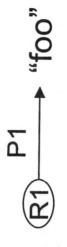

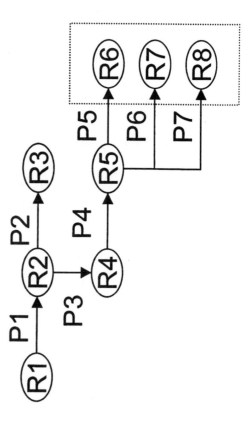

well. The syntax is expressed in XML, which I mentioned a little bit earlier. RDF provides the kind of architecture that will allow stakeholders to define the semantics, whether it is Dublin Core or Global Information Locator Service (GILS) or AACR2 or FGDC—you name it, the stakeholders get to do it. That is a very important aspect of this. RDF has been proposed, and it is in "Last Call" now. If it passes through Last Call, my understanding is that is will become an officially proposed recommendation in the W3C.

The reason for RDF's importance is that it provides a data model—a data model that is very flexible and will allow us to do lots of very good things with it. In its very simplest form, the RDF data model (see previous page) is nodes connected by named properties or "arcs." You have a little thing called R1 on one side. P1 is a property pointing to R2. That is really all it is—an arc and node model. It's very simple—but, of course, it is not that simple because you can do lots of very flexible things with it. The simplest thing you might want to do is a terminal node string. So you can say that R1 has a named property and the value of that named property is foo. You can hook these things together in grafts of arbitrary complexity that become RDF insertions or RDF statements that function as descriptive statements about that resource. *(continued on next page)*

The Dublin Core Data Model
(an application of the RDF data model)

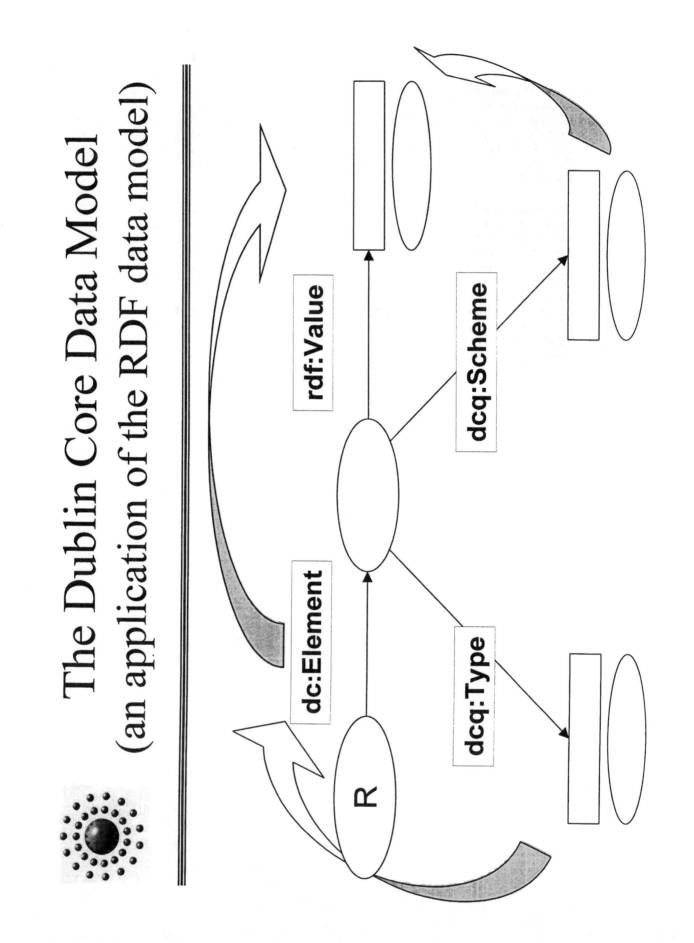

The Dublin Core community, which has had a substantial influence on this model, has its own application of the RDF data model (see opposite page), and it is structured like this: You have the resource on the left side. You have one of the 15 Dublin Core elements that is the named property pointing to an empty node in the middle (we called it a structural or intermediate node—it is just a little piece of structure that allows us to do some more interesting things). On the far right you have an RDF value, which is the value of the property that can either be a string or another node, and which can be further expanded. So, it is a very flexible model.

What do we actually do with the node in the middle? We hang some other properties on it. So, for example, we have something called Type Qualifier, and we also have something called Scheme Qualifiers. These two things are what we find in what we call a qualifier name space for the Dublin Core (DC). That is what I mean by DCQ—Dublin Core Qualifier. A DC element is in the DC name space, types and schemes are in the DC Qualifier name space.

What do these things actually do? A Type Qualifier gives us further information about the characteristics of the element itself, and a Scheme Qualifier gives us further information about the value that we are trying to assign to that element. The purpose of qualifying the element is to further qualify the value to give more information about the nature and the context of that value.

This is the basic Dublin Core version of the RDF data model. (*continued on next page*)

dc:Date

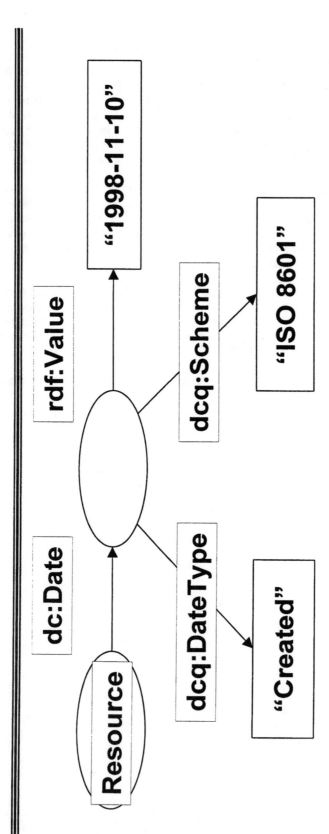

Let me give you an example. One of the top-level elements that has given us a lot of difficulty is the date element. As it turns out there are lots of different kinds of dates, and it is very important to be able to use the date element precisely. Using RDF we want to be able to provide qualifiers to describe much more specifically exactly what we are saying. One of the things we might want to explain is what we mean by the Date Type "created." It is a date of creation, but that still is not enough. Consider this date: 11/10/98. Depending on whether you are in Europe or in the United States, that date means two different things: 11/10/98 either represents the tenth day of November or the eleventh day of October. You won't know which date is meant unless you have a standard that tells you how to take that date apart in an authoritative manner and unless we tell you this standard is the scheme we are using. In this particular case, that standard is ISO-8601. ISO-8601 gives us a standard that says how the dates are arranged, so we can unambiguously take that date apart.

So in this system, we have qualifiers: We have an encoding scheme, ISO-8601. And we have a specified date, which is the date of creation. Using this RDF structure, we have given you a date that is very precise and unambiguous and can be taken apart by people or machines in an algorithmic and reliable way.

RDF can also be used to specify compound values, such as language types, in which case a machine could come in and take this apart and say: I am interested in the value of the subject here, but I am only interested in French, or I am only interested in English, or I am interested in all languages. You can do that, and the machine can take it apart in a way that is unambiguous.

Creator Names also can be problematic unless you know what structure is. We might want to have something called an LCNA—a Library of Congress Name Authority entry for author names. We might also want to have something not used by libraries but beginning to be used by the business community. It is called vCard. vCard is a sort of Internet business card, containing a structured, authoritative version of a name. You can use your own scheme in an RDF format so that you can take apart names in a way that your community understands, but with which other communities will still have a chance of extracting a useful name.

In Summary

Let me finish up here with a summary about Dublin Core and RDF. First of all, DC semantics are fairly widely accepted on the Net at this point. There are several hundred different projects using this in at least 20 different countries, and it has developed a fair amount of momentum. The mechanisms for qualifying it so that it can be used in a much more precise fashion are under development. The infrastructure is evolving rapidly. HTML has been used to encode metadata, but only in a clumsy way. RDF provides us for the first time with a flexible way to do a variety of different types of metadata. The tools to support these kinds of activity are beginning to appear. There are lots of tools that people are developing on their own, and there are also the browser manufactures starting to provide support for RDF in browsers. Interoperability testbeds are underway. One that some of you might be aware of is the CIMI testbed, involving a dozen or more museums and including some natural history museums.

If you want additional information on Dublin Core, we have a brand new homepage. You can get to it in Netscape just by typing Pearl\DC or by typing <http://purl.org.dc>. To learn more about RDF, see the RDF homepage at <http://www.w3c.org/RDF>.

Session 2

The Challenge in Species Discovery and Taxonomic Information

Doing the Impossible:
Creating a Stable Species Index and Operating a Common Access System on the Internet

FRANK BISBY, Director, Centre for Plant Diversity and Systematics, University of Reading, Species 2000

ABSTRACT

The Species 2000 Project is working with some novel techniques in its ambitious mission to create an index of the world's known species. One is the creation of stable taxonomic indexes for individual groups of organisms by the member organizations: the *Global Species Databases*. How may this be done? How may the taxonomy be stabilized yet fluid enough to accommodate change? Another is the creation of a *common access system* to address an array of such databases so that they can operate as a single virtual index covering all groups. If existing Global Species Databases are to be used, this becomes a demanding specification at the computer science level, quite apart from the challenge of forming a seamless index from the components that are compiled independently. The task may indeed be severe, but it is not impossible. Species 2000 can report progress in both areas.

I must admit, I was not initially delighted to receive this request to speak on "Doing the Impossible—Creating a Stable Species Index and Operating a Common Access System on the Internet." Apart from being the longest title I have ever had for a paper given in a symposium, I also felt that this might be a poisoned chalice. But I decided that, in fact, it provided a nice challenge, and I shall try to face that challenge.

Creating Stable Taxonomic Indexes

The first thing you need to know is that I have been working with a team of people around the world who call themselves Species 2000. Our motive is to create an index to the world's species—not by creating one database with a list of all the species in it, but, in fact, by setting up an interoperable system that, using a common access system, will address a central array of taxonomic databases. The second thing you need to know is that we have already made some structural plans regarding how to do that. We are trying to make a stable index—or what we call a Global Species Database (GSD)—for each taxon of organisms.

Clearly, there are many taxonomic databases around the world that have species checklists and taxonomic opinions at their call. Many of those databases are very good databases with excellent data in them. But if you think about taking those databases and using them as the source of information to make a universal list of all organisms, you run into two problems. One is that the data sets overlap. But worse than that, each of them has been internally optimized for one region of the world but not globalized among the different systems. So, if you were to put them together you not only would have to deal with the overlapping species, which might be classified differently in the different databases, but also with the fact that the species may be categorized in the taxonomic structure of families and orders and so on differently. Therefore, you cannot put these databases together end to end. You have to look inside them and rework them.

If you can persuade different communities around the world to create a global index, a global checklist of species for each taxon, then the organization that tries to compile a universal list does not have to understand how each database is structured. They can be put together end to end. Provided there are no overlaps, no demarcation disputes, then that is satisfactory from the point of view of a global list. So, this is the reason why we set ourselves the two tasks that are addressed in the title for this talk. First, how can different groups of specialists create a stable taxonomic index for each group of organisms? And second, how can we create a common access system on the Internet that will allow us to address those components?

My title begins with the words "Doing the impossible." The question to answer is, is the taxonomist capable of producing a stable species list? If the answer is "yes," the next question is, would that list be a useful thing to have? I am going to respond to this with two examples. The first is one that is very close to home. Those of you who know me know that I am a botanist and I work on legumes. For 11 years now, I have led an enterprise worldwide in which we have been creating a Global Species Database for legumes. It is on the Web as Legume Web. It has many faults, this project. It is far from being an ideal, but I can use it as a vehicle for explaining to you how it is that I believe we can make stable species indexes. I will then move away from being egocentric by discussing some of the other models, which will indicate how this is, in fact, a reasonably achievable goal throughout the community.

Legumes: A Global Species Database. With the legume database, we are talking about creating a list of species recognized to exist by specialists. That means that we must include not only taxa and the Latin names of taxa as some people accept them, but also synonyms and taxonomic opinion.

How have we tried to do this for the 19,000 legumes around the world? We have taken it as a two-stage process. For the first stage, we organized regional centers that have been compiling species lists of legumes for their parts of the world, and those lists are the starting material. In most cases the centers use the same software, and in most cases we had extreme difficulty—and still have extreme difficulty—in merging those databases together into one file.

The second stage is to get panels of experts for different groups of legumes. Legumes are normally thought of as falling into 32 tribes of plants. For each of the small tribes or for each of the large genera, we have anywhere from one to four monographic specialists around the world, thus creating a network approaching 100 people whom we contact to try and bring the taxonomic checklist into a responsible opinion.

One job of this network of people is to globalize, to establish a system of genera of the species that will function on all the continents. Of course, the regional data sets sent to us include some local features in the taxonomy. But we have to make sure that the features of acacias, for example, are treated the same way for African plants as they are for American plants as they for Australian plants. For example, one of the Australian acacia experts has decided that acacias should be divided into three genera. That may cause a problem if he has not stated where the African species or the American species would fit in those three genera. We get group panel specialists to say which system will work for the whole world.

Now, of course, the result is an opinion. And there are alternative schemes. The alternative schemes must be cross-indexed in the system through the synonyms, so you can see the data from another scheme if you go in using the preferred or default scheme that we have adopted.

So while we are going for a preferred or usable system, we are also cross-linking the alternatives. This is achieved through panels of experts, who subdivide the various tribes of plants. For example, a friend at the Royal Botanical Gardens is one of four people who work on the *Caesalpinia* tribe. He, in fact, is the one to whom others defer. He recently did his thesis on *Caesalpinia* and sorts that particular genus. So that database has been through two processes. It reflects the local expertise of which species are where, and it captures global taxonomic expertise to bring them together into a coherent system. It is available on the Web, at our Legume Web Service at <www.ILDIS.org>. That is just one example, then, of a team of people from around the world deeply imbedded in the taxonomic profession making a Global Species Database for one group of plants.

Going Beyond Legumes. How can that be accomplished for other groups of organisms? Well, there is not a single route to that destination. In fact, there are various routes. For instance, some organizations appear to me to be working in a region-by-region system. For example, we are talking to the producers of a mollusk database in the U.S.A. and a mollusk database in Paris. In some taxon-by-taxon systems, many of the families have been provided by special family experts putting them into the larger system. The International Legume Database and Information Service (ILDIS) used a combination of these two techniques. Some people start with the names from an index or from the zoological record. So Marshal Crosby, making the mollusk list for the world, started from the names—and, of course, some databases didn't inherit the taxonomy from specialists—and then worked with them to create the database. In the Philippines, experts are working on a fish base, but the baseline taxonomy comes from experts in California. Similarly, a database on bacteria takes its base list of species from the *International Journal of Systematic Biology* (IJSB). So these are different routes by which existing databases or data systems can approach this ideal of becoming part of a world species list.

Now the ideals here are very demanding. Once we thought we would not find one database in the world that met all the demands. We are now talking to 65 such database organizations around the world covering many more than 65 groups. And I have to say that my own project—ILDIS—comes fairly close, but it is certainly not completely there. The one that comes closest in my mind is the world's list of mammals based in the Smithsonian. The only question about it is whether or not the taxonomic expertise put into it is fully global or whether it, in fact, is rather restricted by the set of 20 Americans who developed it. But apart from that, it meets all the demands that I know of for such a system.

So, stable species lists do exist and I would contend that they can be produced and they can be maintained through time. They must be embedded deeply in the taxonomic community so that they can move forward and be fluid. Nobody is talking about their being frozen. Rather, we are talking about their being decoupled. We are talking about their together forming a responsible taxonomic consensus—a practical system decoupled from some of the minutiae of the day-to-day taxonomic debates that move to and fro.

Creating a Dynamic Access System

The second part of my talk is about how we are going to organize these different systems to be available on the Internet through a dynamic access system and what challenges are faced in creating that system. The key word here is *federated* systems. But federated systems are completely different levels of endeavor.

Let us look quickly at the different challenges that make what we were doing seem impossible and that were, to some of us, seemingly insurmountable at the start. I would like to report to you that we are making at least some progress with them.

At the top level, there is great complexity. We—the taxonomic community--are not a multinational organization telling its offices around the world how to use identical software and how to proceed. We are a moving, seething mass of heterogeneous, different databases around the world operating on various platforms and using different database management systems. Of course, this is the classic heterogeneity problem. We have to have interoperability by cross-mapping onto a very simple model at the center to ensure that we can get minimum data to and from those systems.

The Problem of Scalability. We have prototypes working for five or ten databases. Will this extend or operate nicely with 100 or more other systems?

The Problem of Autonomy. Autonomy is another issue. We need a model that makes it possible and desirable for participation by these different projects. We must accept their heterogeneity and learn to live with their autonomist behavior.

The Problem of Stability. Another issue is stability. You might think this is just a matter of there being an ice storm in Montreal or a tornado in the Philippines that puts all the systems out of commission for a day or two. Actually, the most frequent reason for the databases going down is because of internal management problems within multilayered institutions. So, I am at the University. I go away for a week to a conference and I get back and find that our server is down or our server is disconnected. Why? Because bureaucrats in the Computer Service Department changed the allocation of machines and a little piece of paper went around telling us about it six months before and that paper went to the head of the department and not to me. So, I get back and find that the system is disconnected, and it takes me two days to get it back up. Now, this happens in all multilayered institutions around the world. If you are confident that this never happened in your institution, then that is great—but just watch out. That is computer science.

There are other issues to consider with regard to stability, including the issue of interoperability and the question of which standards to use. One of our prototypes provided by the Japanese uses CORBA to link the different databases. It also is necessary to decide whether or not everything goes by a server hub and out to the databases. And this is where the question of stability comes in.

Clearly, we can replicate the servers by having mirror sites. But what about the actual taxonomic databases? At present if you go to the American site or the Japanese site and ask about legumes, you still go to the same server that holds the legume database. If that server is down, you will not get your reply about legumes. We have two ways of dealing with this. We are going to have a backup to the so-called "annual checklist." So, if you cannot get a live version for any sector, you will fall back to a static version. Of course we could also just duplicate each of the databases at the peripheral sites by having a second site holding each database.

The Problem of Taxonomic Knowledge. How are we going to create a seamless catalogue produced from these bits and pieces from different peoples' databases? The answer is that we know a great deal about how different databases vary. We do have a model we are working on, for which the main challenge is getting the name base and the taxon base interfaces to give a harmonious appearance.

The Problem of Demarcation and Overlaps. Of course, some of the databases have duplication. And it is not true that each species that is covered with a Global Species Database is covered only once. So, there are overlaps, and it becomes a question of shading in. For example, we may want, as a Global Species Database, to go to the Missouri Botanical Garden just for mosses and at that particular point in time have the flowering plants shaded out.

Pluralism, of course, worries people a great deal. They are a little bit afraid that our Species 2000 project is going to somehow impose on them, and that everybody will have to conduct research on a fish according to a certain person's system, or legumes according to somebody else's system. What we need is at least one good Global Species Database for each group of organisms. If we have two or three, then is that not a wonderful excess, for then we can then choose among them.

There is more than one world system for mammals, for fishes, and for bacteria. The list does not go a lot further than that for groups that are duplicated. Where we have duplicate groups, then there are at least two different user attitudes: Some people really know which system they want to use, and others do not care. The people who do not care often ask the question: Will you tell us the taxonomy that we can use just to name these organisms (which must be the same as the one you tell the other people down the street)? They need this question answered because if they use the same names, their data will match. So, in areas of taxonomy where there is pluralism, there is pressure for us to get some organization—maybe BIOSIS, which can monitor the uses around the world in the literature—to tell us which taxonomy to use for the default and for the people who do not care. But clearly you want to offer a choice to those people who do care, who want to follow a particular system for fishes or whatever.

The Problem of Missing Sectors. Another problem is missing sectors. The databases that we are working with, if they were full, would cover only 40 percent of the world's known organisms. So there is a remaining 60 percent to be done. We are working very carefully with the Organization for Economic Cooperation and Development (OECD) and with the Global Environment Facility (GEF) to try to make proposals as to how new projects might be started or existing projects might be diverted to achieve Global Species Database status.

The Problem of the Human Element. The human element—the sociology—is enormously important. The great institutions—the Smithsonian, the Royal Botanical Garden, the Missouri Botanical Garden—must come alongside network projects like the ILDIS project I described to you earlier, alongside smaller institutions, and alongside individual people whose whole careers have gone into making one database such as their personal property. All of these different databases have to be used, and we must figure out how to bring these people alongside each other in a federation.

Then there is the question of nationalism and regionalism. Our plan is a global plan, but there are almost no global resources. So, we have to set up Species 2000 Japan. We have to work with the Integrated Taxonomic Information System (ITIS) program here in the States. We have to work with the European Union to try and mobilize parts of the project with regional or nationalistic names on them even though they are part of the global program.

The Problem of Money. Lastly, of course is the question of whether to make things available for free or whether there has to be some cost recovery on the usage of systems. Desires and attitudes vary enormously around the world, and this is very troublesome to all global organizations. We are trying to live with a heterogeneity there as well.

So, these are the challenges that we continue to face. Scalability and autonomy are, in my opinion, more likely to trip us up on the computer science than on the system heterogeneity or the stability, which are our priorities. With taxonomic knowledge, we do know how to handle the heterogeneity. On demarcation, we have some ideas. On pluralism, I think we know how to handle it, but it is a very sticky issue with the taxonomist. The question is whether the taxonomists in a particular group of organisms will allow one system to be used or whether they will insist on slugging it out with alternatives.

Lastly, we are working very hard to draw many institutions together. We are also working very hard in Australia, in Europe, and in the U.S. and North America to make sure that nationalism does not pull us apart. We need to use national and regional funds, but we must aspire to a global program.

Conventions, Standards, and Consensus in Systematic Practice:
How Far Can (or Should) We Go?

PETER F. STEVENS, Professor of Biology, University of Missouri, St. Louis, and Curator, Missouri Botanical Garden

ABSTRACT

Different kinds of standards and conventions are first discussed. The Taxonomic Databases Working Group (TDWG) both endorses the use of particular standards and conventions to help improve interoperability between the various parts of systematics, and also actively promotes their development. Plant taxa of different levels of the hierarchy are in part convention but are not standards. Judicious application of both standards and convention can reduce the labor of describing species. The extent to which standards can be applied to reduce disagreement about the limits of species is discussed; it is argued that taxonomists cherish their opinions in part because of our poor understanding of this most basic of systematic operations. At the level of plant names, the International Plant Names Index (IPNI) aims to become a metastandard by developing bibliographic standards for plant names, initially focusing on a database of well over 1 million names of flowering plants. The database will be replicated, distributed, self-archiving, and will reflect corrections and additions (which can be made directly by anybody in the systematic community) in real time. A prototype module containing author names and abbreviations has been developed. IPNI will both use existing TDWG standards and develop new ones. It is a nomenclatural database, making no judgment on synonymy.

"The nice thing about standards is that you have so many to chose from; furthermore, if you do not like any of them, you can just wait for next year's model" (Tanenbaum 1981, 168).

The goal of this talk is to begin to explore the general issue of the role of standards, conventions and metadata in systematic practice in general and species and their description and delimitation in particular. After a few necessary definitions, I will talk very briefly about the activities of the Taxonomic Databases Working Group (TDWG) in promoting standards and developing metadata. I then will suggest that thinking about conventions and standards helps illuminate the nature of plant taxa, and in particular the constraints on how species are delimited. I then will show how TDWG standards and convention are integral to the developing International Plant Names

Index (IPNI) a database of plant names (initially flowering plants only). IPNI, with its bibliographic information on plant names, kept current and enabling linkages to other kinds of data, provides metadata useful in any biological project that uses the names of flowering plants. The standards developed, and others, can be used to simplify many aspects of systematic practice. Although we should try to standardize much of the routine of systematic work, the use of inappropriate standards can make answering some kinds of systematic questions difficult.

Standards, Conventions, Consensus and Metadata

First, some necessary definitions. A standard, to quote the *Oxford English Dictionary* is an "exemplar of measure or weight"—hence "an authoritative or recognized exemplar of correctness, perfection, or some definite degree of any quantity." A convention, on the other hand, is "a rule or practice based on general consent." The word convention quite often has negative connotations—it is artificial, arbitrary and formal, while a standard refers to something in the real world, or at least something we think is more important. Consensus, "the collective unanimous opinion of a number of persons," is one way in which standards and conventions become effective. Standards in particular come in a variety of flavors, and we can usefully distinguish here between *de facto, de jure,* and formal standards (the last are standards accepted by a standards body like the International Standards Organisation (cf. Mowbray & Malveau 1997)). Standards that deal with "correctness" can be called reference standards; if they refer to rules or actions necessitated by a body of systematic theory, they can be called rule-based standards; and if they deal with "some definite degree of any quantity," they can be called metric standards. These distinctions are not exclusive, but they do emphasize how heterogeneous "standards" are. Metadata are data about data, or data that underpin the use of data in a particular way; and standards and conventions are involved in the development of metadata.

The Taxonomic Databases Working Group (TDWG)

The International Working Group on Taxonomic Databases was set up in 1985 to establish international collaboration among database projects. Its goal is to aid in the dissemination and exchange of information by focusing on the common use and interpretation of terminology, data fields, dictionaries, common logical rules, and data relationships. Basically, it deals with metadata and standards. Initially botanical in focus, it has broadened out over the years, although there is a pressing need to become yet more active.

The role of TDWG is that of a facilitator, and it may evaluate and endorse existing standards or get groups of people together to make new ones. The kind of projects in which it has been involved include defining standards for data collection in economic botany (Cook 1995), geographic names (Hollis & Brummitt 1992), and abbreviations for authors (Brummitt & Powell 1992). It endorses such important standards as a format for recording and exchanging descriptive taxonomic data, DELTA (Descriptive Language for Taxonomy) (Dallwitz & Paine 1986), and the herbaria acronyms used when specimens are cited (Holmgren et al. 1990). Many such standards are in common use, greatly facilitating communication among biologists.

Of course, new authors describe new species for the first time, new herbaria are formed, and so new editions of these standards are produced, or, for the Web versions, they are kept current—and for our future efforts, that is where the emphasis will be. Indeed, with the decentralization now possible with such projects (see below), we need not get into the situation of having an out-of-date standard or a standard that is independently improved by different groups—parallel evolution here, as elsewhere, is the bane of systematics! As the need arises, we can develop new—and extend the coverage of—existing standards. Is there confusion in how botanists and zoologists cite collections? What about author and journal abbreviations and contractions across all groups, not just plants? As lists of taxa (this refers to groups at any level of the taxonomic hierarchy, from kingdom to variety) become ever more comprehensive, these are issues that we may need to consider. Codes of nomenclature are also standards and metadata, and again, there is a need to establish whether there is any call for a unified code of biological nomenclature.

Conventions, Standards, and Systematics

I begin by thinking of the higher levels of the taxonomic hierarchy—classes, families, genera, etc.—in the context of standards and conventions. If taxa at the same rank, e.g., a genus, were equivalent, this might provide some kind of metric for measuring diversity. However, for most systematists higher taxa are simply groups that contain one or usually more lower taxa. They may delimit groups that a systematist for some reason or other thinks are particularly interesting, but that does not convert to any equivalence of groups at the same hierarchical level (Stevens 1997a). There is widespread acceptance of the principle of monophyly, and this means that all higher taxa have to be monophyletic, i.e., contain all and only the descendents of a particular common ancestor, but this is a grouping, not a ranking criterion. However, not only is there still no consensus here, but monophyly is anyway a rule-based, not a metric, standard. Given the constraints of monophyly, it is convention driven by a need to communicate that leads us to give a named group a particular circumscription; we apply names at ranks like order, family, and genus to those parts of a taxonomy that are commonly used in teaching and in general communication between biologists (Angiosperm Phylogeny Group 1998: a phylogenetic naming system will not escape this need to act as a communication system), and so they are in the context a kind of reference standard. But whatever one's systematic philosophy, there is no measurement unit inherent in a biological classification. If I walk two miles, I have unarguably walked twice as far as if I had walked one mile; if my state has 500 genera of plants and yours has 1000, I cannot say that your state is twice as diverse as mine. Similarly, although it may be something of a convention to use numbers of species in estimates of diversity and amount of radiation (systematists have suggested ways of quantifying these), they, too, are a poor metric for this.

What about conventions and these species? Here I touch both on the act of writing descriptions and on how we go about circumscribing species—and I should say that nearly all the descriptive systematic work I do is on tropical plants.

Writing Descriptions Linnaeus used a brief, almost telegraphic style for his descriptions, and he defined and illustrated the terms he used (Linnaeus 1751). Over the years Linnaeus's definitions of shape terms and the like were modified and alternative usages crept into use. Definitions of some shape terms were reviewed by a committee formed under the aegis of the Systematics Association and their consensus published (Anonymous 1962) and adopted by Stearn (1992) in his invaluable "Botanical Latin." These have become reference standards, standards for communication, to be used as a matter of good practice by all systematists when describing plants. Unfortunately, they neither map onto discontinuities in nature nor provide a metric for shape. They are imprecise and even positively misleading if it is assumed that two taxa described as having, say, a differently-shaped lamina apex are thus necessarily assignable to two discretely different shapes, or if it assumed that two taxa with the same shape necessarily do not have discretely different shapes.

That the definitions of these shape terms, although accessible, are difficult to apply without reference to diagrams—yet they generally are so used—points to a problem with many reference standards. Accessibility and ease of use are essential for their adoption, for them to become standards *de facto*. This is particularly true of color standards, such as the set devised by Ridgway (1913) and published in a single edition of 4,000 copies. Its problems were evident by the middle of the century (Hanly 1949), but it is still in use, partly because Ridgway focused on colors common in the living world. But other color standards have inevitably (given the printing history of Ridgway's book, and the fact that the colors there are not all stable) come into use, and these include the Munsell and Royal Horticultural Society color charts, that proposed for British fungi (Henderson et al. 1969), and so on. These later standards are more accessible, although they may focus on different parts of the spectrum. In any case, many biologists prefer to use terms like "red," "violet," and "lilac"—terms in common use but without precise definitions.

Units for measuring size may be arbitrary in the sense that there are all sorts of units used by different cultures or groups. However, inches and centimeters are interconvertible, and they provide a metric by which measurements can be related to one another and manipulated in a way that is impossible with many biological descriptors, which are ultimately reference standards. Biological descriptors refer to a variety of kinds of objects, the extremes of which are terms like "ovule" and "radius"—structures that are thought to have arisen only once in the course of evolution—and "wing", "stipule", and "campylotropy"—for which there is no such evidence. The former often have more precise definitions and are commoner in vertebrate zoology than in flowering plants (e.g., cf. Peters 1964; Wheeler et al. 1993). Reference terms like "acute" are widely used, although not necessarily with identical definitions.

Circumscribing Species I find it unsettling that many of the operations we carry out as we look at specimens and estimate variation patterns—that is, much of systematic practice—amount to a convention, and a largely unanalyzed one at that (cf. Stuessy 1994, who stresses the development of "skills of intuitive pattern recognition," albeit in the context of well-studied temperate groups). The operational species concept many of us use (by "us," I mean systematists in general) is "a species is what a competent systematist says it is" (Regan 1926). This concept—or perhaps more accurately, convention—has been with us for over 150 years (e.g., Stevens 1991, 1997b). In practice this concept/convention has often been used to promote broadly delimited species, with a reduction in the numbers of species recognized being one of its useful results—a rather strange argument, one would have thought. Species are also explicitly based on discontinuities in variation pattern, and there are conventions for how much and what kind of variation is needed to indicate different levels in the taxonomic hierarchy at and below the level of species (e.g., Davis & Heywood 1963; Mayr & Ashlock 1981). But there is disagreement over such conventions, and subspecies and varieties may be differently defined by systematists in different countries (Hamilton & Reichard 1992), or the significance of variation ornithologists had previously called subspecific may be questioned (see Cracraft 1992, on the numbers of species of birds of paradise). It is still more unsettling to one who has long wished for closer links between academia and the museum to observe the lack of connection between those who theorize about the nature of species, a very active area and largely in academia, and those who describe species (McDade 1995), an area that is somewhat in regress and is largely carried out in museums.

A monographer is privileged—he or she can analyze material from throughout the range of a group, judiciously evaluate the variation, and make decisions about the limits of taxa with the "big picture" in mind. But without clarification of criteria for collecting and evaluating data on variation, this privilege amounts to little. I have recently been looking at a widely ranging species of *Rinorea* (Violaceae) growing from Myanmar and Hainan to Borneo (Jarvie & Stevens 1998; cf. Jacobs & Moore 1961). There is not one, but three species—one with two subspecies, and another two species are still to be described. Similarly, in a recent treatment of *Fagraea* (Gentianaceae), 42 species from Borneo are recognized, of which 24 are endemic, while in an earlier treatment the corresponding figures are 14 and 3 (Wong & Sugau 1996; cf. Leenhouts 1962). Importantly, in both cases material seen by the earlier authors was assigned by the later authors to different, and in *Fagraea,* often newly described species; little that was completely new had turned up in the intervening years. But if I ask the questions, Who is right? and why are there differences? it is remarkably difficult to provide answers. We are not sure of whether or not we are delimiting species for a herbarium taxonomist, and we are not sure of the significance of finding locally discontinuous variation that appears to break down in a geographically broader study (e.g., Stevens 1993; Cronk 1999). All too often we seem not to know why (for whom?) and how we should analyze variation (critical comments made by Heywood 1974, about taxonomy are still, unfortunately, all too relevant).

The answers to such questions go beyond the kind of convention and standard I have been discussing, although they start there. We desperately need to articulate what is involved in taxonomic practice if the cherished independence of systematists—the wish each of us has for our own opinions on the limits of species to be taken seriously—is to amount to much. We must work towards clarification of how we collect and analyze data, articulating reference and rule-based standards where necessary, and clarifying and justifying the role convention plays in the whole systematic process.

The International Plant Names Index

Although at the level of species delimitation we are dealing both with unruly nature and unruly naturalists, there are less problematical areas where standards, conventions, and metadata can facilitate the speed and ease with which we do our basic systematic work. The Plant Names Project and its main product, the International Plant Names Index (IPNI), serves to illustrate this.

The names in IPNI will be those currently in the Index Kewensis, based at the Royal Botanic Gardens, Kew; the Gray Herbarium Index, at Harvard; and the Australian Plant Names Index, at Canberra. IPNI will initially include well over 1,000,000 names of flowering plants, and we hope to extend the coverage to all vascular plants in the current phase of the project. In short, it aims to be an authoritative list of all plant names and their place of publication, kept current, freely available and query-able, decentralized, and maintained with a minimum of bureaucracy. It will of course take some time to meet all these ambitious goals. (Further details of the project may be found in Croft et al. (submitted) <http://pnp.huh.harvard.edu>.)

The names will reside in a distributed database, and although only the three institutions just mentioned are involved at present, IPNI is designed to be highly scalable. All new names appearing (including citations of types specimens—types are themselves standards that allow us to relate names to plants with the minimum of ambiguity) will be added from Kew, Harvard, or Canberra and will be accessible as soon as they are added. TDWG standards for geography, abbreviations, and contractions of names and journals, etc., will be followed; these standards, too, will be kept current and generally accessible.

Of considerable importance is the submissions module that has been developed. There are four aspects of the submissions mechanism that I want to mention here. First, although these changes will appear in IPNI as soon as they are made, it will be clear to all users that they have not been checked. Editors, whether of particular taxa, particular types of names (e.g., names described by Linnaeus), or of particular directories (e.g., periodical lists), will check the changes. Second, any and all changes suggested will become part of the permanent contribution history of that record, and this history, too, can be accessed by users. Third, by making it easy for the whole community to submit additions and corrections, the difficult process of editing and verifying the existing entries will be greatly facilitated. Fourth, the submission module itself can be adapted for a variety of uses, so it, too, can become a kind of standard. For instance, it could serve as the mechanism by which names proposed for a phylogenetic naming system are recorded.

IPNI is a nomenclatural list, including the original citation of a name and, where possible, that of its type specimen. Any name referring to vascular plants should be traceable in it, and for most purposes the information it contains will function as metadata, serving to ground names in the literature. To IPNI can be linked images of the protolog, including any illustrations, images of the type, etc. It can be mirrored to institutions and projects, and all projects linked with it will be synchronized with it and kept up-to-date with the information it contains, while corrections to it made in the course of work on any of these projects can be made immediately accessible to all.

Conclusions

Much of the work of describing species and writing floras and checklists is almost formulaic. Reference standards and conventions for journal abbreviations, citation of type and other specimens and of synonymy, etc., are very desirable, and their use should be promoted by groups like TDWG, professional societies, etc. They certainly should become *de facto* standards, if not formal standards, and failure to use them leads to the waste of an inordinate amount of time by systematics. Reference standards may be arbitrary. There may be more than one way of handling journal and book abbreviations and contractions, but so long as the way adopted works, its principles are explicit, and the consequences of its adoption are understood. That is all that matters. Until fairly recently it was a rite of passage for all new flora projects to argue interminably about how names should be handled—should the Australian botanist Ferdinand von Mueller be F. von Muell., F. Mueller, F. v. M., or something else? With a list of author names and abbreviations, this need no longer happen; we can use either a full name or a single contraction. The fewer standards covering such aspects of a species description, the more our work will be speeded up; this is not an area where having several standards is a good thing (cf. the epigraph). Simplification and standardization not only speeds up our work, but it makes it much easier for a student to understand what we are doing. But there are circumstances in which the use of a particular standard may be inappropriate. For writing a flora, the use of plain language and of reference standards such as those in Stearn (1992) is essential, but metric standards are needed for actually deciding on the limits and relationships of species. Here more than one standard is involved. (Note that metric standards can be converted accurately to reference standards, but the reverse operation may well introduce imprecision (see also Heywood 1984).)

I have barely begun to explore the role and interaction of standards, conventions, and metadata in systematics. However, thinking of such issues in the context of systematic practice will help us to understand better what we do, to gather appropriate data more quickly, and will allow meaningful consensus over the limits of the taxa we use to describe the living world—and this makes the important link to projects like ITIS, BONAP, and Species 2000.

Acknowledgements

I thank W. L. Alverson, D. E. Boufford, J. Cadle, N. Cross and F. Pando de la Hoz for helpful discussion. The support of the NSF and USGS (NSF DEB-9726045 and DBI-9808220) is gratefully acknowledged.

References

Angiosperm Phylogeny Group. 1998. An ordinal classification for the families of flowering plants. *Ann. Missouri Bot. Gard.* 85:531-553.

Anonymous. 1962. Systematics Association committee for descriptive biological terminology II. Terminology of simple symmetrical plane shapes (Chart 1). *Taxon* 9:145-156, 245-247.

Brummitt, R. K., and C. E. Powell. 1992. *Authors of plant names.* Royal Botanic Gardens, Kew.

Cook, F. E. M. 1995. *Economic botany data collection standards.* Royal Botanic Gardens, Kew.

Cracraft, J. 1992. The species of the birds-of-paradise (*Paradisaeidae*): Applying the phylogenetic species concept to a complex pattern of differentiation. *Cladistics* 8:1-43.

Croft, J., N. Cross, E. Nic Lughadha, P. F. Stevens, J. G. West, and G. Whitbread. Plant names for the 21st century: The International Plant Names Index, a distributed data source of general accessibility. *Taxon*, accepted.

Cronk, Q. C. B. 1998. The ochlospecies concept. Ch. 11 in: Huxley, C.R., J. M. Lock, and D. F. Cutler (eds), *Chorology, Taxonomy and Ecology of the African and Madagascan Floras.* Kew Bulletin Additional Series, H.M.S.O., London.

Dallwitz, M. J., and T. A. Paine. 1986. *User's guide to the DELTA system.* Ed. 4. Division of Entomology, Commonwealth Scientific and Industrial Research Organisation, Australia.

Davis, P. H., and V. A. Heywood. 1963. *Principles of angiosperm taxonomy.* Oliver & Boyd, Edinburgh.

Hamilton, C. W., and S. H. Reichard. 1992. Current practice in the use of subspecies, variety and form in the classification of wild plants. *Taxon* 41:485-498.

Hanly, D. H. 1949. Robert Ridgway's color standards. *Science* 109:605-608.

Henderson, D. M., P. O. Orton, and R. Watling. 1969. *British fungus flora.* Vol. 1. H.M.S.O., Edinburgh.

Heywood, V. H. 1974. Systematics—the stone of Sisyphus. *Bot. J. Linn. Soc.* 6:169-178.

Heywood, V. H. 1984. Electronic data processing in taxonomy and systematics. pp.1-15 in Allkin, R. and F. A. Bisby (eds), *Databases in systematics.* Academic Press, London.

Hollis, S. and R. K. Brummitt. 1992. *World geographic scheme for recording plant distributions.* Hunt Institute for Botanical Documentation, Carnegie Mellon University.

Holmgren, P. K., N. H. Holmgren, and L. C. Barnett. 1990. *Index herbariorum. Part 1. The herbaria of the world.* Ed. 8. New York Botanical Gardens, New York.

Jacobs, M., and D. M. Moore. 1971. Violaceae. pp. 179-212 in van Steenis, C. G. G. J. (ed.), *Flora malesiana.* Series 1, Vol. 7. Wolters-Noordhoff, Groningen.

Jarvie, J. K., and P. F. Stevens. 1998. New species and notes on Violaceae and Flacourtiaceae from Indo-Malasia. *Harvard Pap. Bot.* 3:255-264.

Leenhouts, P. W. 1962. Loganiaceae. pp. 293-387 in van Steenis, C. G. G. J. (ed.), *Flora malesiana.* Series 1, Vol. 6. Wolters-Noordhoff, Groningen.

Linnaeus, C. 1751. *Philosophia botanica...* Kiesewetter, Stockholm.

Mayr, E., and P. D. Ashlock. 1981. *Principles of systematic zoology.* Ed. 2. McGraw Hill, New York.

McDade, L. A. 1995. Species concepts and problems in practice: Insights from botanical monographs. *Syst. Bot.* 20:606-622.

Mowbray, T. J., and R. C. Malveau. 1997. *Corba design standards.* John Wiley, New York.

Peters, J. A. 1964. *Dictionary of herpetology.* Hafner, New York.

Regan, C. T. 1926. Organic evolution. *Rep. British Assoc. Adv. Sci.* 1925, 75-86.

Ridgway, R. 1912 (1913). *Color standards and color nomenclature.* The Author, Washington, D.C.

Stearn, W. T. 1992. *Botanical Latin.* Ed. 4. David and Charles, Newton Abbott.

Stevens, P. F. 1990. Species: Historical perspectives. pp. 302-311 in Keller, E. F., and E. Lloyd (eds), *Keywords in Evolutionary Biology.* Harvard University Press, Cambridge, Mass.

Stevens, P. F. 1997a. How to interpret botanical classifications—suggestions from history. *BioScience* 47:243-250.

Stevens, P. F. 1997b. J. D. Hooker, George Bentham, Asa Gray and Ferdinand Mueller on species limits in theory and practice: A mid-nineteenth-century debate and its repercussions. *Hist. Records Austral. Sci.* 11:345-370.

Stuessy, T. F. 1994. *Case studies in plant taxonomy: Exercises in applied pattern recognition.* Columbia University Press, New York.

Tanenbaum, A. S. 1981. *Computer networks.* Prentice Hall, Englewood Cliffs, New Jersey.

Wong, K. M., and J. B. Sugau. 1996. A revision of *Fagraea* (Loganiaceae) in Borneo, with notes on related Malesian species and 21 new species. *Sandakania* 8:1-93.

Discover Life in America & the Database Needs of the All-Taxa Biodiversity Inventory (ATBI) of Great Smoky Mountains National Park

JOHN PICKERING, Associate Professor at the Institute of Ecology, University of Georgia; Chair of Discover Life in America

ABSTRACT

Discover Life in America is a volunteer science and education non-profit organization designed to study, use, conserve, and enjoy the diversity of life. Our goal is to forge a partnership among scientists, students, and other citizens both to teach and to learn while doing science. Everyone can contribute to the knowledge needed to better manage and protect biodiversity and thus improve our environmental health and economic well-being. Our first mission is to complete a comprehensive study of all the species in Great Smoky Mountains National Park—an All-Taxa Biodiversity Inventory (ATBI). As we gain synergy from this geographically focused effort, we will share our experience and help studies and educational programs elsewhere. Here I focus on how information technology, including our Web site <www.discoverlife.org>, can help us to coordinate our activities, provide training and research guidance, and collect and disseminate information on the taxonomy, identification, natural history, and ecology of species.

Globally we are faced with a colossal challenge. In the next several decades, we must document and understand the natural history, environmental requirements, distribution, and ecological function of millions of species. If we succeed, we will be able to manage natural communities wisely and continue to benefit from our planet's natural bounty. If we fail, many species will be lost forever, ecosystem functions and services will decline, and our environmental and economic well-being will be threatened. Better scientific understanding and successful education programs could reverse the ongoing, widespread environmental decline. However, the world's scientific and educational communities must make fundamental changes in their modi operandi if we are to succeed. The task at hand is too large for those currently involved in science and education to accomplish. So much information needs to be collected, analyzed, and distributed that we cannot rely on traditional means. We must change our ways, involve the public, and embrace informational technology—most notably, we need to build a trained army of individuals who collect and share scientific information via the Internet.

The number of species on the planet is unknown. Current estimates generally range by an order of magnitude, from 3 to 30 million, possibly more. Yet fewer than 1.5 million species have been named scientifically, and we know little about the biology of most of these. If the current rate of habitat destruction continues, we are likely to lose many potentially beneficial species before they are known to science. Without changing our methods and organizational structure to meet the challenge, there are simply too few taxonomists and ecologists to get the basic information on each species in time to assure that human pressures will not be responsible for mass extinction. We need to develop better ways to allow non-specialists, particularly students, teachers, and amateur naturalists, to supplement the efforts of professional scientists.

Here I consider how we might organize and coordinate such an army of individuals, describing a goal of a new organization, Discover Life in America, to coordinate a large, comprehensive study of all the species in Great Smoky Mountains National Park (GSMNP) in eastern North America. I will address some of the difficulties in mustering students and others to help professional scientists collect quality data and posit possible technical solutions that we may wish to develop to help in our global endeavor.

All-Taxa Biodiversity Inventory of the Great Smokies

Discover Life in America has started an All-Taxa Biodiversity Inventory (ATBI) of the Great Smoky Mountains National Park (GSMNP). The ATBI will collect information on the distribution, abundance, and natural history of the estimated 100,000 species that inhabit the Park. Our goal is to disseminate information that is useful in resource management, science, education, and recreation. In particular, we wish to make detailed information on the natural history and ecology of all species available to the wider, non-specialist audience. We plan to develop interactive identification guides and Web pages for each species. We will make these available through our site's Flora & Fauna section. While completing the ATBI, we will develop methods, train personnel, and form partnerships that will facilitate inventories of other parks and conservation areas.

Our Park offers several advantages for such a comprehensive study. Its geography, geology, and climate have made the Smokies one of the areas of highest species richness in the temperate zone, possibly rivaled in diversity only by parts of eastern

China. It is geographically located near many universities, museums, and other research centers, and it has a large user constituency—an estimated 9 million visitors annually. The Park contains over 500,000 acres, including the largest remaining stands of eastern old-growth forest, which total over 100,000 acres. Its terrain can be rugged and boasts 16 mountains over 6,000 feet.

Of the estimated 100,000 species within the Park, less than 10 percent have been documented to occur within the park's boundaries and many—on the order of 10 percent—are likely to be new species to science. Because of the large number of species that need to be studied and because of the logistic difficulty of sampling such an extensive, rugged area, Discover Life in America hopes to team volunteers with scientists to more effectively complete the study. If one assumes that each scientist on average will oversee the study of 100 species, then it is evident that each scientist is likely to need considerable help in sampling the park to understand the distribution, habitat requirements, and natural history of their organisms. Furthermore, they will need help in photographing specimens, building geo-referenced databases, Web pages, and interactive identification guides for each taxon.

By developing local, national, and international partnerships among educators, researchers, resource managers, and other concerned citizens, the ATBI gives individuals from all walks of life an opportunity to study nature. In helping with the research, school and community participants will get hands-on experience with scientific methods and state-of-the-art technology. Students will do science, use technology, and learn valuable skills, such as how to collect, process, and present information in a meaningful way. They will learn to discover the diversity of life and uncover its wonders. We invite individuals who are interested in contributing to go to our Website at <http://www.discoverlife.org>, register under "Get Involved," and then contact us. In addition to research professionals, we encourage nature lovers from all walks of life—teachers, naturalists, photographers, writers, and others, young or old—to become involved.

Obstacles to Overcome

To enable an individual who is not a taxonomic expert to contribute useful data to the ATBI, we must be vigilant about data quality. We must build the appropriate checks and balances to allow us to understand the source and approximate the level of accuracy of each datum. For an army of volunteers to collect data and present information on a global scale, we are presented with the additional challenge of coordinating, assembling, and presenting their efforts. The World Wide Web is a wonderful tool to assemble and present information—but how reliable is what it yields? How do we oversee the quality of information that we collect and present? Extensive sampling by volunteers could contribute significantly to our knowledge of the distribution of species and of their habitat requirements, for example. Conversely, the inclusion of misidentified specimens into geo-referenced databases could cause considerable confusion about ranges and detract from the value of the ATBI.

The data that we need to collect have a fairly simple structure. For the most part, they pertain to documenting events in time and space. Events such as observations, collections, photographs, sound recording, sensor reading, and molecular and chemical analyses will need to be databased. For each event, critical data will include (1) WHO (or what) collected the information; (2) WHEN it was collected; (3) WHERE it was collected; (4) WHAT it is or pertains to; (5) HOW it was collected; and (6) RELATIONSHIP or link to other events in the data structure. We anticipate using barcodes and other methods to assign a unique identifier to each event. These unique identifiers will allow us to track event handling, such as the distribution of barcoded vials and specimens to taxonomists. They will also facilitate linking parent-child relationships, such as the processing of parasites from a host, and analyzing individual events as members of a set, such as generating species maps from the WHERE of individual specimens.

Although the exact fields and structure of the database have yet to be chosen, we need to address certain issues and select standards to meet our needs. For example, the WHO variable will be critical in determining the level of confidence that we can place in an event's data records. We need to make sure that each WHO participating in data collection and analysis is uniquely identified from other participants. We should also specify WHO's level of expertise and update this level as WHO is trained. Thus, we should be able to put confidence weights on the level of data reliability over time for each participant.

Similarly, how should we standardize WHEN and WHERE across the database? Will date and time be Y2K compatible? Should WHERE be specified in latitude and longitude so that the data are globally accessible, or in UTM coordinates so that they can integrate into the Park's Geographic Information Systems (GIS), or both? How should we document and use confidence intervals for WHERE? Such records will include everything from very accurate GPS or surveyors' measurements to historical information from museum specimens that simply state location as GSMNP. These are questions that need to be resolved. We seek help and advice and do not wish to reinvent the wheel.

We have divided up taxonomic responsibilities into approximately 20 taxonomy teams that will coordinate the activity of their members and oversee and correct the work of the volunteers working with them. These teams are listed under "Who's Involved" on our Website. For each species within a taxon, team members will oversee the answering of questions such as: How do we identify it? What is its name? Or who will name it, if it is new to science? Are we going use the taxonomy in ITIS or the Species 2000 Project as authority files? Where can the species be found in terms of both latitude-longitude and habitat type? How is the species observed or captured? How does it make a living? What is its importance in the ecosystem? What is the effect of rainfall, deforestation, and fragmentation on the species?

For each species we intend to build a homepage with text, images, and, when appropriate, video and sound recordings. Because of the labor involved with building these Web pages, we anticipate that much of this work will be done by students under the supervision of teachers. To date, over 300 pages have been started by students at the University of Georgia and by elementary and secondary students who are participating in our program to enable teachers of minority students to study biodiversity and put their findings on the Web. Ultimately, these pages will be refined and edited under the supervision of taxonomic experts. We also intend to link them to our database, in part so that distribution maps can be dynamically generated.

The primary scientific impediment to our success in studying the planet's multitude of life is our inability to identify it. If we cannot tie event records together with correct names, we will have a jumble of disjunct facts. The participation and training of taxonomists who can put names on species and build identification guides is the first essential step in the process of collecting the information that we need about each species. Because non-experts cannot contribute to the wealth of knowledge about a species if they cannot identify it, we intend to build interactive keys on the Web that will allow students and others to identify species easily, using images and non-technical characters as much as possible. We are developing a software package called "20 Questions." When finished, the goal of this software is to create a tool to identify all species. The computer will ask the user up to 20 questions about a specimen, tell you what you have, and then link to the species homepage. We have developed a demonstration of this technology for species of *Rogadinae*, a subfamily of parasitic wasps (see "Identification Guides" under "Flora & Fauna").

Our database planning is being coordinated in conjunction with USGS-BRD. Our initial plans include using commercially available Biota software to manage data entry and specimen-based event records. We intent to integrate machines running Biota into a network that includes a Unix-based SQL database, so that records can be uploaded and downloaded. Eventually, as we empower numerous volunteers to collect and contribute data, I envision that we will develop the ability to submit data directly through forms on the Web.

Coda

The ATBI is a long-term project that we hope can be accomplished in 15 years. If successful, we will achieve a comprehensive understanding of the species and community interactions within the Great Smokies. In terms of general principles, we will gain scientific understanding on a scale and resolution never attained before from any ecological study. With regard to the Smokies specifically, Park managers will be able to better manage their natural resource using broad-based knowledge of numerous taxa.

If we can successfully develop and implement an information management system that allows non experts to collect useful data on the distribution and natural history of species, we will have a very powerful tool to extend the technology beyond the Park. Ultimately, I envision having a palm-size device that will combine existing technologies so that novices can contribute to inventories as they walk along trails. Such a device might include an interactive key to allow them to identify plants and caterpillars, a global positioning system to record their exact location, a digital camera to take voucher photographs, and the ability to communicate with the Internet from remote locations. With a press of a few buttons, a photograph is automatically sent documenting a WHO, WHAT, WHEN, WHERE, HOW, RELATIONSHIP between a plant and insect.

Yes, the challenge of inventorying life is colossal. But we could complete it in time.

Taxonomic Information Systems—
Stability through Diversity

HUGH WILSON, Professor of Biology and Curator, Departmental Herbarium, Texas
A&M University

ABSTRACT

Biodiversity data are, by necessity, linked to taxa. This linkage is established at the headwaters of data flow—the scientific literature—and retained to the end point in that most clients will query biodiversity data using taxon names. While taxonomic names provide a symbolic "hook" for information linked to a given entity, the overall classification system expresses a nested array of biological relationships among taxa, i.e., a structure that allows interpretation and extrapolation of biodiversity data. This fundamental importance of classification systems as a source of stability and structure is countered by the simple fact that classification systems are inherently unstable. Continuous modification of classification systems is an ongoing response to new knowledge and scientific progress. This changing superstructure for biodiversity data presents minimal problems beyond the digital arena in that data are presented in a fixed (hardcopy) taxonomic context. However, the increased potential for metadata development via digital technologies will not be realized until procedures are in place that allow data placement within a dynamic or fluid taxonomic information matrix. These procedures will be difficult to develop via a centralized nexus of "standardization" or "authority" that carries a limited base of expertise or representation relative to the relevant scientific community. The digital network provides a new medium through which interactive development could be accomplished among a global community of taxonomic specialists. This path of "distributed" development, possibly mediated by extant professional societies, would incorporate the broadest range of expertise and also by default, allow progress toward a dynamic biodiversity data system via consensus-based decisions.

I attended an NSF-funded workshop on roughly similarly topics in 1996, in San Diego, and the result of that workshop was essentially nil. As you can see if you go to the home page describing the workshop, there is really no product. The "product" represented a mixture of grandiose schemes, competing programs, and a lot of jargon. It sidestepped some of the fundamental problems involved with the expression of biodiversity data on the Internet.

So, what I would like to do today is touch on at least one of these problems in some detail. This perspective that I am presenting has to do with my work as Chair of the Internet Communications Committee for the American Society of Plant Taxonomists and also as a functioning member of the Texas A&M working group that is dealing with reporting biodiversity data to the network. I do not represent either group, but my perspective is based on the work that I have done with these groups.

This symposium is concerned with enhanced data flow from various producers of various sorts to the ultimate consumer. The consumer is of utmost importance in the sense that this is where the data are going to be applied. The "metadiversity" notion certainly relates to levels of complexity in linking complex data resources to other complex data resources in ways that are yet to be defined.

Certainly open access is of primary importance. The producers have to have open access to the system to be able to develop data resources, and the consumers—wherever they may be—have to have open access to the product. So, you cannot operate or proceed with regard to biodiversity expression without assuming that it is the diversity of information itself that is of primary consideration. As scientific specialists, we have our concerns about the array of taxa and complex interlinkages and data structures and so on.

The Mission

Our primary mission must be to put fundamental, basic biodiveristy information on the Web and to make that information available for both specialists and nonspecialists to examine. This involves a data "triage." Since there is no way all the information can be put out there right from the beginning, things have to be prioritized. The highest-profile bits of information have to be established as the highest priority. Our discussion of metadata seems to me to be a bit premature when we really have not dealt with putting in the fundamental bits of information that are needed to, for instance, determine the distribution of species X, (a fairly simple problem): What is the distribution of species in genera X across North America? This is a fundamental question for which we really do not have a good answer at this point in time.

Certainly, another assumption is that whatever goes on with regard to metadiversity—or whatever else is going to go on the Web—is going to happen within an environment that is provided by the browser. And that environment requires that the systems established are fast and can deal with whatever problems there might be on the network, thus allowing the user to access both text and image data as quickly as possible. Again, we have to assume that access to the Web sites that express biodiversity data is going to be multifaceted in terms of the user base. Technicians, scientists, and specialists can certainly use the Web, but it has to be designed in such a way that the broadest user base—including users such as decision-makers in administrative positions—can also grasp the information that is provided.

As has been referenced here many times, the applications for this information may not yet be defined. In relation to this, let's look at vascular plants. My area is in vascular plants and I am a bit biased. But the fact is that if you look at any system that relates to biodiversity in general, you are dealing primarily with vascular plants. For example, the Texas Parks and Wildlife Department provides a brief summary of the natural areas of Texas, which are defined in terms of the vascular plants occurring in these regions. Certain plants are, in fact, indicator species. Those that are dominant in certain areas can be used to define regions. Vascular plants also are indicators of diversity, because the relative pattern of diversity expressed by vascular plants is very often concordant with the pattern of diversity that we find in other organisms. You can extend this concept to a national—or even global—level, and biotic regions can be defined by the vascular plants present.

On the World Wide Web, you can go to <http://www.csdl.tamu.edu/FLORA/b98/check98.htm> and find a map that provides a graphic view of relative diversity of vascular plant taxa across the United States, Puerto Rico, and the Virgin Islands. The map is color-coded and illustrates the diversity mapping systems that we have developed based on 70,000 records. It includes not only accepted taxa (about 30,000+) but also geographic checkpoints at the state level for each taxon. These maps are generated "on the fly," and they can be generated for any taxonomic level. You can look at all vascular plants and their subclasses, as well as orders, families, genera, and so on, in this way. It gives you an immediate view of relative diversity of vascular plants across, in this case, the United States. The system can be applied to a single state within the country using a segmented color-coded item. Again, the maps are generated on the fly. There is a counter that racks up the number of taxa, as well as a device that allows the color-coding to be done for California and Texas, pretty diverse states with regard to vascular plants. The point here is that the pattern of diversity among arthropods and whatever else is probably concordant with this pattern. Therefore, vascular plants are fundamental, and you can examine a Web site or an informatics resource and very quickly determine its content by what it has available in terms of vascular plants.

With this particular mapping system, each state is a segment. Not only can it be color-coded depending on how many taxa it carries, but also you can click on a state and get a text listing of the taxa that occur in that state. So, for example, a click on Texas will produce 6,000+ lines—two megabytes of text file—and give you a full listing of the entities in the vascular plant world that occur in Texas. In addition, it is interlinked—that is, these listings are coupled with references to other sources. We have links to fish and wildlife services, vegetation and regional maps for Texas, county-level maps for California, images of varying sorts involved with this other index system, and a map for a given taxon.

The Application of Names

The fundamental item of importance relative to this discussion is the array of taxa. This array provides a "hook" for biodiversity information, metadata, and so on. These individual entities also provide a view of biological structure. The placement of infra-specific groups, species within genera, and so on, is an interpretation of reality symbolized by the application of names.

As a result, the system of classification as expressed here is of fundamental importance. It serves two functions. It gives a picture of biological reality and relationships. It also provides individual hooks for bits of information—whether they be images or other entries for the taxa involved.

So, with regard to taxonomic structure, we have an array of names. There has been a lot of discussion of names here. Names fundamentally are in the public domain. The scientific names are comparable to musical notes in that anybody can access notes and put them together any way they want. The difference with regard to taxonomic structure or classification systems is that the array—the hierarchy that is established by a classifier—is the result of expertise, a lot of work, and personal investment, and is personally expressed. As a result, it is comparable to a score of music, a compilation of music. And as a result of that, it is owned. It associated with an individual.

Taxonomic Structure

Taxonomic structure will vary. There are different perspectives on the array of diversity that one finds in vascular plants or other taxa. This variance can occur depending on the geographic range covered by the system. For example, if you combine North America and Mexico, you get a different picture than you would have for each country separately. It relates to interpretations and applications of the international code of botanical nomenclature for vascular plants. It can change daily on the basis of research, different views generated by data that relate to relationships, and—finally and most importantly—taxonomic opinion. We have the USDA Plants Database, which carries at its Web site over 35,000 taxa of plants (many of economic importance). The classification system expressed there has some synonymy involved—that is, decisions made are based at the USDA. Also, the National Institutes of Health (NIH) has access to genetic information through its Biotechnology Information Center. There is less synonymy here, but there is a full-blown classification at the species level. This is another federal-based item that has a structure, a foundation established locally.

Fully synonymized checklists for vascular plants available on the network today have only one source—the Biota of North America Program in North Carolina. The first display of this information on the Web was produced at Berkeley through the Museum Informatics Program there. A digital checklist provides both mapping and listing. The version is concordant with the published version of the BONAP checklist, which was dated 1994. I learned today that the 1996 version of the BONAP, listed both in terms of the taxonomic structure generated by John Kartesz and the distribution information also generated by John Kartesz at BONAP, is now available.

The U.S. Federal Standard established by ITIS has been referred to here many times as the NBII. I am not sure of the connections between these groups. It is directly associated with the USDA Plants Database, evidently a direct transfer of the BONAP checklist to ITIS. As a result it also is the 1996 version. There were 6,000 changes between 1996 and 1998 for this checklist. But the version expressed at the ITIS site today is two years old, so those 6,000 changes are not expressed there.

The most recent expression of this very critical data set with regard to vascular plant information on the Web is at our site, which does express this 1998 version of the BONAP classification system, including the structure implied by that classification system and the distribution of information. Now a standard is possible.

Agreeing to a Standard

There has been discussion today about following the ITIS nomenclature for the Discover Life in America program. ITIS taxonomy has also been discussed for use in other programs. However, does ITIS represent a valid, legitimate standard that will be followed by those working in the area? There are many difficulties involved. These systems are very complicated, but they are also a moving target. A standard becomes immediately obsolete if it is published in hardcopy. This is because it is under constant revision and constant update, and as data becomes available it is just going to change. That, fundamentally, is the beauty of digital classification systems—that they can change immediately, that they can be updated immediately online. It is a very diffuse target and there are many variants. A lot of difficulties, including authority ownership and general "turf" problems, are involved with the development of the standard, both in terms of the source of the standard and from the perspective of those using the standard.

Finally, with regard just to vascular plants: Putting aside the insects, the viruses, and so on, you are looking at a very large and complex array of biotic entities. You have, for the area covered by the BONAP program (the United States, Puerto Rico, and the Virgin Islands), 30,000+ species organized into 290+ families. And there are variants available within any element of that hierarchy. So, it is a difficult task and not one to be quickly sidestepped if you are considering expression of metadata or any sort of data as a function of vascular plants.

In terms of expressing this information on the network, there are various options. I don't pretend to offer up a solution to the problem, but basically if something is going to be done that is functional, it will have to move beyond talking, jargon, and competing centers of development. It is going to have to be inclusive. You cannot have one person—John Kartesz at the BONAP program in North America—providing a standard for the global user base. It is not going to work and it is not going to be acceptable. You have to tap in to the full community of active folks in plant taxonomy. There has to be some sort of input involved. The computational system is set up in such a way that movement with regard to classification is a doable item on the network. It certainly is not an impossible task. And certainly any effort to develop a standard should focus on the fact that it is a reference and that the user would benefit if, in areas of controversy or uncertainty, different optional alignments could be expressed, both in terms of the classification and the underlying associated data.

Just looking at distribution, you can imagine what has to be done. But it can be done computationally to show the distribution between a species and a subspecies, depending on the rank of the entity. Certainly, with regard to anything that is produced by the federal government or any publicly supported entity, open access needs to be defined to include anybody who wants to download the information in a form that can be incorporated into whatever task is to be performed.

A Role for Professional Societies

You can't have the individuals or groups that are providing this fundamental bit of information be invisible at the site presenting that information. There has to be some sort of remuneration within the commerce of the Web that is relevant to contributors. And certainly the full community, again, has to be involved in the enterprise. Certainly a possible path for development—a path that we have recently proposed to NSF be at least explored through the Web site of the American Society of Plant Taxonomists—is to first of all focus on the Internet as a medium, not only for expression of information but also to use as an "Internet Commons." The term "Internet Commons" has been applied here as a common medium through which an active group of specialists can work through the network to develop, maintain, and curate these sorts of classification systems.

Institutional or governmental centers?—they certainly have been tried. And other patterns of funding will continue to be tried. But I don't think they are going to be successful in terms of expressing biodiversity information in a useful and updateable way. If this effort is distributed among specialists, I think it has a much greater chance of success. Examine traditional infrastructures that are available today that allow, facilitate, and are preadapted to this sort of enterprise. Certainly professional Societies should be mentioned here—for example, the best expression available is the American Society of Mammalogists. Such professional groups are composed of people who are actively engaged in a specific enterprise, taxonomists with expertise who are familiar with the nuances of these systems and their subparts. So, professional societies are essentially, from a cultural point of view, preadapted. All that is required is whatever modifications are needed to allow them to move into this arena to try to pursue this sort of activity.

So, basically you have these large taxonomic groups. Many professional societies have a direct link to not only individuals, but also facilities, areas that house specimens. They have people accustomed to curating these materials. You see the emergence on the Web of these societies, who are creating a Web presence. These societal Web sites serve as interactive nodes for various things, such as membership directories. But, certainly this enterprise could be expanded into developing content for these sites. You have again the tradition established at the societies for hardcopy publication, submission of articles, peer review, etc. It is part of societal activity at this point in time. You have societies that have been in existence for decades. Therefore, you have the potential for the permanent transfer of responsibilities through generations, through cohorts, and so on, already in place with professional societies. You have, most importantly with regard to the social parameters of science that have been mentioned here, a society ready to distribute responsibility, data resources, and credit among a membership of participating individuals, not centered with an agency or a commercial indexing enterprise.

ITIS,
The Integrated Taxonomic Information System

BRUCE B. COLLETTE, Senior Scientist, National Marine Fisheries Service
Systematics Laboratory

ABSTRACT

The Integrated Taxonomic Information System (ITIS) is a relational database of scientific and common names for plants and animals. The use of consistent names of species is fundamental to successful management of biological systems. ITIS provides a standardized vocabulary for this purpose and integrates the scientific results of the world taxonomic community into a coherent list of biological names. ITIS was designed to replace the flat file of scientific names maintained by the U.S. National Oceanographic Data Center (NODC). ITIS currently contains about 266,000 names of plants and animals and is accessible on the Web at <http://www.itis.usda.gov/it is>. ITIS is up-to-date for North American vertebrates, vascular plants, and crustaceans. ITIS staff are reviewing and editing names transferred from NODC and have added high-priority names such as fish species covered in FAO world catalogs. Through the continued cooperation of its partners, ITIS will make a significant contribution to the scientific infrastructure that is fundamental to the conservation and management of the world's biodiversity.

First I would like to say a few words about the Integrated Taxonomic Information System, or ITIS. ITIS is a unique government organization because it is a non-bureaucratic. It has no director and no direct funding. It exists only because the people involved had a vision: that we need a standard, yes a standard, name—not as an expression of taxonomy, but as a way to get from one database to another database. So, for the purpose of communicating between databases, we have to agree on a name. It would be nice if it were the "right" name, but the important thing is to have the same name so that someone can get data about a species from all your databases. And that is simply what ITIS is all about—a way of doing this.

It is not the same way that Frank Bisby spoke of. We are coming from different directions and hopefully we will meet in the middle. One of the reasons that ours is different is because we started with an existing database of hundreds of thousands of names that had already been entered. This was the National Oceanographic Data Center (NODC) database, which we loaded and now need to modify.

An Introduction to ITIS

What I want to do this morning is tell you a little about the ITIS project, including the key components of interrelationships with other projects, where we are now, and where we are going. ITIS is an online database (see <http://www.it is.usda.gov/itis>) built through partnerships with the world taxonomic community, sponsoring agencies, and organizations. Our goal is to provide on the Web quality taxonomic information about all organisms from both aquatic and terrestrial habitats. (There are, according to various accounts, 300,000 to 400,000 names available now.) Our original focus is North America because the governmental agencies involved are North American. But where databases are available, like for mammals of the world, we go global immediately.

Creating a Standardized List. We believe that informed decisions for managing our biological heritage can best be made with easy access to the wealth of information already existing about plants and animals. The problem is communicating between databases. As I said before, we have to agree on the same name so that we can get into each other's databases. In fact, we started as an organization because several federal agencies responsible for managing the nation's biological heritage found that they had information stored under different names about the same organisms, so they could not communicate with each other. This was on both the federal and the state level. We needed interoperability.

As a result, our goal is to standardize credible lists of species names, which have unique identifiers. This falls within the recommendation of the National Research Council and other agencies that have said that taxonomy is important if we are going to manage biodiversity. I once spent 10 minutes trying to explain to Jim Baker, the head of the National Oceanic and Atmospheric Administration (NOAA), why there is not a list. There are, of course, lists of lots of things—but we don't even have a list of commercial species within the United States. Thousands of taxonomists have been working on this for hundreds of years, and we still have a long way to go. Depending on the source, there are from 6 million to 40 million entries we need to make. The names are in Latin. The original descriptions are dispersed among thousands of biological journals, from obscure societies and little museums, and in all languages. The only thing you can read in some of them is the Latin.

Rules to Follow. We have rules of nomenclature. We also have separate rules for zoology, biology, and bacteria in constructing the infrastructure of ITIS. It was necessary that the business rules for each of the codes were integrated into the structure so that the names would not violate those codes. Yes, classification is constantly changing, and it has to be constantly updated. But that is the beauty of the Internet—it can be updated.

The History of ITIS

ITIS actually began in 1972 in the Chesapeake Bay region, when the Virginia Institute of Marine Sciences started one of a lot of local codes. This was then taken on by the National Oceanographic Data Center. NODC is responsible for archiving physical chemical data, including biological data.

This was in the 1970s, and computer fields were limited, so it was not a good option to put in the entire species name. A code was better. So, a flat file, a so-called intelligent number system, was devised. The first number is the phylum, the second number is the class, and the third number is the order. This works okay up to a certain point, but then it collapses because you have too much data. Further, the emphasis was on quickly putting the names in the database because the data were available. Employees were charged with getting names in quickly, and this meant that many of the names entered were unreviewed.

In 1985, EPA entered into a partnership with NOAA. This then broadened to include what is now the United States Geological Survey (USGS). In 1992 there was formal commitment to replace the code. As a result, in 1993, the real effort started to develop a relational database based on a system of classification, so that, for example, if you wanted data on a given species and there were taxonomic problems with identification, you might be able to go up a level in the relational database structure and get the data on a generic level.

Where We Are Now

We went online in 1996, and it became necessary to migrate the old National Oceanographic Data Center database into ITIS. This means we inherited some good data and some bad data. This also means we now have a big cleanup job. So when you go to our Web site and you see bad data, it is because we have not yet cleaned it up. The reason is some people were using those names and those codes, and they can continue to use them. We will create links so you can type in the old name, the scientific name, or the common name and the system will tell you the currently accepted scientific name. There is also a "change link" so that you can get back to the original taxonomic serial number. So, where we are right now is getting new data and cleaning up our old data. In this sense we need help from the systematics community.

Partnerships. Our partners include the Department of Agriculture, NOAA from the Department of Commerce, the USGS, EPA, and the National Museum of Natural History. We are directly linked to the KDI project in the University of Kansas, and recently we have added Canadian participation. These are active partners that are participating as we develop our program.

ITIS as a Relational Database. The system is built around a relational database. The database includes scientific names, the authors, the dates in a single classification, a unique identifier, and a taxonomic serial number (TSN). In addition, there are associated data, some of which are obligatory and some of which are "nice-to-know" data that we put in when available. There is an online system that can be queried. Reports can be asked for. There is a system that allows you to compare two lists of names if they are in the proper format. In addition, you can download the data. In fact, if you don't like our particular system of classification, download it and change it. It is there for people to use.

Taxonomic Workbench. We also have a taxonomic workbench, which is designed to enter data. We are still working out the best procedures to make this more interoperable, to make it more accessible to people in the field, and to make corrections. Right now all updates and changes funnel through us.

This is a simplified database, consisting of a scientific name with a number for computer purposes—the taxonomic serial number—behind it. Synonyms are linked to it. There is a record of change-tracking from the time a name is originally entered.

Every time there is a change there is a reason for the change. There are publications sited. There is a series of vernacular names linked, and it is indicated if these are approved by some organization or other authority. There is a lookup table of authors of publications and of species. There is a comment field for anything else that is not required but about which we have information (for example, is it an endangered species?).

Our Homepage. Visit our homepage to see what we have to offer. You'll find you can query the database by typing in a common name or a scientific name. You can generate reports. You can extract the scientific name and other data from ITIS. You can download anything you want and modify it any way you want. You can compare different databases because when you have local lists from different places, there are going to be a lot of matches (and some non-matches—you actually might want to focus on those non-matches and figure out why they are not matching).

You also will see on the homepage places to pull up publications, experts, and names. Credibility can be found in the right-hand corner. It also will alert you regarding whether the data have been reviewed. If they have not, be cautious—we haven't gotten to that record yet. Remember, we don't have millions of dollars and hundreds of people, so we have not yet achieved the goal of updating all the data. But we will get there. In fact, you can help us by visiting our site, then telling us how you think it could be improved.

Reaching Our Goal

One way we're trying to reach our goal is to take some of the small amount of money that is available and contract with systematists to produce lists for groups that are important. For example, we have a contractor working on a beetle list for North America. And we have an algae contract.

In addition, we are particularly interested in finding old-time taxonomists who still have lists of species on 3x5 cards. We want to make sure that we can get that information captured electronically while these people are still alive. Taxonomy is itself an endangered discipline. In many groups there is only one expert in the entire world. If we don't get that information now, we will have to do it all over again, which is not very cost effective.

We also have people to evaluate the data. Many of these are systematists based at the Natural History Museum of the Smithsonian. Many others are, and will increasingly be, in other parts of the country and from other parts of the world. Experts will review the data and make a rational decision on which name to use.

We have a data-development team that is trying to obtain new sources of data, new lists, just as Frank Bisby does for his distributive system. We acquire the data from whatever source we can get, but then it has to be developed. It has to be formatted. It then must undergo peer review. Hopefully, it is certified. Then it is loaded and managed online.

All of this is accessible on the Internet. We realize we cannot make changes as fast as we would like. There are some glitches and problems in development, as there are in any large system. But we still have lots of names up there, and names for many important groups are in very good condition.

We also plan to interact with different groups. Information presumably will flow out from ITIS to groups like the public and science writers, people who want the correct name for an organism for a high-school report or a story they are writing. This is the place to get that correct name.

We are trying to be representative of good systematics, but we also have to be practical and results have to be immediate. We have to manage our resources now—not with tomorrow's taxonomy, but with the information we have right now. We cannot wait for perfect taxonomy. We have to make some decisions to give you some standard names to enable you to move back and forth between the databases right now.

Interaction with the systematics community is essential. The data stewards come from the systematics community. The data sources come from the systematics community. And peer review is provided by systematists.

We are in cooperation and coordination with a long suite of organizations including Species 2000, CONABIO in Mexico, and FAO, which produces aquatic species catalogues on taxa of importance. FAO covers mostly food fishes, but they include turtles and other organisms. All the names of all the organisms of the FAO catalogues are in, updated, and correct in the list. Bit by bit we will move through and get the rest of the names updated.

In addition, we have been endorsed by the National Performance Review and Access America. We have space at the National Museum, where we are in direct contact with the largest group of systematists in this country. We have a data-standardization process. We have hundreds of thousands of names in there. We have been recognized by Vice President Gore with a Hammer Award for Interagency Cooperation for making information available at a really cheap cost. There is very little direct funding money. As I said before, it is a volunteer effort.

Where We're Going

So, where do we go from here? We have to finish cleaning up the data. We have to expand the geographic and taxonomic coverage. We have to redo the Web page to make it easier to retrieve information. We have to become a bureaucracy, because at some stage the buck has to stop someplace and somebody has to be in charge.

We also need somebody to encourage the sponsoring cooperating agencies to contribute more money so we can get the job done. We need to expand partnerships with various organizations. We have to expand our relationships with the systematics community. When I say these things, some of my taxonomic colleagues won't talk to me because they think I am trying to make the ITIS system a standard. But it is not a standard—it is just a means for helping people move among and use various databases. It is just a method of communication.

Session 3

The Challenge in Earth Observation, Ecosystem Monitoring, and Environmental Information

The Challenge in Earth Observation, Ecosystem Monitoring, and Environmental Information

ROBERTA BALSTAD MILLER, Director, the Center for International Earth Science Information Network (CIESIN) at Columbia University

ABSTRACT

This presentation will discuss the challenges inherent in developing information systems that encompass the vast quantities of data and information from diverse sources necessary for research and policy on biodiversity and ecosystems. These challenges fall into three broad areas: data integration; data access and dissemination; and public information. Examples will be drawn from environmental data systems and tools in use or being developed.

It has been a very interesting day thus far. We have had people discussing what should be done, people discussing what will be done, and then people discussing what is currently being done. It is that last category that I think we will take further today with what really is a very outstanding panel reporting on some systems efforts both at the national level and international level.

But first what I would like to do is look at the PCAST report of the Panel on Biodiversity and Ecosystems, in historical perspective. Then I will address three major challenges that are raised by that report and that we need to deal with in responding to the report. Those challenges, I would argue, are the challenge of data integration, the challenge of data access and dissemination, and, finally, the challenge of public information.

Background

The PCAST Panel on Biodiversity and Ecosystems emphasizes the need to use data and information resources for monitoring ecosystems and for integrating data. What the panel members had in mind when they wrote their report was economic data and biodiversity data for providing policymakers and the public with information for resource management. All of this is important. But the desire to build links among scientific research, data management, and public policy is not new.

National Income Accounts. In the 1930s, the economist Simon Kuznets, working at MIT, developed the National Income Accounts, which were time series data of economic activity (in terms of productivity) in all sectors of the economy. His goal in doing this was to improve our understanding of the economy and to provide a means of measuring change in productivity in various sectors. National Income Accounts are the economic indicators that still affect economic policy and, some would argue, are responsible for our economic prosperity in the period since then. I think this can be seen as a very successful attempt to link the scientific research in economics with information series and public policy.

Social Indicators. There was a second attempt also. This attempt took place in the late 1960s and the late 1970s. Taking off from the idea of economic indicators, there was in this country—and in a number of other countries—something called the Social Indicators Movement. The Social Indicators Movement was based on the recognition that what is most important in national policy is not economic in nature and that, while economic indicators are themselves useful, they are not enough. National policy needs to be informed by statistical data on both tangible and intangible changes in the society.

Tangible kinds of indicators that were discussed included education test scores, infant mortality rates, literacy levels, and unemployment statistics. Intangible indicators included topics such as health and well-being and confidence in government. (If you think that confidence in government is not very important, look at the United States and Russia today and see how important confidence in government is for the smooth working of a country and, in particular, an economy.)

Economics vs. Social Indicators. There are significant differences between economic and the social indicators. The economic indicators have a common metric: They use dollars and cents. Everything is expressed in money. As a result, the economic indicators are additive. You could add these indicators together and get a gross national product.

Social indicators are different. They use diverse metrics. You don't measure literacy, unemployment, and confidence in government along the same metric. They are very, very different. As a result, social indicators are not additive. They are all separate. There have been attempts to combine various kinds of indicators into a composite indicator. (One of the more well-known attempts resulted in the Indicator of Development, which I believe was composed of literacy, infant mortality, and education of women.) But in almost every case, the additive social indicators left out something. When you combine social indicators, you lose information and detail. Consequently, social policy based on these additive indicators did not work terribly well.

The Current Situation. Today, we are facing similar problems in some respects and different problems in other respects. We need data series that will help us in research, in policy, and in resource management. But the circumstances today are very different than they were in the '30s or in the '60s or in the '70s. Biodiversity and ecosystems are complex systems. They are not closed systems. They are affected by economic activities. They are affected by social, demographic, and cultural activities and phenomena. They are affected by politics and by public policy, including treaties, regulations, war, foreign policy, and transportation policy. They are affected by physical and environmental change at regional and global levels. Then, of course, there are the biological functions that take place within this broad, shifting framework of many other types of change.

A second difference in the situation today is related to advances in information technologies. We have the capability to obtain and save vast quantities of information—probably much more information than any one person could use. So, part of the problem is that we have an embarrassment of riches. The problem addressed by this meeting is to bring order to all this information. But policymakers are not going to be able to deal with the vast quantities of information that scientists can deal with or that data managers are going to be able to deal with. The translation from science and data management requirements to the policy framework has to be a matter of imposing order on that chaos.

A third difference from earlier attempts to create data series for public policy is the growing emphasis upon *public* as well as *policy* information. In the 1930s, Simon Kuznets did not worry about informing the public about environmental indicators. This was—even then—a public policy issue but not something about which the public was concerned.

Things are different today, and such issues must be addressed by this group and by others who wish to respond to the PCAST Panel on Biodiversity and Ecosystems.

The Challenge of Integrating Data

As I noted at the start, there are three challenges for us to accept. First of all is the challenge of data integration. We have already heard a great deal about the data problems of biodiversity. But it is a lot more complicated than data. In a very real sense, biodiversity is about people. Biodiversity is about economic markets, and biodiversity is about global environmental change. In order to understand biodiversity, you have to have data integration. You have to pull data on all of these together into a single data series or a single database or a single type of data. This is true whether you approach the topic from a scientific, a policy, or a public information perspective. Because the science of biodiversity involves so many fields, the data series themselves have to involve multidisciplinary data.

Integrating multidisciplinary data is not an easy task. For example, you may have to compare or combine remote sensing data with population data, with transportation data, with in situ data in order to have the background to deal with certain kinds of land-management issues. We don't have a common metric. We are not like the economists in the 1930s and thereafter. We don't have dollars and cents that we can use for all of these data series. Space—spatial representation—frequently becomes the framework for integrating the data.

The Problem of Space. But space also creates a problem in data integration, because the unit of analysis or the basic spatial unit differs for the three major types of data that I am talking about. Remote sensing data is provided to us in an image, and that image then is superimposed with an imaginary grid. Scientists use that grid to analyze images.

But socioeconomic data are collected in political jurisdictions, and those political jurisdictions never approach a grid (except for a few places in the Midwest). Jurisdictions are determined by historical forces, historical practice, or historical agreements. Jurisdictions also can be determined by rivers or by, in some cases, the shifting boundaries created by war, politics, and treaties. All socioeconomic data that are collected by the government are collected for political jurisdictions. So you have to break out of the tyranny of those political jurisdictions in order to put the data in a framework where you can use them with the gridded data that are available through remote sensing.

To complicate things further, you have ecosystem data. Now, ecosystems don't translate easily to a grid or to a political jurisdiction. So, you have still a third geographical area that you have to put together when you are integrating data. Therefore the data themselves often need to be transformed before they can be integrated and used together. This is a really difficult task.

Examples of Integrated Data. What I want to do now is give you a couple of examples of integrated data. One example is the newly created gridded population of the world map. It is roughly a five-minute-by-five-minute grid, and, obviously, the areas must differ up at the poles. The map is imperfect, but it is being corrected right now. In addition, parts of the map are better than others. However, this map marks the first time we have ever been able to produce population data that wasn't expressed by national boundaries but instead by the grid. Of course, you don't want to lose the national boundaries, because that is where the laws and the regulations are enforced. So, you need to move between those two means of representation. In fact, at CIESIN, we have also gridded the Mexican population on a one-kilometer-square grid. These data are all available online.

The next example is a program that we maintain online called the Demographic Data Viewer, or DDViewer. This provides you with mapping capability for the U.S. Census. You can map the entire country, a state, a county or group of counties, and you can even map counties across state boundaries. And since census databases are created from massive state databases, to be able to cross these state boundaries is quite a feat. You are able to go in and select the unit you want to map. You select the variables that you would like to have on the map and it goes down to the census-block group. You can specify the parameters of what you are doing through a program. Then you basically press the Map-It button, and you get your data instantly. Again, it is a way of visualizing demographic data, population data, and census data in a different way so that you can integrate them with various kinds of information. It enables you to get away from the tyranny of the political jurisdictions in the display of socioeconomic data.

Still another product that we maintain online is something we call DDCarto that translates census data to other kinds of units. From the counties and the states, you can translate data to zip codes, you can translate data to congressional districts, and you can translate data to eco regions. Therefore, you can move from one kind of geography to another kind of geography.

It is this kind of work that needs to be done for data integration. It is as much data preparation and data development as it is data analyses. And yet, if you are going to integrate disparate types of data and if you are going to provide data for public policy and public information, you have got to go through these exercises and you have to transform your data.

The Challenge of Data Access and Dissemination

The second challenge that needs to be addressed is the challenge of data access and dissemination. This is something that we have talked about a number of times already today. People have talked about the need for interoperable metadata. People have talked about the need for common metadata standards. People have talked about the need for distributed information management systems. These topics are going to be addressed in very experienced and able detail by the panel today, so I am not going to go into too much detail now. I would emphasize though that distributed information systems for biodiversity must link with multiple kinds of data. It is not enough simply to have biodiversity or biological data. You have got to link into the socioeconomic data and the global-change data.

Let's look at the data and information system from the Socioeconomic Data and Applications Center (SEDAC), which is part of NASA's Earth Observing System. Because many of the data on socioeconomic factors have to be pulled from many different sources, the SEDAC search system provides a means of searching multiple data catalogues, either singly or all at once. You can search it through a structured system, through a key word, and through a geographical interface. This is a metadata search tool. You are not searching the data themselves—you are searching the metadata to identify metadata that might be of interest. We do have a version of this that allows people, particularly in developing countries, to do an e-mail search of this catalogue, because although many of the people who use it do not have the bandwidth for full connectivity, they do have e-mail available.

The Challenge of Public Information

The third challenge that is raised by the Report of the PCAST Biodiversity and Ecosystems Panel is the challenge of public information. There are a number of reasons to focus on public information: The panel recommends it. The convention on biodiversity recommends it. Agenda 21 recommends it. A host of other public reports recommend that a data management strategy must include a public information component as well.

But another reason for doing so is because the technology has a bias for public dissemination. The days when information was placed in libraries or provided only to those who had a "need to know" are fast disappearing.

A third reason for emphasizing public access, as well as policy access and scientific access, is related to democratic traditions. This is an argument that comes out of the earlier Social Indicators Movement. One of the leaders of that movement, Sten Johanson, a Swedish sociologist who was in charge of the Level of Living study in Sweden, argued that in a democratic society, a government had a duty to inform (to give data to) its citizenry on public policy, and, furthermore, the citizens had a right to the kind of data that would enable them to evaluate how well they were being governed. For the first time in history, we have the technological capability to make this happen.

Biodiversity and ecosystem research can have indicators, can have a steady stream of public data because, again, the technology has changed. We have moved from the book to the electronic medium. But there are some requirements that this technology lays on us. First, it requires having a user interface that is very friendly. Not everyone is going to be technologically sophisticated. Computer data programs must be easy to use.

Second, I would argue that there should also be multiple means of dissemination of this information. There should be computers and electronic information systems. There should also be computers with printing capabilities available in public information centers or public information places. I am thinking of libraries, civic buildings, and the contemporary market place: shopping centers, convenience stores. If there were computers there that had data available and a printing capability, even someone who wasn't able to run the computer could get the information he or she needed and walk away with a printout.

Still another aspect of providing indicators for public policy is providing training. It is going to be easier, obviously, for younger people than older people, but some kind of training program is a valuable and logical part of the public information program.

In Summary

In summary then, one of the central recommendations of the PCAST Panel on Biodiversity and Ecosystems is to translate scientific research into data that can be used in monitoring ecosystems, in managing biodiversity and ecological resources, and in forming public policy. This will only happen, I would argue, if we are able to improve our capacity to integrate data, if we are able to document and disseminate the data, and if we are able to make the resulting data and information available to both policymakers and the general public.

Locating Biodiversity Data Through the Global Change Master Directory

LOLA OLSEN, Project Manager, NASA Global Change Master Directory

ABSTRACT

The Global Change Master Directory (GCMD) currently holds descriptions for approximately 7000 data sets held worldwide. The directory's primary purpose is for data discovery. The information provided through the GCMD's Directory Interchange Format (DIF) is the set of information that a researcher would need to determine if a particular data set could be of value. By offering data set descriptions worldwide in many scientific disciplines—including meteorology, oceanography, ecology, geology, hydrology, geophysics, remote sensing, paleoclimate, solar-terrestrial physics, and human dimensions of climate change—the GCMD simplifies the discovery of data sources. Direct linkages to many of the data sets are also provided. In addition, several data set registration tools are offered for populating the directory. To search the directory, one may choose the Guided Search or Free-Text Search. Two experimental interfaces were also made available with the latest software release—one based on a keyword search and another based on graphical interface. The graphical interface was designed in collaboration with the Human Computer Interaction Laboratory at the University of Maryland. The latest version of the software, Version 6, was released in April 1998. It features the implementation of a scheme to handle hierarchical data set collections (parent-child relationships); a hierarchical geospatial location search scheme; a Java-based geographic map for conducting geospatial searches; a Related URL field for project-related data set collections, metadata extensions (such as more detailed inventory information), etc.; a new implementation of the Isite software; a new data set language field; hyperlinked e-mail addresses; and more. The key to the continued evolution of the GCMD is in the flexibility of the GCMD database, allowing modifications and additions to be made relatively easily to maintain currency, thus providing the ability to capitalize on current technology while importing all existing records. Changes are discussed and approved through an online "interoperability" forum. The next major release of the GCMD is scheduled for early 1999 and will include the incorporation of a new matrix-based interface, a

> rapid valid-based query system; improvement in the
> operations facility—important for future distributed options;
> new streamlined code for greater performance and
> maintainability; improvements in the handling of seven
> current fields proposed through the interoperability forum (at
> no expense to the data providers); and the release of
> DOCmorph, a more robust version of DIFmorph to translate
> many "standards" multidirectionally. Issues and actions will
> also be addressed.

The Global Change Master Directory is a directory of data sets on Earth science, including broad coverage of the atmosphere, oceans, biosphere, and land. It connects users to 24 sites fairly evenly distributed around the world among those that maintain global data sets.

This is a project that began at NASA and continues to be supported by NASA. The original directory focused on remote sensing data. However, it has grown to be much more than that. It is now a system that holds data set descriptions for earth science data.

My comments today will focus on aspects of the GCMD that might apply to anyone developing a system of metadata records.

User Working Groups

First, I would like to stress the importance of having a science user working group. One needs to focus on those who will use the data system. The GCMD has two ecology-related advisors involved in our current user working group, and I want to emphasize just how important the group's input has been.

User group members often ask interesting and fundamental questions: For example, one member of the user working group asked us to estimate the number of data sets in the world. Here we were, designing a system and talking about scalability! Did we know what we were scaling to? Did we ever think about how many data sets there really were? I independently asked the science coordinators on the project to estimate the number of data sets. At the time we were working on the Environmental Task Force efforts, so we made an estimate of DoD data sets. The estimate they determined for biological data sets was 3.5 million! But after listening to this morning's talks, I contend that there actually are even more than that. Of course, the total depends on how you count data sets and how they are aggregated.

Our user working group recently asked another interesting question: Do we know how many of our users are actually getting to the data sets? Our answer was "no." Now we are tapping into the links so we can get a better idea about how many users are accessing those data sets.

Registering Data Sets

Users are not only important in helping to design (and redesign) the system, but they also play a direct and fundamental part in database building. Users register their own data sets and provide the metadata record on the GCMD using a Web form. The main questions are: What? Where? When? Who? With this information, we gather what is basically needed for someone to begin searching.

Data Fields. There are 32 fields of information that can be stored. Not all are required, and some are quite new with our latest version. Two new ones are the Related URL, which links users to data sets or extended descriptions, and the parent-child aggregation option.

There is nothing about the way the fielded data are stored that mandates the output format. The metadata record can be displayed as a GILS, NBII, or FGDC record.

We believe that the set of 32 fields (known as the Directory Interchange Format, or DIF) is the necessary set of fields for the user to determine if a particular data set is a candidate for a desired application. It currently has multidisciplinary capability, and it is alive and evolving as there are new needs and new capabilities. All the modifications are decided through an interoperability forum, where the participants discuss their needs.

In addition to the data-set descriptions, there also are fields for sources, sensors, campaigns, and other data center information, along with modification tools for supplementary information.

Getting Scientists to Register. One of the staff members recently published a paper about why scientists aren't writing metadata. Of course, there are many reasons. However, one important reason is that the scientists did not believe they would be credited for their work. We are hoping to promote the use of data set citations. The current data set citation will be modified to comply with the new standard citation being proposed by the International Standards Organization (ISO).

Searching the Directory—User Interfaces

We have been working to simplify the directory search. The current search interfaces have been modified for this particular version of the directory. One is the Guided Interface, in which valid terms for all the parameters are listed in pull-down menus. Anytime changes are made to the "valids," they take effect here.

Another interface is based on the Isite search engine software, which is Z39.50 compliant. Since Isite permits numeric searches, you can do temporal searches for date ranges and spatial searches. You can also search for data in specific fields. The parent-child capability implemented through the "Guided Search" using the database has also now been implemented through Isite.

There are two experimental search interfaces for which we are seeking user feedback. One is based on science keywords. We have noticed that several other groups have adopted this particular interface, because it is a simple way to help users to look for data sets. The database is searched via topic, term, and variable—a hierarchical set of Earth science keywords. The keyword list has remained stable over time. We attribute this stability to a set of 14 rules for adding or modifying the keywords.

The other interface that has inspired us to do some additional work is one that was developed with the Human Computer Interaction Lab at the University of Maryland. A paper that was written about this interface was called "The End of Zero-Hit Queries." As you select your options, this interface shows you the number of data sets that are left in that particular category. One can visually watch the number of data sets to view change as one selects and de-selects by temporal and spatial coverage. We have extended this concept for the next version of the directory by taking all the fields that have valid values and putting them in a matrix interface, so that all the fields can be used. The user always knows how many data sets are left in any combination of parameters that you choose.

Who Uses this System?

We can't know "exactly" who uses this system. However, we do collect metrics that indicate the "domain" name for unique users—those who have gone at least beyond the homepage. The "domain" indicates whether the user is a foreign user, a commercial user, an educational user, a government user, or a military user. We also track the number of DIFs or the data set descriptions accessed. Soon we will have a quick look at who is actually getting to the data. Usage continues to increase, and we are recording access by more than 17,000 users per month.

Homepage Options

In addition to offering access to the GCMD, our homepage offers other options. One of the options is the Global Change Calendar, which is a listing of all the conferences for which we have information. This is one of the offerings that we at NASA contribute to the Interagency U.S. Global Change Research Programs' Global Change Data and Information System. This list is also maintained with the help of system users. So if you are sponsoring a conference and want to advertise it, you can register it here.

Another link from the homepage is to the interagency U.S. Global Change Research Program. One of two choices to note here is the Global Change Research Information Office (GCRIO). The GCRIO acts as a user-support arm for the Global Change Data and Information System. That work is very important and now includes information on the U.S. National Assessment.

The last link I would like to mention is to Committee on Earth Observation Satellites (CEOS) International Directory of data sets. In this case, there are mirror sites that also host the data set information in this directory.

Information on Archiving Workshop

I would like to mention an important data archival workshop that was just held by the Data Management Working Group of the U.S. Global Change Research Program. The information will be out on the Web within the week. <http://gcmd.nasa.gov/dmwg98/>

The Committee on Earth Observation Satellites Working Group on Information Systems and Services

GERALD BARTON, Physical Scientist with the NOAA Environmental Services Data and Information Management Program (ESDIM)

ABSTRACT

The Committee on Earth Observation Satellites (CEOS) addresses coordination of the satellite-Earth observation programs of the world's government agencies responsible for civilian Earth observation (EO) satellite programs, along with agencies that receive and process data acquired remotely from space. The Working Group on Information Systems and Services (WGISS) addresses the information systems and services that help CEOS agencies achieve this coordination and that enable ease of access by users and potential users to the EO data holdings of members worldwide. The Catalogue Interoperability Protocol (CIP) is being developed by the Protocol Task Team within the Committee on Earth Observation Satellites to facilitate the access, searching, and retrieval of Earth observation data. Several CD-ROM packages of environmental data have been prepared to demonstrate the usefulness of environmental data sets. The AVHRR 1 Kilometer project, involving scientists in many countries, uses data from the NOAA Polar Orbiting Satellites. The International Global Observing Strategy (IGOS) has developed a set of pilot applications, such as the CEOS Disaster Information Server that has current satellite-derived information about drought, Earthquakes, fires, floods, oil spills, tropical cyclones, and volcanic ash. See the CEOS WGISS Web page at <http://193.36.230.105/wgiss/ >

I am going to talk about the Committee on Earth Observation Satellites (CEOS), with a focus on the Working Group on Information Systems and Services (WGISS). This was a requested talk to show the international aspect of what we are doing in data management.

Who We Are

I am with the National Oceanic and Atmospheric Administration (NOAA). NOAA has many parts. I am associated with the National Environmental Satellite Data and Information Service. For those of you in the United States, we bring you the weather satellite pictures that come to you every day. NOAA also includes the National Weather Service and the National Marine Fishing Service.

A lot of biological work goes on at the NOAA National Ocean Service, particularly in the coastal environments.

There also is the Committee on Earth Observation Satellites (CEOS), which addresses the coordination of satellite-Earth observation programs of government agencies around the world. The kinds of satellites we are talking about here are the weather satellites, the Landsat kind of satellites, radar satellites, and so on—not specifically the communication satellites.

The Working Group on Information Systems and Services

The Working Group on Information Systems and Services (WGISS) is a working group of CEOS that helps the agencies achieve coordination and enables ease-of-access by users and potential users to the Earth observation data held by people around the world. CEOS itself was started in 1984. The group recognized the multidisciplinary nature of satellite-Earth observation and the value of coordinating international mission plans. It now has a broad framework for coordination across all space-born Earth observation missions. The WGISS was established as a CEOS working group. (There actually was a working group on data that existed for a long time. It was changed to WGISS just for a different focus and to reestablish things in 1995.)

One primary objective of the WGISS is to optimize benefits of space-born Earth observations, especially through cooperation in planning and the development of data products, formats, services, applications and policies. (This involves lots of data management.) Another objective is to aid members in the international user community by serving as the focal point for international coordination of space-related Earth observation activities, especially those related to global change, and to exchange policy and technical information to encourage compatibility among space-born Earth observation systems currently in service, as well as among the data received from them. So, it is not only to coordinate what is going to be done and how the Earth is going to be observed with different satellites, but it is also to use the data from the satellites.

The WGISS has grown to encompass the agencies responsible for Earth observation programs along with agencies that receive and process data. It also includes other organizations, such as the World Meteorological Organization Global Climate Observing System, which now has affiliate status in the CEOS. These other organizations are actually incorporated into the CEOS as affiliate members and attend meetings both at the plenary level—there is a plenary meeting in India quite soon—and also at the coordination-group level and at the WGISS levels and at the working group levels.

Approximately 40 Earth observation missions have been launched since the establishment of CEOS. Fifty more are planned for launch within the next five years, and a further 16 are already planned for the following five years. So, there is a lot of coordination involved. The points of contact for the Secretariat are at the European Space Agency (ESA) in Paris and at the Japanese Space Agency in Tokyo. There are many international aspects to this.

Subgroups of WGISS. There are three subgroups within WGISS. There is a Data Subgroup, there is a Network Subgroup, and there is an Access Subgroup.

The **Data Subgroup** is there to enhance the complementarity, interoperability, and standardization of Earth observation data, and to undertake tasks to foster the inner use of data, ensuring compatibility of data content, formats, and tools used in the generation of the data products. So, this group gets down to the nitty-gritty of the data, how things are transferred, what things should look like, and what the fields should contain.

The purpose of the **Network Subgroup** is to provide coordination and cooperation on network architecture for electronic access to Earth-observation data worldwide. An example of what happened recently as a result of this group's efforts is the establishment of high-speed networks between Japan and the U.S. to enable transmission of satellite data back and forth. This network effectively got rid of the delay you usually experience when you are addressing information on another continent. For example, I was just over in Japan two weeks ago for a CEOS meeting, and access to information in the U.S. was just as if I were in the U.S.

The **Access Subgroup**—the main work of data and information management—is the WGISS group itself. We have two major goals for the WGISS. The first goal is that it enable Earth-observation data and information services to be more accessible to data providers and data users worldwide, especially through international coordination. The second goal is that it take into account the requirements of users and CEOS participants and undertakes tasks to develop or demonstrate improved methods and tools for locating, advertising, accessing, and exchanging information. In the process of achieving these goals it serves as an international forum about the development and operation of catalogue systems and catalogue system elements.

Task Teams. A number of task teams also exist. Just to show you the diversity of the topics, the CEOS International Directory Network is a service that is available worldwide. The Global Change Master Directory is replicated in two other locations on the globe—one in Italy at the European Space Agency and one at the Japanese Space Agency in Japan. They are complete replicates. The original idea was that users in different parts of the world could save the communication time by going to the location that is closer.

There also are coordinating nodes and a number of cooperating nodes. My NOAA directorate is a cooperating node. The Canadian Center for Remote Sensing (CCRS) also is a cooperating node. In fact, there are many of them around the world, so people can get to the different directories on the International Directory Network.

The CEOS Interoperability Extension is a testbed for catalogue interoperability techniques and protocols. It allows various browse techniques so you can get samples of data and actually look at them online.

Land Stations

Land stations can sense one kilometer when the satellite is overhead. It was an international effort to go to those land sensing sites that get the one-kilometer data, to assemble the data at a few locations, and to maintain that data set so that you can look at all the land surfaces over the Earth over time.

One of the archives is at the USGS Data Center in Sioux Falls, S.D. It is a very, very nice project. You can get vegetation data there for areas around the world and retrieve it in a time-series way.

Other Features

I want to also mention the International Global Observation Strategy (IGOS), on which CEOS is working. There are six areas for the six pilot programs. Another project we are doing in NOAA under Helen Wood, who was the former chair of WGISS, is a pilot project on natural disasters. There is a nice homepage for it that looks at hurricanes, at flooding, at fires, and so on.

CEOS also has a CD-ROM. In an example, the CD-ROM showed a city's development over time. It showed population-growth and land-use changes for a 20-year period in a geographic GIS database and also with satellite data superimposed upon it. It also has case studies that talk about the science of remote sensing. It has data sets. It has satellite systems. And it has lesson plans on it, which is very nice. You can do it by location. You can do it by topic. There has been a lot of work in this area using Landsat data and other remote-sensing data through some of the international groups. There is another CD-ROM, too, that is being developed in India, and that CD-ROM will be more a tutorial CD-ROM and a demonstration of both Earth observing satellites or satellite remote sensing data as well as GIS data. These CD-ROMs demonstrate capabilities using satellite data.

The Global Information Locator Service

ELIOT CHRISTIAN, Computer Specialist, U.S. Geological Survey

ABSTRACT

Eliot Christian is co-leader of the Environment and Natural Resources Management Project within the G8 Global Information Society initiative. This project reached an international consensus on standards to support locating environmental information, whether held in libraries, data centers, or published on the Internet. Eliot describes the international work on the resulting Global Information Locator Service.

I am going to talk about the Environment and Natural Resources Management Project of the G8 Global Information Society. You heard this referred to in the prior talk as the "G7"Information Society, but Russia has now been added, at least for the purposes of the Global Information Society itself, making it now "G8."

In 1995, the information technology ministers met together. The idea was to engage in north-south dialogue about what is happening—particularly in terms of sociological impacts—as we move to these new technologies. These are some of the things they said they are going to do:

1.   Promote interconnectivity and interoperability
2.   Develop global markets for networks, services, and applications
3.   Ensure privacy and data security
4.   Protect intellectual property rights
5.   Cooperate in applications research and development
6.   Monitor social and societal implications

In addition, they decided there should be pilot projects to demonstrate the capabilities of these new technologies and infrastructures. These pilot projects would be organized under 11 themes:

1.   Global Inventory
2.   Global Interoperability for Broadband Networks
3.   Cross-cultural Education and Training
4.   Bibliotheca Universalis (Digital Libraries)
5.   Electronic Museums and Galleries
6.   Environment and Natural Resources Management
7.   Global Emergency Management
8.   Global Healthcare Applications
9.   Government Online
10.   Global Marketplace for Small and Medium-sized Enterprises
11.   Maritime Information Systems

The first one (Global Inventory), headed in Europe, sits on top of the others and provides an inventory of all the pilot-project activity. Others are managed by different people in different nations.

The Environment and
Natural Resources Management Project

The one for which the United States is responsible is Environment and Natural Resources Management (ENRM)—number six in the list above. I am co-leader of that project plan. Essentially the idea here is to try to come up with consensus on an international basis—much like we are doing at this meeting—regarding the sort of standards that would have to be in place to create a mechanism for people to find the information of interest, in this case, for environment and natural resources management. In addition, we are to build a prototype of a virtual library of data and information on that topic.

Participants. These are the nations who have been fairly active participants: Australia, Canada, Finland, France, and Germany. International organizations active in our program include the European Commission, the European Space Agency, the UN Framework Convention on Climate Change, the United Nations Environment Program, and, especially, the European Environment Agency.

Project Structure. The G8 group is a politically motivated organization. As a result, the term "expert" doesn't mean what you and I think the term means. Instead, it means a person without a political portfolio, a person who cannot make policy. The term does not ensure that the person really understands the topic that is being considered. However, I would say that everybody in the ENRM group did actually come as "experts," in the way we think of experts. Many of them knew very little about information infrastructure but were knowledgeable in environment or natural resources management.

This—and all of the G8 projects—were specifically time-limited. We are under a mandate to not create new bureaucracies, so we cannot go on forever. As a result, we are now moving toward the twilight of the project. We will have another meeting in January (1999) to pull the final project report together.

Working Groups. Three working groups were set up for the ENRM project. Each group had a different focus.

The Meta-Information Working Group was where we pulled together the people who wanted to talk in technical terms about these topics. The European Commission and the European Environment Agency headed that working group. The group had to determine how to come to consensus on standards so it could create a model for this information technology piece. We adopted as a model the work that had started in the global change community, working through a group called the Interagency Working Group on Data Management for Global Change, or IWGDMGC (an acronym someone reinterpreted as, "I Wish God Didn't Make Government Committees"). This group advocated the standard that had already gotten fairly wide play—that is, a profile of the Z39.50. My group elaborated a specific usage guideline for the Global Environmental Information Locator Service (GELOS), and it also developed a collections policy. The collections policy, together with the technical standards, determines the basis for deciding if something is in or out of the system.

Climate Change Working Group was the second working group. Led by Switzerland and the Secretariat of the Framework Convention on Climate Change, this group accomplished quite a lot, including:

- coordinating digitization of national communications;
- exploring its role in promoting "green technologies;"
- exploring collaboration with UN agencies that promote Internet access;
- exploring greater linkages with developing countries, climate change communities, and national focal points; and
- promoting GELOS.

The group also promoted the interoperable system that we had built as a demonstration prototype, if you will, of the idea of using common standards.

The Biological Diversity Working Group, the third of the groups, was led by Germany's Federal Agency for Nature Conservation. This group put together a Web page, began compiling funding sources, worked on common standards, and, again, tested and refined the GELOS server.

The Global Environmental Information Locator Service (GELOS)

Let me talk a little bit more about this prototype—the Global Environmental Information Locator Service. This prototype was developed primarily by the European Commission's Center for Earth Observation, in Italy. The records that are included in this GELOS system describe many types of information resources. For example, you have calendar entries about upcoming events. You have entries about experts. You have entries about remote databases that are accessible. All of these entries are commonly searchable, based on the set of Z39.50 standard entries attributes. So, for example, you can search using a "title." It may be the title of a meeting. Or, it may be the title of a book. The system will recognize all things that are titles.

The Biological Diversity Working Group also focused on defining the semantics of the underlying system. You can put many different user interfaces on top of this—or maybe the users get to design their own interfaces (there are many that have been built in this way as well). As noted earlier, the primary capability is for people to register data sets or themselves as experts or themselves as people who want to be notified when things happen, and so on.

GELOS searches can be done by geographic location, by keyword, by free text, or by a combination of these criteria. In addition, you can fan out this search, if you will, distribute it out over the Internet to a wide variety of other databases. The ability to conduct such a distributed search is made possible by our use of a common standard, Z39.50. Z39.50, used with a profile like GILS (Global Information Locator Service, a.k.a., Government Information Locator Service) or FGDC's Geospatial Profile, is what makes this all hang together. I have a list of things you can get to with this standard—about 700 different resources. One is the FGDC Clearing House, which in turn points to over 90 different resources that are searched. Another pointer is to

CIESIN, which, again, uses the same Z39.50 standard and fans out to around 20 different countries. There also is a supersearch available on GELOS.

Looking to the Future. As I said before, the G8's work on the Global Information Locator Service is being wrapped up. We are looking to move sponsorship to the United Nations Environment Program (UNEP). So far, the UNEP is very positive about this possibility. However, its recurring question is, "You mean we really don't have to spend any of our money to do this?" But that was the way we operated under the G7. These are just participating nations contributing what they will. There has been no funding for this. It is just the nations sending people, and, in our case, the European Commission in particular putting out resources to build the software. Thus, this has been a grassroots effort.

The Global Information Locator Service (GILS)—An Analog

The thing that was adopted by the G8 was a search interface—not a user interface, not a records format, not a database scheme, not a common piece of software. It was this notion of a common service for searching. That search interface is GILS.

I would like to talk a little bit more about Global Information Locator Service (GILS), for I know there is a lot of misunderstanding about it. If you walk up to a help desk, there is somebody there to answer questions. GILS is sort of a help desk. It is a service that says, "You can talk to me about the following things: I know people's names, I know their addresses, and I know their expertise." So we have a vocabulary that we both understand. You can say, for example, "I am looking for somebody who is an expert in biodiversity and I would like his name and phone number because I want to contact him." The help desk attendant then supplies an appropriate name and phone number. That is what GILS does.

In order to have this conversation in the first place, we both have to be talking the same language, such as English. That is what Z39.50 does. It gets us to the point where we are talking the same language. Then GILS says, "Oh, since we have a vocabulary. I know what you mean when you ask about names, addresses, and subject expertise."

We have heard it said that some things have GILS records in them. But there is no such thing as a GILS record. GILS is the search interface. It says, "You can talk to me about these things," and it writes down the answer for the user. It has delivered something to the user in the context the user requested.

Let's stop for a moment and look behind the help desk window. What are those helpers really doing? In the material world, the people at the help desk have a bunch of books on the shelf, where they can find the name. But they might have to go over to a professional society to find additional information requested. In fact, if you really look behind the scenes, you find out that there is no such thing as a record that will supply all the information requested.

But you as a user really don't care how the helper—be it a human or a search engine—finds the answers to your question. As a user you just are asking your question to an interface. The fact that it uses a DIF, for example, doesn't matter to you. In fact, the search interface of the Global Change Master Directory is GILS-compliant. CIESIN is GILS-compliant. As a user, you don't need to care. You wouldn't know. It is hidden from you.

An even better example is that there are services that are really just referrals. So if you ask to see their databases, they have none. Instead, when you ask a question, they decide who would know the answer to the question, and only at that point in time do they actually develop any data. But again, at the interface level, it really doesn't matter to the user what's going on behind the scene.

So the point of GILS is, if we could just have people all agree on a common search service, everyone could have any user interface they want for their own system. It could be for kids in the Globe Program. It could be for professionals. That is why we say GILS is just a search interface, but it happens to be a very good one. That is why we adopted it for GELOS. It could also serve as a general standard to assure interoperability in other types of systems.

Beyond Metadata: Scientific Information Management Approaches Supporting Ecosystem Monitoring and Assessment Activities

ROBERT F. SHEPANEK, Senior Scientist and Director of the Information Resources Development Staff (IRDS) in the National Center for Environmental Assessment (NCEA)

JEFFREY FRITHSEN, National Center for Environmental Assessment (NCEA) of the U.S. Environmental Protection Agency's Office of Research and Development

ABSTRACT

We present an integrated vision for scientific information management approaches supporting long-term monitoring and assessment activities within the USEPA's Office of Research and Development (ORD). This vision was developed based upon lessons learned from the implementation of several scientific information management systems and from development of the ORD's strategic and implementation plans for scientific information management. The vision reflects that effective management of scientific information must address technical, cultural, and management challenges. Technical challenges include management and integration of metadata, data, and the modeling, analysis, and visualization tools used as part of assessment activities. Cultural challenges relate mainly to the protection of intellectual capital produced by individual investigators. Management issues include commitment of adequate resources for systems development and operation, support for related policies and procedures, and appropriate incentives for involvement by staff and project participants. Past experience with EPA and other organizations have shown that the management issues are frequently most limiting to successful implementation of integrated information management solutions. USEPA ORD's vision for information management addresses the following technical challenges: developing directories of environmental resources collected and maintained by multiple organizations, providing access to descriptive information (metadata) sufficient to support secondary use of those resources; integrating data collected at multiple spatial and temporal scales; and integrating data resources with analytical tools and models. Metadata efforts have focused initially on the development of environmental resource directories enabling users to find data of potential interest, and development of detailed catalogs of descriptive information that enable users to evaluate the use of data as part of some assessment activity. In ORD's strategy, the concept of a data directory has been extended to include analysis tools, models, documents, and multimedia products to better reflect the complexity of environmental inventory and monitoring activities. Additionally, the strategic vision expands the focus of technical efforts such that various levels of metadata can support integration of data and data systems and integration of data with modeling, analysis, and visualization tools. This type of integration becomes useful for integrated assessments of biodiversity and is exemplified by integration of project-specific systems with a common data dictionary, or a common reference database for taxonomy, such as the Integrated Taxonomic Information System (ITIS). Effective information management approaches supporting monitoring and assessment activities must also recognize that there exist significant cultural challenges that must be met to ensure success of a long-term monitoring project. The cultural challenges relate to the sharing of data, loss of control of the use of the data, and realizing credit for collecting data, or adding value to data. ORD's vision for information management addresses these challenges by leveraging technology to restrict access to data and information as assessment products are developed, and proposes an incentive-based approach to catalyze sharing of data.

The title of today's talk is, "Beyond Metadata: Scientific Information Management Approaches Supporting Ecosystem Monitoring and Assessment Activities." What we will be talking about is the need to—as much as possible—leverage the use of information technologies to support all aspects of the environmental assessment process.

Information Diversity

In order to set the stage and put this topic in context, I would like to describe ever so briefly the scientific information management environment and what are we dealing with when we are talking about scientific assessments. First of all, we are dealing with information diversity. We are dealing with a lot of different types of information—not just biodiversity. But even if you are just looking at biodiversity, we still have to bring in a lot of other types of data in order to deal with the subject.

Environmental assessments are becoming much more multidisciplinary. In many of the government agencies, we have to consider environmental assessments in the context of combining ecology with human health. And all of a sudden, we have a whole mess of data that we have to pull together. The big challenge in terms of information management here is to manage many small pieces of information and a few very large pieces of information.

90

We also have the scale problem when we do an environmental assessment. For example, we can start off with large remote sensing data sets. These are large-scale data sets that may need to be combined with regional monitoring studies in order to conclude something about status and trends in the environment.

But even if we stop there, we still don't have the full picture, because we haven't yet considered the ecological processes. Therefore we have to go down to some site-specific intensive studies. It is the combination of these three types of studies—large-scale, regional, and site—that makes a complete environmental assessment. This is not just a message from the EPA—this is the Committee on the Environment and Natural Resources Monitoring Framework that came out in 1996. The Framework is a federal monitoring strategy to combine these three levels of data in order to do environmental assessments. It is actually pretty complex.

Systems Diversity

In addition to information diversity, the other thing that we have in the scientific realm is systems diversity. I am not talking about ecological systems here—I am talking about data systems where we have multiple information management systems. These systems are all individually developed for individual organizations and they, by-and-large, don't talk to each other. So the challenge here is to develop and provide interoperability between systems and with reference databases.

If I am developing a database for Project A here and another one for Project B there, then one of the things that I want to bring is some consistency in terms of the way I name data elements. If I refer to water temperature in one way for one database, for example, then I should refer to it in the same way in another database. At the least, we must have some sort of translator in-between the two databases that can interpret what has been stored in each.

We have heard before about the Integrated Taxonomic Information System (ITIS). One of the uses of ITIS is to promote a common way of naming the same taxa or taxon. Well, our databases in Project A and Project B, therefore, ought to refer to this reference database of taxonomy in the same manner so that Project A and Project B are calling the same species the same thing. Similarly, we have the same problem with chemical names.

The final complexity here is we have a very distributed workforce. Gone are the days of the individual investigator in academia coming up with some grand discovery and publishing it. No. Now we are forming research teams that transcend organizational and geographic boundaries. And the participants in those teams bring to the ball game their own information technology, their own information management environment. This means that there is by necessity another level of integration required. The challenge here is to link heterogeneous environments.

Three Challenges for Scientific Information Management

This situation brings up various challenges for scientific information management, and we categorize them into three big categories. We have the technical challenges—those that are related to the management of metadata and the tools needed to complete assessments. We have the management challenges—those that have to do with providing adequate resources—we are always asking for more money, right?—and also the support for policies and procedures to make the information management systems work. (Remember, a system is comprised of people, software, and hardware. If management is not enforcing the procedures, then people are not part of the equation there.) And, we have the cultural challenges. The cultural challenges relating to scientific information management have to do with the protection of the intellectual property rights of authors. If we don't acknowledge that, then we are going to be developing systems that don't work.

Cultural Challenges. Let me start with the cultural challenges. The cultural challenges basically are to provide protection for the actual property rights of others. If I as an investigator have collected a chunk of data, I usually want first publication rights to those data, because my career depends upon getting the results of my work published in a journal. If we don't acknowledge that, then we are not going to have buy-in at the principal investigator level. At the same time we are going to have to promote data-sharing and, to a certain extent, change the thinking of the scientific community. What we need to do is achieve recognition that the publication of metadata and data are as important as the publication of a journal article. One way to achieve this is to work with the scientific societies, the professional organizations, peer review panels, and so on, to reinforce the fact that there ought to be "brownie points" given out for someone who publishes metadata as well as data. Because until they get that credit, until the principal investigator can say, "Hey! I got something for that," they are not going to do it. Earlier someone mentioned a publication that came out a few months ago that said exactly those things. And to reinforce that, one of NASA's campaigns came up with a few "commandments" for their working group. I will share just a couple of them:

1. Thou shalt make thy data available even unto thine enemies. (Now that is promoting data-sharing!)
2. Thou shalt release thy data from bondage. (How many times have we heard about a guy still sitting on the data two years after the research is completed? Just hasn't published yet—and that doesn't help the community.)
3. Thou shalt not covet thy neighbor's data until they have had a crack at them.

You may laugh and it may sound trite, but you know, we do have those impediments that keep some scientists from using the information management systems that we develop.

Management Challenges. Some of the management challenges involve pleas for more money, commitment of adequate resources, and various publications advocating that 10 percent to 20 percent of the research budget ought to be allocated for information-management activities. Management challenges are probably seen more in the beginning of a program and less as time goes on. We need support for related policies and procedures, and we need appropriate incentives for the involvement of staff and project participants. Again, this aspect relates to the need for management to acknowledge that you published your metadata.

Technical Challenges. I classify the technical challenges into two different types of needs. First, we need tools to help users find relevant data and information in a distributed environment. We need to provide adequate descriptions of data so that a user can judge whether he or she can use those particular data for some particular use (often a use that was not considered by the guys who originally collected the data). And secondly we need to provide access to that metadata and the other resources.

Most of our scientific information management efforts so far have focused on those two needs, but there are some additional technical challenges. We need to develop approaches and standards that facilitate data integration. This will allow us to pull together data from multiple data sets and have information technology help with that process, instead of having to change the headings in your spreadsheet, for example. We need to enhance the interoperability of data systems. We must develop and use some sort of intelligent agents that can bring together information from multiple databases so that data integration is not a lot of laborious work on the part of individual investigators.

We are obviously providing some model and analysis and visualization tools now. However, there has to be an integration of those tools with the data themselves. In other words, choose your data set, choose your tool, and information technology can bring them together. I am not saying that we have all this developed, and I am not saying we have all the answers. But this is the vision of where we want to go. And I think information technologies can be used to support more of these kinds of activities, which are part of the assessment process.

EPA Efforts in Scientific Information Management

Within the EPA we have recently developed an implementation plan that spells out a vision for information management within the office of Research and Development. The plan encompasses the next three, four, and five years, so not everything is in place yet. But the major crux of it is to basically leverage information management technology to support all aspects of the assessment process. Part of that is to adopt or develop (but hopefully adopt as much as possible) approaches, standards, and procedures to maximize the integration of data, data systems, modules, and other analysis tools. We are using information technology to make this assessment activity more efficient.

We also are trying to integrate as much as possible our efforts with ongoing national and international efforts, because the EPA as an agency realizes that we can't do it all, we certainly haven't done it all, and—to some extent—we are behind organizations like NASA and NOAA in having effective data-management policies and systems in place.

This vision of the EPA's Office of Research and Development (ORD) attempts to address the technical management and cultural challenges that I have already discussed. This vision is developed and guided by the newly formed ORD Science Information Management Coordination Board, so that there is actually an organizational entity within our shop that is trying to pay attention to what information resources management should provide to support the types of activities that EPA has to conduct. If you wish, you can download the strategic plan from the Web page (<http://www.epa.gov/ord>).

What we are trying to achieve in terms of scientific management systems is an end result that combines these five elements: a **metadata directory** (how do I find something and describe it?); a **data format wizard** (how do I bring together various types of data that are in a distributed environment?); a **geographic module** (how do I deal with data that has some sort of spatial context in terms of management and reorganization?); a **statistical module** (how can I pull statistical routines and combine them with data?); and a **modeling module** (how do I pull together all those various modules, atmospheric depositions, ground water infiltration, agricultural run off, and so on, with the data that I have?). In application, what we envision is that at the start of a project the principal investigator would come along, enter their project description, and then begin to discover the background material needed to start the project using the metadata directory. As they pull together data they would use something like the data format wizard for the collection and integration of data. As they got into the analysis they would use the other modules, such as the geographic module, the statistical module, and the modeling module, to analyze and add value to the data they pull together. Finally they produce the report, putting another entry back into the metadata directory that essentially tracks the project from there. Thus, the metadata directory as we conceive it is fairly robust, representing various types of metadata objects, data sets, databases, projects, modules, documents, and even multimedia material.

Recommendations

I would like to close with a few lessons we have learned from going through the process of trying to understand the scientific information management environment. I will present these in the form of recommendations. First, I would put forward three general recommendations: 1) view information management as more than just storing or capturing data sets and distributing them; 2) use an incremental type of process—start with the metadata, go to the data, add on the tools, and so on; 3) use the best practical technology. (Using state-of-the-art technology usually means someone gets caught on the bleeding edge and it is tough to be there, so opt for practicality.)

The 20-Year-Rule Recommendation. Data are a resource that needs to be protected. A lot of money goes into collecting data. Some experts speak of the idea of "data entropy," where the value of data is very high as the principal investigator collects it. Gradually the value tapers off and goes off into nothingness as distance and time gets put in-between the data collection effort and later steps. Data entropy doesn't have to happen if there are adequate metadata. We think in terms of a 20-year-rule. The 20-year-rule simply asks: Will someone 20 years from now, not familiar with your data, be able to use and understand the data solely with the metadata that you provided?

I submit that there are *not* a lot of records out there that could pass the 20-year-rule. But if we could create such records now, we would avoid data entropy in the future. We need robust directories of environmental data information and tools—the types of things that represent more than just data sets. And the metadata standards that we use need to be developed based upon the needs of science, which may mean not built from top down. With metadata, we need to build basic, starting with the basic entry, such as title, abstract, contact, description of themes, spatial and temporal extent, and so on.

Network Architecture Recommendations. A few words about network architecture: We have all come to the conclusion in the field that we need to implement some sort of hybrid of centralized and distributive approaches. A purely centralized approach does not work, and a purely distributive approach does not work either. We probably, at a directory level, need to restrict network nodes to summary-level metadata. Detailed metadata and the data themselves are probably best stored close to the originating sources. So there is some need for data archiving facilities.

Management Recommendations. Some suggestions for management: Plan for and provide adequate resources. Again, it sounds like I have my hand out, but we have all been involved with projects that were at some point in time inadequately funded. In addition, management needs to provide incentives for data-sharing and publication. It also must get people to use the systems that we develop, share the vision for an integrated information management environment, and promote collaborative efforts.

Within the EPA, for example, we have an Ultraviolet Band monitoring program, as well as other atmospheric monitoring programs. Wouldn't it be neat if they were developing an interoperable type of data system? Well, before we weren't, but now we are. We need to link administrative management and scientific systems to reduce the burden of preparing data documentation. For it *is* burdensome. It does take time. If you describe the project once for the budget people because you are about to go out and spend extra dollars, for example, can't you use that description as part of your description in your metadata system?

Cultural Recommendations. Perceived threats to loss of intellectual property can impede the use of IM systems. I think mostly those threats are overstated and overemphasized, but they are real. They keep people from using IM. Data-sharing as an approach needs to be promoted, because data-sharing can lead to mutual career advancement. I am reminded that the most influential or the most interesting scientific advancements often are those that are as a result of merging two fields.

In addition, publication of metadata and data should be recognized as a worthwhile effort by peers. That idea is currently supported by several journals, including those published by *The Ecological Society of America, The American Geophysical Union,* and *The Geological Society of America.*

Publishing Good Metadata. Finally, publication of good metadata minimizes inappropriate use, another concern that scientists have about giving up their data into a system. The highest priority, though, in terms of doing environmental assessments, is to develop good directories of environmental data to help us find the information that is already out there.

Environmental Metainformation in the Work Program of the European Environmental Agency

STEFAN JENSEN, Project Leader, European Topic Centre/Catalogue of Data Sources (ETC/CDS), European Environment Agency

ABSTRACT

In 1996 ETC/CDS started operation under the task and vision to build a metainformation system on the environment on the European scale on behalf of the European Environment Agency (EEA). Following the guidance of G7 metadata initiative, the ETC/CDS advisory committee and the EEA representatives involved—building on thorough experiences in developing a metainformation system on the environment for Austria and Germany—the CDS fields and data model was developed and agreed upon. Technically, it is based on the GELOS standard—adding some optional fields through national demand. To meet the need for a multilingual environmental thesaurus, GEMET was built by merging existing European thesauri and adding translations for missing languages. The main purpose of the thesaurus was defined as indexing metainformation. Customers of the systems are seen to be the EIONET, the general public, and national initiatives. From this ground, software development results in a flexible input tool (WinCDS) and a state-of-the-art retrieval tool (WebCDS). For thesaurus purposes a maintenance tool as well as a simple "thesaurus browser" (ThesShow) is available. Metainformation collection started in 1997 with other ETCs and EEA, following a supply-driven approach (to register available and used sources). Only after agreeing on the selection criteria early in 1998 could they be used to follow a demand-driven collection approach. Interpreting the vision as the call for supplying—sooner or later—a seamless access to all kinds of environmental information through a catalogue, the GELOS+ fields are shaped according to recommendations from American and European standardizing bodies (both currently merging into the international ISO 15046-15). This enables appropriate description of spatial environmental data. This goes parallel with the implementation of spatial visualization and query of metadata in the CDS software. Collection by now results in a database with 1280 data sources and 550 addresses. Taking for granted that filling and updating of the catalogue will be a core activity of the ETC/CDS in the years to come, several crucial decisions need to be made. The maintenance of these sources is currently hampered by the lack of binding updating obligations and some changing policies. The EEA's strategy of a "European Reference Centre on Environmental Information" must be used to overcome these shortcomings by: clearly defining the role of CDS as the entry point (catalogue) for retrieval of quality-assured environmental information; identifying the integration with EEA data warehouse and EEA GELOS server; involving the ETCs in a constant process intensively using the selection criteria for national data collection. The interest of the majority of the member states in the usage of the CDS or a similar approach shows the opportunity to use it as a harmonizing approach to manage both their own business case in metainformation and their European reporting obligations. To further support this, reporting obligations from EU legislation are currently added to the database. Beyond this, the CDS system will develop into a distributed environmental information system that forms an entry point to various environmentally related sources, located at distributed providers—no matter if these are information from space or from Earth science, from mapping authorities or from monitoring networks—bridging the gap between public science and administration, between Europe and its regions, as well linking to global services.

My name is Stefan Jensen. I am the project leader of one of the nine European Topic Centres set up by the European Environment Agency. The European Environment Agency (EEA) was installed in 1994 in order to do reporting on the state of the environment.

The Organization

The European Observation and Information Network was established through the work of the EEA. As I mentioned, the network consists of nine Topic Centres. Most of them are subject-oriented. For example, one deals with nature conservation (this is where the biodiversity aspect would fit in). One deals with air pollution, one with soil, and so on. All the major topics are covered. Our Topic Centre—the Catalogue of Data Source (CDS) Topic Centre—deals with the information aspects of the network. One of our principal tasks is to gather metainformation, or metadata, in order to facilitate access to information collected by other partners in the network. This Topic Centre is an organization consisting of nine active partners from four European countries—Austria, Germany, Italy, and Sweden.

The work functions like this: There are 15 member countries in the European Union. But we are working with 18 countries (extended by Iceland, Liechtenstein, and Norway) at the moment. These countries named 18 National Focal Points. In addition, for each of the Topic Centres you find in the member states a so-called National

Reference Centre (NRC). The NRCs carry out the work in individual topic areas. So the core of the network consists of about 200 contacts involved in the work.

Then there are other institutions, such as scientific organizations, that are named by the member countries and that play an important role in environmental reporting. These other institutions are also part of the network and, to different degrees, they are involved in the current work.

The Task

Our task is, speaking on the meta-level, to create a European-wide metainformation system on the environment.

We began this task in 1996 by conceptualizing and implementing a common data model, a common language. The next thing was to promote the new data model to institutions that were not involved in this process. This initial effort also addressed the issue of existing national environmental information systems—metainformation systems—within the member states (which are, to a certain degree, already available, although the vast majority of the member states do not have them yet).

Next came the development of some pieces of software--first for data collection and second for the retrieval of data. For example, an important issue in Europe is the fact that there are a total of 13 languages that need to be addressed. So it was thought to be beneficial that building a multilingual environment be a part of the work.

The development of selection criteria was another issue we had to address. When we started data collection, we had not yet set selection criteria. As a result, we had to define some selection criteria based on the kinds of sources we were using.

We are continuing to collect data. We also have to maintain the meta-database, and we have to supply access to distributed systems, which we are now only starting to do. So at the moment, we have no distributive system yet. But like the Global Change Master Directory in the U.S., we have one database that is currently used.

The User Groups

Who are the user groups? Some of the user groups, including the EEA, the Topic Centres, and the National Focal Points, are pretty obvious as core users. But other users are not so clear. They include institutions running national systems (national metainformation initiatives), other institutions working in the field, and the "general public." There certainly are various other institutions that might be interested in these kinds of data, but we are still in a learning process about them and other potential users.

The Data Models

What is our data model? Where are we building on? We are building on the Global Environmental Information Locator System (GELOS) described earlier in this conference by Eliot Christian. We took the GELOS element set and had member states add certain fields, which were not made mandatory. Neither are the fields we added mandatory. However, we do have certain mandatory fields, and we encourage our users to fill in the mandatory fields. We also encourage the use of these mandatory fields in the construction of the software. Still it is possible to register the entries without mandatory fields, but I have seen this in only a couple of applications. If the information is really too thin—if, say, you have only three or four fields filled in—then it might not be very useful, and what you get out of the system may not be what you thought you were going to get.

We are also conducting various standardization initiatives, which allow us to at least meet Level I requirements (Level I requirements mean that you only cover first entries). We use other standards to build a thesaurus.

As with GELOS, Z39.50 will also be our protocol for accessing distributed systems. We are running profiles such as GELOS on it. But at the moment we are using GELOS not for a distributed system but for a description of elements we use in one database. SGML is the current data exchange format. I can see from the discussion here that XML is probably the next-generation format for such things, but SGML is a good start in moving toward XML.

Metainformation

I would like to reflect briefly on our experiences with metadata and why we introduced this kind of metainformation. I think that metainformation is relevant to a pyramid full of sources, including databases, stations, documents, maps, images, tools, and projects. The top of the pyramid is the locator system—the entry to this information—the tip of the iceberg. The bottom of the pyramid is founded by the access to the data themselves.

CDS-Based Harmonization

Our system is called CDS—Catalogue of Data Sources. We see that there are some national metainformation systems around in Europe that have a very high level or degree of detail but still do not cover everything. This is why we concentrate on a common subset to all of them.

Harmonization is, therefore, an issue. What we have achieved in this area is that member states are adopting the data model for the design of their national systems. You can imagine that each country has its own specialties and, like some people working with biodiversity, I imagine each country will have its own specific ideas. For example, some would like to have specific fields about plants or specific fields about beetles, and so on, just to describe the individuality of the source. Something like this is happening here as member states build on the CDS, including GELOS.

However, there are some countries that stick very closely to what we are doing. They are building their national metainformation systems on our software, which is based on MS ACCESS. They can easily change and adopt the software to their needs.

The CDS also is used in some supranational projects. One example is the Alpine Convention, which can be described as a biodiversity convention for the Alpine region.

Tools

We are also building various tools. One tool I mentioned already is a thesaurus, which can be used for indexing and retrieving metainformation. The one we are building is just a general thesaurus, so it is not a thesaurus on biodiversity. If you look into it you might find some terms out of your field, but it will probably not meet all the specific needs of individuals and scientific domains. However, the general thesaurus is a starting point and includes quite a number of terms (5,400!) in—at the moment—11 languages. (Greek and Islandic are currently missing but should be included by April 1999, by which time we want to finish the thesaurus.)

Software developments have resulted in a flexible input tool—WinCDS. We also have a state-of-the-art retrieval tool—WebCDS. This WebCDS tool is based on JAVA, which many of our clients are not able to use effectively because of firewall problems. Win CDS allows the usage of Structured Query Language (SQL) databases, and it has an easy search interface for HTML customers.

Criteria and Priorities for Collection

Now about the data that is in such a system: It was decided by the EIONET group, by the member states, and by the European Environment Agency that we should have at least a small central catalogue with core information where a certain level of quality control can be applied. This catalogue will include the following information:

- The Directory of EIONET partners
- Items produced by the EEA/EIONET
- Data requested by the EEA/EIONET on a regular and scheduled basis
- Data deliveries to the EU as a result of legislative reporting
- Data requested by several international bodies
- Environmental databases operated by international organizations and environmental conventions
- National State-of-the-Environment Reports
- National Environmental Monitoring Programs
- National Environmental Resource Libraries
- National meta-databases or reference databases on the environment

WebCDS Content

What is at the moment contained in this catalogue system? Here are the environmental themes and their percentages:

- environmental policy (20%)
- information (8%)
- water (8%)
- pollution (7%)
- general (6%)
- legislation (5%)
- biology (5%)
- air (4%)
- administration (4%)
- natural areas, landscape, ecosystems (4%)
- rest (29%)

Themes like those listed above, which are the most popular themes, are a part of the general thesaurus. The 5,400 thesaurus terms are assigned to 40 themes. The terms are used for the indexing; then you can assign them to the themes. The themes identified here also show that at this stage there is some focus on an administrative catalogue, since it includes quite a bit of environmental policy information.

Session 4

Building the Infrastructure

The Metadata Challenge for NBII

ANNE FRONDORF, Program Manager, National Biological Information Infrastructure,
U.S. Geological Survey's Biological Resources Division

ABSTRACT

This presentation will briefly review the development of the
National Biological Information Infrastructure (NBII) to date
and describe key recommendations of the PCAST *Teaming
with Life* report relating to development of a "Next
Generation" NBII. Some of the challenges involved in
developing and implementing metadata standards and tools
for the NBII include: the need to address a very wide
variety of data types, information products, and analysis
tools within the NBII infrastructure; the need to provide
metadata approaches that help link the biological
sciences/biodiversity conservation community with other
related communities (e.g., geospatial data and library
communities); and the need to develop approaches and
tools that not only lead to production of high-quality
metadata but that also are understood and accepted by
those who will need to enter the metadata.

Today I want to summarize briefly the work to-date in building what currently is the
National Biological Information Infrastructure (NBII). Then I will look at some of the
major infrastructure-related challenges that are facing us, particularly as we work
toward the goal of the next generation NBII as described in the PCAST report.

Part of the charge that was given to the original National Biological Survey—when it
was first created by Secretary Babbitt and predating our merger with the U.S.
Geological Survey—was to help to create a national partnership for sharing biological
information. That idea of information sharing was the basis of what we have tried to
do to date in NBII.

The philosophy behind NBII is to help build a distributed federation of biological data
and information. The standards, the policies, the rules by which we would all agree to
work together—these are the underpinnings that make it possible to collaborate in a
distributed way and allow us to have discovery, retrieval, and integration of data

across different sources. Perhaps most importantly, they also allow for the application of biological data and information to the real questions on which we are focusing.

In this talk, I will focus on two areas of the NBII program that are most pertinent to the reason we are meeting here this week. The first area is the diversity of the content, because obviously that diversity of content has significant implications for how we put the infrastructure together—particularly on the metadata side. It also has implications for how we look at metadata standards, tools, techniques, and approaches.

The second area is the ongoing NBII commitment to link with and build on existing, parallel, infrastructure efforts in other communities. You have heard about several of these efforts—both at the national and international levels—at the meeting this week. The NBII focus in this regard has always been to help create a bridge between other infrastructure efforts (which represent other views and other communities) and the biological sciences community. That has been the philosophical commitment that we have had in working on the NBII.

Building the NBII

Our approach has been to be very inclusive in terms of looking at the content of NBII, which, of course, means looking at databases, data sets, a variety of information products, and analysis tools to use on data. Some of this NBII content comes from USGS biologists, who are out on the ground doing biology. Some comes from our many partner agencies and organizations outside the USGS.

The USGS North American Breeding Bird Survey is an example of this diversity. This is a program run by our Patuxent Wildlife Research Center. This program has very valuable long-term data sets. It includes over 35 years' worth of data on over 400 different species of North American birds. The center obviously has very valuable data that it is trying to make more accessible through the NBII. The center also provides information products derived from the data sets, such as maps of bird distributions for individual species.

Involving State and Federal Agencies. Other key biodiversity data producers that we want very much to engage in this effort include state agencies—most importantly, the state fish and wildlife agencies and the state natural heritage programs, because those two groups together collect, maintain, and provide a very large amount of very valuable biodiversity data. These data are maintained in diverse formats that may vary from agency to agency and state to state. All this is a big challenge for us. How can we work collectively with those groups at the state level that really are great developers and repositors of biodiversity data and link them into this bigger effort?

Collections and Museums. Obviously natural history collections and museums are tremendous producers and maintainers of biodiversity data. What we have tried to do at NBII is work—wherever we have the opportunity to work—individually with particular museums or collections to help them be in a position to make more of their biological specimen data accessible, as well as help them look at these issues strategically. We are working with our partner agencies—including federal, state, and non-government agencies and organizations—to see what we collectively can do with the collections and museums to help put those institutions in a position where their data are more accessible, more interoperable, and more applicable for resource management decisions.

Directories. Directories of biodiversity or biological science experts can also be another really valuable information product if you think about federating them and making them accessible for different people to use and access. The Taxonomic Resources and Expertise Directory is one example. This is a cooperative project among the federal agencies that work together on the Integrated Taxonomic Information System (ITIS) and the Association of Systematics Collections (ASC). Basically, we have created an online directory of taxonomic specialists for North America that includes information on their areas of taxonomic and geographic specialty and that is available for people to find and use as a resource. We now have about 1,000 different specialists listed there. Experts can both enter and update their data online that way.

Analysis Tools. Another important part of the NBII content is tools for biological analysis. The idea here is that we want to be in a position not just to let people find data and information more easily but also to find and share analytical tools—such as ecological models or GIS applications. These are tools that people can use to get to the point at which they are actually answering a question or producing a result. We can use the federation to share the tools just as you can use the federation to share the data. We have a component of NBII where we are working to make biological analysis tools available for people to find, share, and use. And we are working to populate this component with more tools and make it an important part of the NBII.

Partnerships to Build the Infrastructure. I have gone through these areas of content very quickly. But my goal was to emphasize that what we are talking about are communities—communities either of producers and suppliers of data and information and tools or communities of customers or users. Whatever we are talking about—state agencies or technical-report writers or modelers or some other group—these are all communities that we have to involve in building the infrastructure.

With regard to metadata, for example: We need to have approaches to metadata—whether you are talking about metadata for technical reports, metadata for analytical tools, metadata for data sets, metadata for information products, metadata for directories of experts—that cover all those aspects of the content. And we want to try to do this in a way that engages all the various communities and makes them want to be part of the broader endeavor. Only with the involvement of all communities will we be able to provide the common framework that knits all information together and makes it possible for someone to find museum specimen data, satellite imagery data, an ecological model, and a technical report that all relate to the very specific question that a person has to answer. That is the goal that we are trying to reach as we work with our partners to help build the NBII.

Linking NBII with Other Infrastructure Efforts

Now I want to discuss the importance to NBII of linking with and leveraging existing, parallel infrastructure efforts in other communities. I am going to use as an example just one infrastructure effort, the National Spatial Data Infrastructure (NSDI). Obviously part of that content I just described were biological data sets that are spatially referenced (e.g., bird distribution). That is why it has been such an important part of our focus to help make a linkage with spatial data initiatives. Again, our goal has always been to try to be a bridge between the biological sciences community and other communities (such as the geospatial data community). By supporting collaboration between the NSDI and the NBII, we can help make that bridge and, by doing so, hopefully build support for both the NSDI and the NBII.

The Federal Geographic Data Committee. Within the Federal Geographic Data Committee, which coordinates the NSDI, we have established a Biological Data Working Group. This Working Group has members from several federal agencies, as well as some non-federal partners, that are working together under the structure of the FGDC to look at ways to help ensure that we are doing our utmost to increase sharing and access of biological spatial data.

We are also working through the FGDC standards process to try to build some federal data and metadata standards that we can use in the NBII. The first thing we have done in that regard is a metadata standard for NBII. We did this by developing a biological profile of the existing FGDC geospatial metadata content standard. This profile includes the entire FGDC geospatial metadata standard and adds some elements to it, so that hopefully it is more pertinent or meaningful to the biological sciences community. For example, we added some elements about nomenclature and taxonomy, which the spatial standard doesn't really cover, since that is not what it is set up to do. This is a good example of the kind of bridge we are trying to build to link biology back to the spatial data community.

Clearing House. Another way we are working with the NSDI is through the Clearing House. We have an online NBII Metadata Clearing House, created along the same lines and procedures of the NSDI Clearing House. We operate as a node off the NSDI. Again, we have extended our Clearing-House function a little bit to allow people who are looking for metadata and data sets to search on those additional biological metadata fields that we have added in our biological profile. So, in a way we have taken the NSDI and biologically enhanced it. To me, this is a very visible example of bridge-building between biology and the spatial data community.

Cooperative Funding Efforts. We also cooperate with the NSDI to help fund non-federal projects (with state agencies or universities) that are, again, helping to build the NSDI and NBII. This has been a very successful partnership—one that allows you to actually "see" some of those bridges being built. For example, I have seen instances in which a state fish and wildlife agency or a state heritage program, in order to make this project work, will join forces with an organization like a state's Geographic Information Systems Council—two kinds of groups that might not normally have a lot of interaction with each other at the state level. By helping provide money and by looking for projects that link biology and spatial data, we have hopefully encouraged some groups at the state level to start making some connections.

Again, I want to emphasize that although I have used NSDI as an example of linking to other infrastructures, that is only one example. In fact, a huge part of the NBII effort involves looking for ways we can link with other infrastructure efforts, both nationally and internationally. One other example is the Global Change Master Directory. The NBII Program has a cooperative relationship with NASA's Global Change Directory. Again, we pull resources together, and that has allowed us to find and document biodiversity data sets and then make those data sets accessible through both the Global Change Directory and the NBII.

Essential NBII Infrastructure Components

Now I would like to identify a couple of key NBII infrastructure elements. The first is the development of a controlled biological vocabulary. This means having a consistent, standard reference of biological terms that is available for people to use—both on the supply side, to use in describing data and information products, and on the demand (or the customer) side, to use when one is searching for information. This is the kind of key contribution on which we can all work together.

The second important component of the NBII infrastructure is a standard reference for biological nomenclature and taxonomy. For the NBII, this reference is the Integrated Taxonomic Information System (ITIS). I know you heard about ITIS yesterday from Bruce Collette. But I will just add that since we started work, the NBII program has been a very strong advocate and supporter of ITIS, because as far as we are concerned, having a common frame of reference that is scientifically credible for species names is a linchpin concept to make all of this work. The species names are what locate us in a biological data world.

The Effect of the PCAST Report on NBII

The PCAST report has definitely laid out some challenges for the advancement of NBII. I just want to touch on two major ideas that I think have implications for the kinds of things we are discussing here this week. The first is the PCAST recommendation to significantly increase the biodiversity and the ecosystem data and information content of the NBII. We have really only scratched the surface of the diversity and the extent of content that we need to include. To advance farther, we really must increase our investment in and funding for all those different kinds of communities that I identified earlier as the producers and maintainers of biodiversity data. To make that happen, we must continue to focus our efforts on involving those communities in both the design and the building of the infrastructure. Again, we need to help them see themselves within that broader picture.

The second big focus of PCAST was the idea of a next-generation NBII and the fact that we want to increase the amount of research and development funding that is focused on biodiversity information science and biodiversity computer science. This will support the idea of true interoperability of all this distributed content—we eventually want to be truly interoperating all these data and all these information products, all these tools.

Challenges Faced by NBII

The greatest challenges faced by NBII are encountered as we look for ways to link together all interested stakeholder communities—communities that represent aspects of the totality of biodiversity data and information and analysis—communities such as state agencies, museums, collections, library communities, and spatial data communities. We need to try to engage all these communities, even if they do not totally agree on all the aspects of our work in terms of building the infrastructure.

In terms of metadata, we need to be thinking of ways to make metadata standards that are modular, so that we can link things together across communities. The metadata standards and approaches also should allow people to prepare high-quality metadata. Yesterday, Jeff Frithsen spoke of the "20-year-rule." I have a slightly different—and personal—take on what quality metadata are under the 20-year-rule. My idea is that you want to have metadata that are good enough that someone with whom you may never come in contact can use your data for some application that you yourself would have never imagined. I think that when we are in a position to let people really create quality metadata and when we give people usable metadata tools that make sense from their perspective, we will be well on the way of reaching our goal.

The National Spatial Data Infrastructure: Coordinating Geographic Data Acquisition and Access

JOHN MOELLER, Staff Director, Federal Geographic Data Committee

ABSTRACT

Our nation's communities are addressing a wide range of complex economic, social, and environmental issues. Geospatial data plays a key role in helping communities synthesize information relevant to these issues. Unfortunately, data are often difficult to locate, obtain, and integrate. Geography creates the unifying element that brings people together to identify key issues, develop a vision, set goals, and determine the actions necessary to improve their community. Coordinated geospatial data from all levels and sectors that is produced, integrated, and made readily available to all citizens can empower communities to move toward consensus rather than conflict. Also, consistent, reliable means to share geospatial data among all users could result in significant savings for data collection, enhanced use of data, and better decision-making. In April 1994, Executive Order 12906 was issued, which called for the establishment of the National Spatial Data Infrastructure (NSDI). The NSDI offers a mechanism to link technologies, policies, standards, and resources necessary to improve the way geospatial data is acquired, stored, processed, disseminated, and used. The Strategy for the National Spatial Data Infrastructure, published in April 1997, creates a vision of the NSDI that "current and accurate geospatial data will be readily available to contribute locally, nationally, and globally to economic growth, environmental quality and stability, and social progress." This vision will be realized only when federal, state, local, and tribal governments and the private sector and academia are working collaboratively to develop integrated geospatial data and promote better access to this data to improve the decisions affecting the nation's communities. The Federal Geographic Data Committee, chaired by Secretary of the Interior Bruce Babbitt, provides federal leadership for the development of the NSDI and promotes the coordinated development, use, and sharing of geospatial data on a national basis. The development of the NSDI has responded to a set of needs and interests common to geospatial data producers and users. Development and implementation have involved activities by federal agencies and many organizations outside the federal government. It includes a series of evolving, common practices to meet some basic needs of organizations and individuals; to know the characteristics of data—this is accomplished through the implementation of a data documentation standard known as the FGDC Content Standard for Digital Geospatial Metadata; to find and access data—the vehicle to do this in the NSDI is called the Clearing House; to have some common sets of data to use as building blocks—these basic geospatial data sets are known as Framework and are intended to provide a foundation on which organizations can build by adding their own detail or use to orient and compile other data sets; to transfer and integrate data among users and providers—this includes standards for common data classification systems, data content and data models to facilitate data development, sharing, and architectures and technologies that enable data sharing and improved geo-processing (Data standards activities are facilitated by the Federal Geographic Data Committee and technology standards are being addressed by the private sector); to leverage our resources invested in geographic data—no one organization can build the NSDI and many cooperative efforts are underway across the nation to make geospatial data more available and usable. These actions have resulted in considerable progress but much work remains. The 1998 report from the National Academy of Public Administration "Geographic Information for the 21st Century" follows a 1993 study by the NRC, "Toward a Coordinated Spatial Data Infrastructure for the Nation," and endorses vigorous development of the NSDI. As part of stronger efforts to achieve smart, sustainable growth in cities, suburbs, and rural areas, Vice President Gore recently announced several initiatives to help communities gain access to and participate in the NSDI. The need for geographic information is booming—some have called it a geospatial revolution. The improved use of geospatial data and geographic information technology can help our nation improve the opportunity for all citizens to participate in community-driven solutions while better meeting crucial Federal responsibilities. For additional information and more detailed descriptions of the National Spatial Data Infrastructure and the many activities it involves, contact the Federal Geographic Data Committee (FGDC) or one of the many stakeholders who participate in its development and implementation. The FGDC hosts a Web site at <http://www.fgdc.gov> that provides a wealth of information and specific materials to help implementers and also direct links and contact information to other stakeholder organizations that can help with implementation issues.

We have been discussing the linkage of biological information, using the link of the NBII to a global biological network as one example. Across the globe, there are a number of nations—at least 24 to 30 countries of which we are aware—that are either building spatial data infrastructures or discussing the needs and opportunities for developing a global spatial data infrastructure. In fact, next week in Australia there will be another conference to talk about working together to construct at least the beginnings of a global spatial data infrastructure. Today, I would like to talk to you about such an infrastructure: the National Spatial Data Infrastructure.

Geographic Information and the National Spatial Data Infrastructure (NSDI)

First, let's think about the importance to geographic information, particularly as it relates to communities. These communities can be thought of as towns, cities, counties, and so on. But they also can be watersheds, biological communities, ecosystems—anything that has a geographic component and base to it.

In a political context, geographic information in this country has historically been held by communities. Geographic information has long driven decision processes at the community level, where it is used to figure out issues like how and where to develop road networks. But as we have moved to more a centralized government, with increased power of state and local governments (a move aided by the computer revolution), we have seen that much of the local data that had historically been used by citizens in communities began to be removed from the communities. However, I think that now, with today's political environment and technology environment, such trends have been reversed. We see that more and more communities today have the necessary tools and technology, as well as the continued interest, to have that data and information restored to them to be used in dealing with issues that are important to people at the local level. In fact, Mark Shaffer, Assistant Secretary for Water and Science within the Department of Interior, has pointed out that we can think of geographic information technologies as Jeffersonian technologies. In other words, these are technologies that facilitate the democratic process, that begin to bring people back in touch with the place where they live and back in touch with the information and decision processes associated with where they live.

So geographic information is important. Place matters. We all live somewhere, we all work somewhere, we all play somewhere. So, this information is really important both to us as individuals as well as organizations, and I think we are seeing more and more recognition of the value and importance of place. In 1998 there was a study done by the National Academy of Public Administration that looked at geospatial data for the 21st century. In that study, researchers identified geographic information as being a fundamental underpinning for about 50% of all U.S. economic activity. They identified 12 major sectors that relied on geographic information in dealing with issues important to those sectors and those sectors comprised about 50% of our gross national product. So economically geographic information is important.

Government activities in counties, cities, and states are geography-based and so geographic information likewise is important to them in meeting their responsibilities. I think we will see continued trends in that direction as governments take a cross-jurisdictional approach to various issues. For example, rivers flow through communities—they don't very often start and stop within the same community. Ecosystems—or almost anything else that you want to talk about—almost always begin and end in different kinds of administrative jurisdictions. This creates the need for a common understanding among jurisdictions. This common understanding is a fundamental geography of where we are, the capabilities that exist within that particular place, and the common understanding of the potential solutions on which we can focus. Likewise, in the devolution of government, more and more of the focus is being placed back on communities and community solutions. And so we see that geographic information is becoming more an integral part of place-based government. However, effective, placed-based government requires that more and more of that information be available—not just to governments and a few select organizations, but also to all citizens.

What we found, as I am sure many of you are aware, is that geographic information is difficult to use. It is difficult to find. And if you find it, it is hard to integrate. In addition, much of the data are not current, not documented, or not complete. Hence, we have the establishment of the National Spatial Data Infrastructure.

The Vision of the NSDI

In April, 1994, Executive Order 12906 was issued. It established the National Spatial Data Infrastructure as an initiative to try to bring about better coordination, better sharing use, and better dissemination of geographic information. The basic purposes of the Executive Order are fourfold:

1. One purpose is to advance the goals of the National Information Infrastructure and to build on the emerging network and improved information technology capabilities that are available within the country.
2. Our second goal is to reduce duplication of effort that takes place in collecting and using geographic information. In the early 1990s, there was a quick survey done of federal government geographic information activities, and it was estimated that at that time federal agencies annually spent about $4 billion on geographic data. We know that there is a lot of overlap and duplication. In addition there is no good estimate of the amount of money expended by state governments and local governments, but I am willing to guess that if we collected that information, we would find that it is several times that which is expended at the federal level. So, there are a lot of dollars going into geographic information. And there is a lot of duplication that can be avoided, which would allow us to make more efficient use not only of the data but also of the economic resources available to us.
3. Third, we could get more effective management by all levels of government if we can move toward this vision of greater sharing, access, dissemination, and use of geographic information.
4. The fourth goal of the National Spatial Data Infrastructure is to find ways to improve how we acquire, distribute, and use geographic data and geographic information.

The vision that was established for the NSDI—a vision that was reaffirmed in 1997—is a lofty vision: It is to have readily available current and accurate geospatial data that will contribute locally, nationally, and globally to sustainable development or to economic growth, environmental quality, and social progress.

What is the geospatial data to which NSDI's vision refers? What are some of the kinds of information that are being incorporated into the National Spatial Data Infrastructure, and what kinds could be incorporated into it in the future? Geospatial data includes field-measurement information, or information about the natural or built environment. Species, habitat, streams, water quality, and transportation networks all are kinds of field-measurement information. Geospatial data also includes remotely sensed information. This is information that comes from airplanes, satellites, or any kind of platform that collects remotely sensed images. Map information—information that has historically been stored on maps, held on maps, or that you can think of placing on a map in the future—is part of geospatial data as well. And so is a lot of data—data about biology, land records, land ownership, social information—any data that have connections to place. These data have been spatially referenced but have been stored in a variety of different media in records in museums, records in county courthouses, and in records held at other places. So, all information that has a relationship to a place—that is on, above, or below the surface of the earth—can be envisioned as becoming part of and being available through the National Spatial Data Infrastructure that is being constructed.

Components of the NSDI

Now I would like to speak about the principal elements that we are considering as we build the National Spatial Data Infrastructure.

The Framework. The first element around which we are building is geographic data, geographic information, which will form what we call the framework. What we have found through research is that anybody who is building a Geographic Information System (GIS) has need for some basic core data. Research has shown that there are anywhere from six to eight fundamental data sets that almost everyone uses when they begin to build a geographic information system or begin to build geographic data sets. As a result, we have identified seven basic fundamental layers as framework data sets—core "building blocks" of data—that will compose the National Spatial Data Infrastructure. The intent is to build these skeletal framework data sets consistently and seamlessly across the country so that they can be used as building blocks for anyone developing spatial data; as a way to add further attribute information; and as a referencing network or as a framework to tie other geographic information. Those seven framework data sets within the NSDI are:

1. digital ortho-imagery;
2. elevation data;
3. geodata control;
4. hydrography, or the basic outline of the river and water network of the country;
5. a basic transportation network;
6. administrative boundaries, such as county, city, and state jurisdictions and boundaries of large federal holdings, such as national parks, national forests, military reservations, Indian reservations, and other administrative boundaries; and
7. a basic land survey network in the western part of the United States that would include the public land survey system and other, similar kinds of basic land registration networks that may already exist in the eastern part of the country.

Metadata. Metadata is fundamental. A basic description of information is critical for people to be able to access, understand, and begin to use spatial data sets.

The Clearing House. Within the National Spatial Data Infrastructure we are trying to establish a network of interconnected geospatial data providers to have universal access to geospatial information. Right now if you went out on the network and just did a search for vegetation through one of the other basic, commercial search engines, you would get back all different kinds of information. What we are working towards is the establishment of this network of interconnected nodes that serve geographic information and that give people the ability to go to one place—the Clearing House—and do one search of all the spatial data sets that are registered through the Clearing House.

In providing for search and access methods through the Clearing House, there are some fundamental steps that involve metadata. The first—and the most difficult—step is the preparation of new metadata, the documentation of the sets. There is software available for validation and staging, through which you can run your metadata records. It will tell you if there are errors and give you keys to correct those errors, so that you will have a valid metadata record that can be inserted into the Clearing House and that will create the capability for using the Clearing House as a search method. Publication would be in a Clearing-House node, with user access provided through the Clearing House and through the software available for implementation of the NSDI Clearing House.

This is a growing network. It has been in operation for about three years. Within the past year we have seen a doubling of the number of nodes that are available on the network. We are now at about 90 to 95 nodes that serve metadata. But more and more of the nodes are actually beginning to serve the data themselves, so you can access and extract the data directly from the NSDI Clearing House.

The Development of Standards. A fourth component is the development of standards. Within the NSDI there are two different types of standards that are being developed—technology standards and data standards.

In geoprocessing technology standards, the leading organization for development is the Open GIS Consortium. This is a group of about 140 organizations, about 100 of which are technology providers, hardware/software companies, telecommunications companies that deal with geospatial information. They are working on interoperability standards so that this vision of "plug-and-play" geoprocessing technologies and the ability to move data sets and the applications of information from one vendor platform to another will, in fact, become a reality. We are not there yet, but in the next couple of years we see these interoperability specifications really moving to where they will become mainstream and available through the venders.

On the data side, the Federal Geographic Data Committee (FGDC) is providing the leadership for geospatial data standards and data management standards, such as transfer standards, metadata, and content standards. We have between 22 and 24 subcommittees or working groups within the FGDC, and many are dealing with data-thematic content or classification standards. The Biological Data Working Group, for example, is working with biological standards.

There are 10 standards that have been approved, and there are another 25 standards that are in some state of development by FGDC subcommittees. The intent of the standards-development process of the FGDC is to develop standards that will be useful for any level of government, any level of academia, or any part of the private sector.

The Executive Order calls for federal agencies to implement standards as they are approved by the FGDC. But implementation of standards is voluntary outside the federal government. Therefore, we are encouraging the subcommittees and working groups to involve interested parties—not just from the federal government but from all levels of government and from all sectors—in the development of standards so that, hopefully, these standards can be useful and applicable across all sectors.

We are also working to link the FGDC standards activities to other national standards development work and to international standards development work. So we are in the process of developing a harmonization or a cross-working mechanism with the International Standards Organisation (ISO) process so that we won't be duplicating steps if we move an FGDC standard into the national arena or into the international arena. That seems to be going quite well right now.

Partnerships. The last part that is really fundamental to building the NSDI is partnerships. No one organization or entity really has the financial resources or the mission capability at this time to collect all the geospatial data that it needs so the organization can deal with the mission activities or the decisions that it must make. So we see partnerships, such as the partnership with the NBII, as being a fundamental cornerstone of building the space. We are working with as many organizations as we can across the country to try to figure out the roles that different sectors can play in helping build the NSDI.

The NSDI and the
Federal Geographic Data Committee (FGDC)

The Federal Geographic Data Committee (FGDC) was established in 1990 by an order of the Office of Management and Budget and further reaffirmed in the Executive Order of 1994. It was given the federal leadership position for coordination of federal agency activities and the responsibility for trying to bring together all sectors across the country to work together to build the NSDI.

Organization. Right now the FGDC consists of 16 cabinet and executive level agencies at the federal level, as well as the bureaus and sublevel organizations within those cabinet-and executive-level agencies. It includes organizations such as the EPA, the Department of Interior, the Department of Agriculture, the Department of Commerce, the National Science Foundation, the Department of Defense, the Tennessee Valley Authority, the Library of Congress, the National Archives and Records Administration, and a number of others.

But broader than the federal level, what we are also trying to do is involve as many stakeholder members or stakeholder organizations as possible in the development of the National Spatial Data Infrastructure. For example, we have partnerships with the National Association of Counties, the National League of Cities, with the International City/County Managers Association, with the Open GIS Consortium, and with the University Consortium for Geographic Information Sciences. A partnership has also been created with the National States Geographic Information Council, an organization that represents probably 45 or more state GIS coordinating councils and a very effective organization at trying to bring together state coordinating bodies to get their involvement in the development of the spatial data infrastructure. I think states are becoming very, very effective now in coordinating geographic information within their jurisdictions.

115

FGDC has benefited from the very effective chairmanship of Secretary Babbitt. Mr. Babbitt is knowledgeable about the need for geospatial information and the importance of both geospatial information and biological information. He was the one who handed out the Hammer Award for the ITIS project. He has been very, very supportive of data management and data coordination activities, because he sees this information as something that can help the department, the federal government, and—in fact—the whole nation in dealing with its science issues, as well as in dealing with the need for better land use and natural resource management decision processes. Within the FGDC, we have standing orders regarding the steering committees Mr. Babbitt chairs—we schedule those committee meetings only when the Secretary can attend. He runs the meetings. And he does a very effective and articulate job of talking about metadata. It has been wonderful.

FGDC Metadata Standard. We do have a metadata standard within the FGDC. Its basic purpose is to organize our internal investment in spatial data by providing ways to inventory, to have quality information that is available to others, and also to provide information that can help others in processing and interpreting data that they get in a transfer. The standard was called for in the Executive Order, and it was adopted in 1994 as the format for federal use (although one of the challenges remains getting organizations to actually implement the metadata standard as they develop new spatial data sets). The metadata standard also can be used as the search vocabulary in the Clearing House.

The FGDC Metadata Standard has a lot of data elements. It also has 10 sections that organize different components of the standard for navigation and organization. Some of these sections are mandatory components and are really important for transfer and for basic understanding of what is contained within a spatial data set. Those are things such as identification, reference information, citation information about a data set, the basic kind of abstract information, the time period to which the data set pertains, and contact information.

One of the things that we are working on is improving the FGDC metadata standard. FGDC Metadata Version 2 was passed in August, 1998, and allowed for extensions, additional profiles, and other things that enable the building of a biological profile. Similarly, a cultural and demographic profile is being developed.

We are also working at the international level in the development of an international metadata standard. That standard is built fundamentally on the FGDC standard and the U.S. will be developing a profile that will pretty much follow the same standard elements that the FGDC has developed, so that the investments that people have made in the FGDC standard will be preserved. We will be working to provide a transition to the international standard, so no one will lose work that has already been done.

The NSDI and the NBII

We have already heard about the National Biological Information Infrastructure (NBII). I would just like to touch on a couple of points again to show that the NBII and the NSDI are compatible, that the ways they have been developed support and compliment each other. As you know, the NSDI focus is on spatial data and information, while the NBII focus is on biological data. Those biological data that have a spatial component are being included in the NSDI. As the NBII is being developed, it is intended for that information to be accessible and available through the National Spatial Data Infrastructure. Both of them are conceptually quite the same. Both deal with diverse content, diverse communities and groups of users, and distributed networks. In addition, both are looking to build on common standards, to increase accessibility and use, and to create partnerships.

The biological data activities within the National Spatial Data Infrastructure include biological metadata, the profile of which is an extension of the Federal Geographic Data Committee (FGDC) standard; the FGDC Biological Data Working Group, which is looking at the need for and promoting the development of biological standards; and extensive work of the biological community with other FGDC working groups which encompasses groups such as earth cover, vegetation subcommittees, hydrographic or water data subcommittees, and other subcommittees that have a relationship to and a bearing on biological information.

Challenges for the NSDI

The NSDI is intended to promote access to data and to facilitate sharing for decision processes. One challenge that we face is regarding metadata. Metadata is critical for access, understanding, and use of data. But it still needs a lot more work, a lot more involvement and participation of people from all levels of government and of specialists in all different communities in the development of the metadata records.

In addition, we see geographic information becoming increasingly vital to the decision-making needs of the community, and we need to continue to expand tools, technology, and information to support the communities. As I said, many organizations are not yet making the needed investments, particularly for legacy information.

I find it interesting that often, state organizations or non-federal organizations that voluntarily adopt metadata and the principles of the NSDI are doing a better job than those that are required to collect metadata. The lesson we can learn about mandatory versus voluntary participation and the correlation to acceptance of standards is that we should focus on making the case based on standards as a good business practice and that managers need to be involved. We need to bring our managers, our executives, into the process, because they are the ones who really can support and encourage organizations in better data management, and they are the ones who will use it in decision processes.

As we face these challenges, we must remain aware that it is the strategies that address the decision-making needs of communities and organizations that are the strategies we have seen being the most successful. Such strategies will help us move forward even more quickly.

If you wish to find out more about NSDI, you can visit our Web site at <http://www.fgdc.gov>.

Digital Libraries Research and Infrastructure

STEPHEN GRIFFIN, Program Director, Division of Information and Intelligent Systems at the National Science Foundation (NSF)

ABSTRACT

The Internet and World Wide Web have demonstrated that scholars, students of all ages, and the general public have a boundless appetite for information of all types. Millions now regularly use the Web as a primary source of information and also as an inventive medium for communicating and sharing knowledge, enabling new relationships, collaborations, and intellectual communities. The Digital Libraries Initiative (DLI), funded by NSF, NASA, and DARPA from FY94-98, supported pioneering exploration into issues of organization, access, security, and use of distributed-information resources. The six DLI projects addressed a broad range of fundamental research: new document models, video capture and cataloging, geographic data spaces, image retrieval concept spaces, agent-based synthetic global economies, and new tools for classroom education, to name a few. [National Synchronization Home Page: <http://dli.grainger.uiuc.edu/national.htm>] The Digital Libraries Initiative-Phase 2 (DLI-2) sponsored by NSF, DARPA, NLM, LoC, NEH, NASA from FY1998-FY2002 and other agency partners will look to support new areas and dimensions in the digital libraries information life cycle, including content creation, access, use and usability, preservation, and archiving. DLI-2 will also look to create domain applications and operational infrastructures and understand their use and usability in various organizational, economic, social, and international contexts. <http://www.dli2.nsf.gov/>

I would like to begin by telling you that I am from the National Science Foundation (NSF). The NSF is a government agency. Frequently people get us mixed up with the National Academy of Sciences, so I just wanted to say that we are an Executive agency, very much in the same scheme of governmental management as other independent agencies.

The organizational structure of NSF is that of a common bureaucracy. Bureaucracies are easy to laugh about. But they can seriously get in the way of getting things done, particularly in interdisciplinary programs. That is something about which we have thought very hard regarding the Digital Libraries Initiative (DLI), for not only is it interdisciplinary, it is inter-everything. How does one, therefore, map support for an inter-everything set of activities onto a very tightly structured hierarchical set of organizations—a set of super-organizations—that are established purportedly to promote these sorts of things?

The Digital Libraries Initiative is the focus of my talk today. We have two phases—Phase 1 and Phase 2—and I would like to present them both.

The Digital Libraries Initiative-Phase 1

Phase I officially ended at the end of August, 1998, although most of the sites still have their testbeds and their Web pages up online. It was a fairly modest program cosponsored by the National Science Foundation, the Defense Advancement Research Projects Agency (DARPA), and the National Aeronautics and Space Administration (NASA) to try to put together some technology testbeds and some programs of basic research. Make no mistake, the Digital Libraries Initiative was an information technology program. We provided no money for content.

The research that was involved in the Digital Libraries Initiative projects could be characterized as 90% digital, 10% libraries (that did not escape everyone's notice). We think that we had some very successful technology projects. Over the course of the four-year term of DLI-1, as our thinking matured and evolved, we came to the conclusion that developing digital libraries technologies needed to proceed within consideration of multiple contexts, including content, social, domain, applications, and international. A technology-centric program would not be as successful. We feel that the DLI-Phase 1 projects were exceptionally successful in adopting and working within broader perspectives.

We have put in $24 million over four years, and the cost sharing varied between 100% and 200% per project. So government investment was effectively doubled and tripled.

There were six projects, all based on a similar project model and each led by one of the following universities: the University of California at Berkley, Stanford University, the University of California, Santa Barbara (whose testbed was closest and most germane to geographic information systems), the University of Illinois, the University of Michigan, and Carnegie Mellon University. We managed to broaden the scope of the projects, increase the level of government investment, and actually further our thinking about what we were doing by building partnerships with people who had other values and other insights and other perspectives on the idea of a digital library. I think we had, in all, over 100 partnerships of many different types. Some corporations would give funds to the projects. Some would supply services or other resources, including staff.

Some of the most productive forms of partnerships were in the exchange of staff. Some of the companies paid for researchers from their research laboratories to spend a year at a university. Even in a globally networked world, there are some things that can only be achieved when people are face to face, sitting together around the same table. So, I think this exchange of personnel was extremely valuable. We hope to expand this concept and start exchange programs with visiting scientists.

The Digital Libraries Initiative-Phase 2

In February of last year, based on the recognized success and achievements of the Phase-1 projects and other community efforts, we put together a second phase to the initiative, a phase we creatively called Digital Libraries Initiative-Phase 2. In this phase we broadened the program in a number of ways, particularly in terms of content use and usability. Once again the technology only gains meaning when it is placed in an environment where people use it to work on information of value and interest to them. The problems associated with that makes it very difficult to, for example, persuade the computer science community that it should use some of its efforts and resources to assist other communities. Believe it or not, I cannot make, without some scrutiny, an award to a biologist. This is because it would be noted in this community, where people keep very close track as to whether your program is funding the people they believe it is supposed to fund. So one of the real challenges to the Digital Libraries Initiative-Phase 2 is to construct new funding schemes that will desensitize this issue.

Partnerships for Phase 2. The core sponsors of the Digital Libraries Initiative-Phase 1, NSF, DARPA, and NASA, are joined in Phase 2 by the National Library of Medicine, the Library of Congress, the National Endowment for the Humanities, and the FBI. We have partnerships established with a number of other agencies, including the Smithsonian, the National Archives, and the Institute for Museum and Library Services.

I believe strongly that digital libraries research and development activities must be carried out in places other than university laboratories. We must have activities that we support in venues other than university research and computer-science laboratories. We must have activities supported in museums and in libraries, wherever they may be. As a result of this conviction, our new program made very substantial changes in the documentation. In Phase 1, competition was open to universities. In Phase 2, this competition is open to both universities and non-profits, thus multiplying the number of eligible proposers by a significant amount. We also are trying to make the Digital Libraries-Phase 2 attract a much broader sponsorship across the federal government and the private sector by trying to encourage other people to join in the funding of projects that come out of our competition.

Narrowing the Technology Agenda. In addition, the technology agenda is narrowed. We have discovered during Phase 1 that certain technological areas are more important to the digital libraries than others. So, we have a narrower technology focus. We are pushing extremely hard to develop and to enhance research activities related to developing content and collections. We are also pushing hard within our organization to fund digital libraries infrastructure.

Phase 2 Programs. Digital Libraries-Phase 2 has two deadline dates—July 15, 1998, and May 17, 1999. The response to the July 15th date was amazing. Although we have not yet entirely reviewed all of the entries, we already know there were 220 proposals requesting $400 million! (We don't have $400 million yet, but we always have hope.) I will give you a rough proposal profile by content: About 25-30% of the proposals were actually in fundamental research core IT technologies. About another 25-30% were in domain areas combined with core technological research, which is what we want. That would be in GIS, in biology, in physics, in mathematics. There are all sorts of disciplinary applications begging for technologies to help them. Twenty-five percent of our proposals had to do with medicine and health. And surprisingly, almost as many—25%—had to do with the arts and humanities, including proposals for building digital libraries for dance, music, various sorts of ethnographic studies of every sort. It is really wonderful to read these proposals, and we are all just absolutely thrilled by the richness of the offerings.

About three weeks ago, I announced another program to be added onto Digital Libraries Initiative-Phase 2—the Program for Digital Libraries International Collaboration. It has become increasingly evident that doing this locally really makes no sense. So we released a program announcement that we will fund U.S. teams to collaborate with non-U.S. teams. There are no country quotas. This program is, I think, extremely elegant in its simplicity. There are no requirements other than collaboration with a non-U.S. team to be eligible for funding.

Just as a little experiment, about a year ago, I started adding languages (in addition to English) to my Digital Libraries Initiative homepage. Now, I have it in nine languages, five alphabets, and three different character systems. The point is that knowledge about whatever topic is encoded in many, many different ways. The non-English portion of the Web is increasing at a much faster rate than the English portion of the Web. In fact, the whole notion of semantics can only make sense when you think of it in terms of information being expressed in different languages, because of their varying capacities for encapsulating and communicating meaning and different types of concepts and perspectives.

This provided some justification for launching the international program. Additional justification came in the form of the success of five NSF-European Union working groups that we fund jointly with our Division of International Programs. The five working groups are in the midst of producing a final report. I believe there is a draft report out and available on the Web now, and I think it will also be distributed in the next few weeks. We are quite excited about the international program.

I will wrap this up just by telling you an anecdote. One of the things that I insisted on in the international program was that the currency of comparability of effort was not going to be money. In other words, we don't expect non-U.S. research groups to put in the same monetary amount as U.S research groups. Of course, non-U.S. research funders can put in the same amount, or they can put in more (and I think that many of them will). But they also can put in less. It is the comparability of effort and a really good collaboration that is what we are looking for.

I think the thing that made this idea light up in my head occurred about a year ago, after I joined a telecommunications working group meeting in Russia. On the flight back, I discovered that my seatmate also worked for a nonprofit. I discovered that she and others were working for a Washington, D.C.-based conservation organization that was funding biodiversity studies in Ukraine. When I asked her about the costs of her program, she explained that they gave grants for some Ph.D. researchers from countries in the former Soviet Union to work collecting data at Ukraine sites for a year. The grants, she explained, cover all the researchers' salaries, all their expenses, all their accommodations, and so forth. I asked the size of the grants, and she responded that they start at $500 a year and go up to $5000 a year! This anecdote illustrates why comparability in currency is something we have to think about very carefully. And that is one of the reasons we are looking for international collaborations in different ways.

Session 5

The Metadata Challenge for Libraries

Building Digital Libraries for Metadiversity: Federation across Disciplines

CLIFFORD LYNCH, Director, the Coalition for Networked Information (CNI)

I am going to make some fairly wide-ranging comments this morning, and I am afraid I am going to ask more questions than I am going to answer. But hopefully this will set the stage for some more detailed discussion of metadata issues later in the panel. It also, I think you will see, will connect very strongly with some of the comments that Steve Griffin was making about the evolution in thinking in the new phase of the NSF, ARPA et al. Digital Libraries program.

The Vocabulary of Our Industry

One of the things I want to do is probe at some words that have been used a lot today. We all feel good about these words, but the definitions can get vague. Lead candidates are digital library (what on earth is a digital library?), interoperability (something we all know is a good thing, but we are not exactly sure what it means), federation (another term that we use rather glibly that is similar in meaning to interoperability), and infrastructure (a very relative term, with one person's infrastructure being another's application).

Digital Libraries. The idea of a digital library really emerged in the late 1980s. I think it's clear to everyone that digital libraries are going to be key components in the networked world and will play very significant roles in efforts such as the biodiversity program that is our focus here. But there is still a very real conceptual debate about what a digital library is and how it fits into the broader environment of networks, network services, application support services ("middleware"), and the applications themselves; there's also debate about the roles that they play with respect to organizations and individuals. For example, in an expansionist sort of mode, one can view a digital library as the manifestation of an extensive system (infrastructure?) of digital storage repositories and the tools to organize, search, and navigate them. It is the organizing interface that puts all of these data at your disposal. Another more limited way to view a digital library is as a storage system; it is simply as an infrastructure component that houses data and that can be drawn upon to get work done. In this latter view one thinks of digital libraries as components that may be built on by applications that actually serve users—particularly in very complex, integrative, multidisciplinary environments.

One of the big, open issues today is how passive or active the digital library should be. There is one view that says digital libraries are mostly about housing data and are mainly passive; they react to user queries. There is another view that says that digital libraries ultimately become work environments; they are about making decisions, about doing analysis, about getting work done—and in that sense, digital libraries may be far less passive than some of their physical predecessors, such as print collections. They may really start moving in the direction of data-analysis environments, collaboration environments, and computer-supported work environments. In that sense, they may be the manifestation of an active kind of infrastructure and an environment for doing work.

We must think about the definition of digital libraries as we consider their roles here.

You heard earlier that the first round of NSF digital libraries was mainly about information technology. I think the kinds of things that researchers were calling for in the second round were much more about operational systems and sustainable-content bases. I also think there are questions going beyond the social and institutional roles of digital libraries, and those questions are going to really emerge over the next few years as we gain more experience with operational systems.

Interoperability and Federation. When we think about the issues involved in biodiversity, we have as big a sweep and diversity of content as any pursuit I can imagine. The range and number of information sources and computational resources that need to be woven in here is quite stunning. It includes geospatial information and remote sensing. It includes systematic and molecular biology resources. It involves environmental data, like the EPA and pollution data. It involves both the published and the gray literature from a huge number of different disciplines.

The range of data includes lots of multimedia—not just in the sense of numeric data sets or of combinations of video, text, and images, but also of spatially organized data as a basic data type. Spatially organized data will be critical, particularly as we try to understand the effects of climate change and the effects of various building and population shift activities on the biological world. We need to recognize that spatial data is going to get more and more complex, because it is going to move in the direction of time series of spatially organized data. We are very interested in how things change over time, and the quality and availability of data varies wildly across time.

That is another component here that is very, very different from, for example, thinking about libraries that work off the traditional publishing process, which in a very real sense has not changed in several hundreds of years. Articles are articles, text is text.

But now we see new generations of sensors and other technological advances improving our data, very steadily, decade by decade. We also see huge blank spaces, gaps in the data, gaps that are very significant. In addition, and unlike traditional libraries, we find wild variation of conceptual organization as we move from resource to resource.

One of the central challenges we face here is how to link together—or interoperate or federate—all of these very different resources. It's not clear what our expectations—at least our realistic ones—really are in this area. We know that we can give some very superficial coherence to much of this information by making it available through a Web browser; we probably cannot devise a single universal data model that covers all of the resources that we'll need to investigate and manage biodiversity. This is an area that calls out for more consideration.

Consider what we've learned in the library community about the difficulties of federation. On a conceptual level, library catalogs are fairly consistent as we move from place to place. Certainly, we all have enjoyed the experience of being able to walk into various research libraries and do our work. After all, one card catalog is pretty much like another.

But building a high-quality federation of library catalogs using technologies like Z39.50 has been a startlingly difficult problem—a problem with which the research library community has been struggling for over a decade now. Some of this has to do with the multiplicity of vendor systems available, coupled with the fact that the vendors are not necessarily eager to interoperate elegantly. Some has to do with the insistence by various institutions on the continuance of various local idiosyncrasies. Regardless of the cause, the fact of the matter is that construction of this federation has been hard.

When we start talking about the reach of data that I have been describing, the concept of federation becomes remarkably complex. In fact, it is not at all clear what those sort of global data models are that would allow us to accomplish that federation. The kinds of work going on in metadata standards has given us the beginnings of a definition—at least for discovery and retrieval purposes. But we know, particularly in dealing with geographic data, that we must go a lot farther than simple discovery and retrieval—there are extensive manipulation and presentation concerns that come to light. If nothing else, some of the descriptive metadata approaches let us treat the resources as a collection that can be searched consistently and systematically, even if they may have to subsequently be used sequentially or in smaller groups of similar resources that are more amenable to federation.

Infrastructure. The fourth candidate for my list of conveniently ambiguous terms is infrastructure. We have certainly heard about the construction of all manner of infrastructures in the initiatives around spatial data (think of the very phrase "National Spatial Data Infrastructure," for example) and around biological diversity data. I think that infrastructure is a sort of wonderful catchall term, but we need to start thinking much more about what we want from the overall "system"—be it applications, infrastructure, or whatever—and what the components in this system are and how they interact and connect with each other. We also need to recognize, I think, that infrastructure is a moving target—once we understand a network service, and it becomes ubiquitously available and widely used, and stable—we tend to consign it to infrastructure, and in particular new people who are learning the network regard it as infrastructure, because for them it was always there and they can count on it.

Metadata Issues

We know metadata will be an essential tool. Let me turn to some issues around metadata at a high level.

First, I think it's important to say that I think that it's often unhelpful to talk about metadata as a thing without context—it's information that exists and is being exploited to make something happen: resource discovery, federation, management and presentation of a digital object, electronic commerce, whatever. Our decisions about metadata need to be guided not by metadata "theology" but by the demands of the activities that we need to support.

Metadata Use Across Communities. One of the metadata issues we must consider is the correlating and using of metadata for multiple communities. We have content that is shared in common by different communities—but the communities are describing the content for different purposes. All of a sudden we are faced with the very real challenge of using these multiple, independent metadata sets together in the kind of multi-disciplinary research about which we are talking. There are some conceptual models for this, such as the Warwick Framework and the Resource Description Framework coming out of the World Wide Web Consortium. But right now a lot of this is still architectural modeling. We have very limited experience in marshalling this sort of thing for actual retrieval across disciplinary communities.

Metadata: More than Data Elements. Another consideration about metadata: Metadata is not just data elements. Those data elements are populated by vocabularies. We have heard earlier in this meeting about various efforts to develop controlled vocabularies to populate those sorts of data elements. In fact, this is not just a commonplace activity in scientific nomenclature within disciplines. It is also, for example, long-standing practice in organizing literature from various disciplinary points-of-view. For example, think about the work the National Library of Medicine has done with medical-subject heading schemes to organize the literature of Health and Life Sciences. Think about the work that organizations like the Institute of Electrical Engineers and others have done in the vocabulary for the broad engineering disciplines.

Therefore, one of the things we face in this kind of multi-disciplinary work is inter-linking—for the first time—these controlled vocabularies. All of a sudden, these vocabularies are not just books. They are databases that act as "traffic cops" and interchange points and translators. We really have very limited experience with these kinds of multilingual, multi-terminology information resources, which, I believe, are going to be a very key component of this sort of multi-disciplinary information system. We need to explicitly recognize that along with primary information and metadata, there is going to be a need for a whole set of system components that manage vocabularies, gazetteers, thesauri, and similar tools and maintain mappings among them; these are going to be services in their own right. And if these are going to be general-purpose servers on the Net, then we need to think about the protocols or other service interfaces that applications will need in order to integrate their use.

Critical Evaluation of Metadata Costs and Results. Historically, we have taken this odd view of metadata, in which we first define the right metadata and then we try to build the accompanying systems. Automation of the library catalog offers a wonderful lesson for us here. As you know, there was this sort of proper description that was manifested in card catalogs and later in the digital bibliographic records that were used to print catalog cards when shared copy cataloging became a reality. Then systems came into place that allowed us to automate the card catalogs. We built these retrieval systems, called on-line catalogs, and very rapidly discovered that we didn't know what to do with some of the data elements in the bibliographic record that were so carefully and specifically tagged and differentiated one from another and recorded. At least some of the information there made absolutely no difference to the retrieval process, at least as far as anyone could tell.

Metadata is a really big investment. For example, the museum, archival, and special-collections world is now facing the enormous challenge of digitizing all of the treasures it has been holding in physical form. It is not uncommon in those projects to see budgets in which the generation of the metadata to describe the things that are being digitized is up around the same level of investment as the digitalization itself!

Metadata is really expensive, both to create and to maintain. This cost must be considered as we learn more about what does and doesn't make a difference in the use of metadata, and we need to reflect this evaluation back in our ongoing processes and standards for creating metadata.

Other Concerns

I want to end by raising a few more questions about digital libraries, about scope, and about federation.

The Issue of Published Literature. There is an enormous published literature out there. Some of this is so-called grey literature—technical reports, policy statements, and so on. A lot of it is the traditional journal literature that has been coming out through traditional published journals. This literature also needs to get inter-linked into this giant system. The inter-linkage of published literature suddenly gives this project a very different character.

Some of the numeric and remote sensing databases, or the molecular biology databases are public domain or quasi-public domain. These data are fairly accessible and are often viewed as the "collective property" of the scientific community. But when we start looking at the whole body of published literature, we have a much broader range of ownership, economic models, and control concerns regarding those linking processes. It is not just the journal literature. It is the abstracting and indexing databases that organize that journal literature and make it coherent. It is also various kinds of handbooks, encyclopedias, and other reference materials that are likely to evolve into very complex databases, which again are linked to these vocabularies, which in turn are linked to these sorts of data sets. These are going to be significant parts of the system. And we should not overlook the fact that some of the vocabularies themselves are commercial properties.

The Economics of Data. All of these databases operate under different economic and business models. Therefore, we need to think about the experience of the user who is wandering around in this system. For example, for a given project, you discover some federal-government geospatial data that you can download for free. You find some journal literature. You rummage around in an encyclopedia of plant types. Some of the material you have used is commercial, while some might be supported by a university or a scholarly society.

How will the economics of this work? You can take the obvious easy-out and say, "A screen will pop up and ask you to enter your credit card number." In fact, that is not the way things are working right now. If you look particularly at the university community as it moves to use literature that is increasingly in electronic form, you find site licenses that entitle members of university communities to utilize this material. You also find very difficult problems regarding authentication and access management and regarding how you demonstrate you *are* a member of one of those communities. We need to think rather carefully about the sort of economic and business models that are going to infuse the user's experience in transversing the infrastructure we are building, particularly as we look at it in the broadest sense—as a place to make decisions, to do analysis, to do research, to do work, to capture an understanding.

Ownership Issues. Ownership and data sources also are going to be extremely varied. There is federal content; there is international and foreign content; there is state, local, and regional content. And remember that while there is a pretty well-established policy about how federal data are managed, paid for, and distributed, there are 50 different state policies. In addition, cities are making up policies on their own, and some cities are looking to these as significant revenue sources. So, we have a very complex patchwork of policies about access and ownership that we need to consider.

Many data sources are non-governmental. Some of these are for-profit publishers or data suppliers with fairly well-established commercial motivations and business approaches, but we also need to recognize that universities, state libraries, museums, scholarly societies, and other groups are going to play a role here. It's much less clear what sort of ownership and economic models are going to become prevalent here.

We also need to recognize that many researchers are going to want to be able to integrate private, unreleased data with the "public" (either free or commercially accessible) information resources, but they will need to do this in a way that protects their private, unreleased data. And these arrangements will need to be flexible enough to facilitate constantly changing inter-organizational research collaborations.

The Issue of Scope. There is also a question of whether digital libraries are not only places to passively house, archive, and preserve data, but also places to use data, to understand data, to reason about data. What role will digital libraries play in the publishing process? Are digital libraries within this infrastructure going to become ways for people to publish databases, to publish research reports? How will the system relate to the grey literature as this grey literature changes character and moves into electronic forms? And will people be able to contribute to and comment on material that is already housed there? As collaborative analysis activities take place more in the electronic environment, will digital libraries include the records of these activities? These also are important questions to consider.

Legal Questions. There also is the significant issue of legal publication of record. Much of the work in the environmental, biodiversity, and spatial data communities interpenetrates with a lot of legal issues about land use, about environmental impact, and so on. In addition, some of this material is going to be material of record, so we need to deal with questions about source integrity and authenticity. And, although this is properly a matter for another talk, we have to work out the assignment and funding of responsibility for archiving all of the data for the long term.

When we talk about metadata, there is a tendency to focus very heavily on description for discovery, because we have been so challenged by these problems of federation and interoperability. My view of metadata is considerably broader and also encompasses metadata for making assertions about source, provenance, authenticity, and integrity—the whole range of things that comprise terms and conditions of use. All of these are going to be quite critical as we go on to build systems to support biodiversity.

Conclusion

I hope the questions I have raised will be useful in forming our discussion about the sort of scope and direction of the biodiversity infrastructure (or system, if you prefer to leave the assignment of roles to infrastructure as an open question) and about the role digital libraries play in infrastructures. I have to stress that there is no right answer here—it is not as if somebody had the definition of digital library and we just have to look it up. It is a question, to some extent, of what we choose to label as a digital library and how we sort the cultural and economic baggage and traditions associated with the labels we choose. But I think that these sorts of questions—questions about where work happens, where analysis happens, about our expectations in terms of interoperability and federation, and how those relate to data management and archiving—are going to be very critical as we go forward.

The Metadata Challenge for Libraries: A View from Europe

MICHAEL DAY, Research Officer, The UK Office for Library and Information Networking (UKOLN), University of Bath, Bath, BA2 7AY, United Kingdom <http://www.ukoln.ac.uk/ > e-mail: <m.day@ukoln.ac.uk>

ABSTRACT

The effective management of networked digital information—including resource discovery, the management of access based on rights information, long-term preservation, etc.—will increasingly rely on the effective development and use of systems that can collect and use appropriate metadata. This paper will outline an approximate typology of metadata formats and discuss the importance of metadata interoperability from the perspective of selected European metadata initiatives—including the BIBLINK, Cedars, DESIRE, and ROADS projects.

Introduction

The effective management of networked digital information—including resource discovery, the management of access based on rights information, long-term preservation, etc.—will increasingly rely on the effective development and use of systems that can collect and use appropriate metadata. This paper will attempt to introduce some issues relating to the metadata challenge for libraries from the perspective of some European metadata initiatives.

A Typology of Formats

The first thing to note is that metadata formats are diverse in their nature and implementation. A *Review of Metadata Formats*, carried out for the European Union-funded DESIRE (Development of a European Service for Information on Research and Education) project, identified and described over 20 formats that were in use (or under development) in 1996, and additional formats are in use or under development (1). Lorcan Dempsey and Rachel Heery point out that many subject communities and market sectors are strongly attached to their own formats:

> ... considerable effort has been expended on developing specialist formats to ensure fitness for purpose; there has been investment in training and documentation to spread knowledge of the format; and, not least, systems have been developed to manipulate and provide services based on these formats (2).

For these reasons, this 'format diversity' is likely to be perpetuated over time and, indeed, new metadata formats will periodically be developed to address the perceived needs of other subject domains and communities. There are tensions between this continuing drive for specialist formats and any requirement for a level of interoperability that would permit adequate resource discovery across subject domains and information types.

In order to analyse the different metadata formats in existence, the DESIRE study produced a typology of metadata based upon the underlying complexity of the various formats (Figure 1). According to this typology, there is a continuum from simple metadata like that used by Web search engines, through simple structured generic formats like Dublin Core to more complex formats which have structure and are specific to one particular domain or are part of a larger semantic framework. Examples of these more complex formats are the MARC formats used by libraries and formats based on the Standard Generalised Markup Language (SGML).

Band One	Band Two	Band Three	
(full text indexes)	(simple structured generic formats)	(more complex structure, domain specific)	(part of a larger semantic framework)
Proprietary formats	Proprietary formats Dublin Core IAFA/Whois++ templates	FGDC MARC	TEI headers ICPSR EAD CIMI

Figure 1. *Typology of metadata formats, adapted from Dempsey and Heery (1998)*

Band One formats are relatively unstructured and are typically extracted automatically from resources by Web search services. There is no widely used standard format. Band Two formats tend to have some structure but are simple enough to be created by non-specialist users. These formats do not tend to contain elaborate internal structures and do not easily represent hierarchical objects or complex relationships between objects. Formats in this band include ROADS templates used by some Internet subject services and simple Dublin Core (DC). Band Three formats contain more descriptive information, both for resource discovery and for the larger task of documenting objects or collections of objects. They contain more structure than those in Band Two. A variety of formats exist in this category, including the family of MARC formats used by the library cataloguing community and SGML-based initiatives like the Text Encoding Initiative (TEI) header, Encoded Archival Description (EAD) and the format being developed by the Consortium for the Computer Interchange of Museum Information (CIMI).

The DESIRE report concluded that format diversity would remain. "Vested interests, competitive advantage, integration with legacy systems or custom and practice will always mean that there are differences of approach."

Interoperability

This existing diversity of formats has major implications for interoperability. One response to this problem is the production of metadata crosswalks (or mappings) between one or more formats. At a very basic level, crosswalks can be used as a means of comparing metadata formats and their potential for interoperability. They can also, however, be used as the basis for the production of a specific format conversion program or, potentially, for the production of search systems that would permit the interrogation of heterogeneous metadata formats.

Interoperability, in this context, requires the adoption of core metadata formats, like that proposed by the Dublin Core (DC) initiative, to act as intermediaries for semantic interoperability between heterogeneous resource description models (3,4). Stu Weibel suggests that the promotion of a "commonly understood set of core descriptors will improve the prospects for cross-disciplinary search by unifying related attributes" (5). With specific reference to Dublin Core, Weibel suggests that one approach to interoperability in a heterogeneous resource description environment would be to map many description schemas into a common set (like DC) which would give users "a single semantic model for searching" (6). Crosswalks from Dublin Core to a variety of other metadata formats, including GILS, ROADS templates, USMARC have been produced with interoperability issues in mind (7).

Heterogeneous Resource Discovery

The MODELS Project. The MODELS (MOving to Distributed Environments for Library Services) project is funded by the Joint Information Systems Committee of the UK higher education funding councils under its Electronic Libraries (eLib) programme. MODELS was motivated by a recognised need to develop an applications framework to manage the rapidly multiplying range of distributed heterogeneous information resources and services being offered to libraries and their users (8). It was felt that, without such a framework, networked information use would not be as effective as it could be. MODELS essentially provides a forum (primarily in the form of a series of workshops) for exploring shared concerns, addressing design and implementation issues, initiating concerted actions, and working towards a shared view of preferred systems and architectural solutions. Resource discovery issues have featured widely in MODELS discussions. For example, the MODELS 2 workshop was simultaneously the OCLC/UKOLN Warwick Metadata Workshop (now known as DC-2) that developed the concept of the Warwick Framework (9).

The MODELS 4 workshop concerned integrating access to resources across domains (defined as institutions, disciplines or regions) and identified a systems framework that would use a layered approach to cross-domain resource discovery. At the highest layer, the system could utilise a simple generic metadata format (like Dublin Core) for basic resource discovery. At lower layers of resource discovery, the same system could be configured to use descriptive information from domain-specific metadata formats. Rosemary Russell characterises this as enabling a user, "in a single search environment, to 'drill down' or move progressively through a hierarchy of increasingly rich and specialist metadata as they ... [move] through a continuum from resource discovery to resource evaluation, access, and use" (10).

The Arts and Humanities Data Service Resource Discovery System. An example of this layered approach is a resource discovery system being developed for the Arts and Humanities Data Service (AHDS) in the UK (11,12). The AHDS consists of five subject-based service providers that (amongst their other responsibilities) need to operate within a resource description context specific to their own subject domain. For example, the Oxford Text Archive—the AHDS service provider for literary and linguistic texts—would normally describe resources using Text Encoding Initiative (TEI) headers (13,14). The AHDS are implementing a resource discovery system that will provide unified access to the resource description systems of the service providers using Dublin Core and a Z39.50 gateway (15).

European Dublin Core Implementations

The Nordic Metadata Project. Interoperability issues have been to the fore in early European Dublin Core implementations. The Nordic Metadata Project (funded by the Nordic Council for Scientific Information—NORDINFO) has produced a variety of Dublin Core tools including the development of a metadata aware search service (16). The Nordic Metadata toolkit includes a utility called *d2m*, a Dublin Core to MARC converter which will convert Dublin Core metadata embedded in HTML into various Nordic MARC formats and USMARC (17).

BIBLINK: Linking Publishers and National Bibliographic Services. A different approach to interoperability is embodied in the BIBLINK project, which is funded by the Telematics Applications Programme of the European Commission (18). This project is concerned with the development of a custom-built software system (the BIBLINK Workspace or BW) that will convert metadata produced by publishers—in the form either of an extended DC known as BIBLINK Core (BC) or a SGML header—into the UNIMARC format (19). UNIMARC records will then be converted into the formats (usually MARC) used by the participating national bibliographic agencies who can then enhance them for inclusion in their national bibliography and (potentially) for returning to the publisher.

***DC-dot*: A Dublin Core Generator.** Another Dublin Core tool that has been developed is *DC-dot* (20). *DC-dot* is a metadata generator that will retrieve a Web page and automatically generate Dublin Core metadata suitable for embedding in the <META> section of HTML pages. The tags can additionally be edited using the form provided and converted to various other formats (USMARC, SOIF, IAFA/ROADS, TEI headers, GILS or RDF), if required.

Internet Subject Services and the ROADS Project

The ROADS (Resource Organisation and Discovery in Subject-oriented services) project is funded by the JISC under eLib (21). The project provides software tools and support for the creation of Internet subject services or information gateways. Services that use ROADS use a simple metadata format (ROADS templates) adapted from Internet Anonymous FTP Archive (IAFA) templates but the software itself has been designed to work with interoperability as its primary focus (22).

A basic requirement for ROADS-based services is that they are able to interoperate amongst themselves. In project terms this is referred to as cross-searching. For this, ROADS (version 1) makes use of the Whois++ protocol—a means of making structured information available from physically distributed servers (23). The ROADS software uses Whois++ to query (and retrieve information from) distributed servers containing structured descriptions (ROADS templates) of Internet resources.

In addition, ROADS (version 2) makes use of the centroid facility of Whois++ to facilitate query routing between servers. A ROADS 'index server' will periodically visit selected ROADS subject services and generate an index summary (or centroid) for each. This centroid will contain all relevant index terms in that database so that an initial search of the index server will determine which of the subject services will have information that matches a given query. If desired, the query can automatically be passed on to all of the subject services whose centroids indicate the existence of relevant index terms and the relevant templates returned for display to the end user (24). Demonstrations of ROADS cross-searching (*CrossROADS*) using Whois++ and centroids have been made available on the Web (25).

ROADS-based services have great freedom with regard to which software tools they choose to implement and the ways in which they can configure their interfaces. Services can even create new ROADS template-types based on their own requirements. In order to help preserve a minimum level of interoperability between ROADS-based services and to help cross-searching, the project has set up a metadata registry—the *ROADS Template Registry*—to record information about all template-types in use and their associated metadata elements (26). In addition, the project has developed some generic cataloguing guidelines in an attempt to help ensure that the information content of ROADS templates remains broadly consistent (27).

The ROADS project also has an interest in wider interoperability issues. It is felt that in some situations it would be desirable to make ROADS databases available to end-user clients (and intermediate systems) that use the Z39.50 search and retrieval protocol. To this end the project developed an experimental Z39.50 to Whois++ gateway. The gateway functions as a Z39.50 server, accepting queries from Z39.50 client systems. It then converts them to Whois++ queries and passes them to the ROADS server. As results are returned by the ROADS server, they are converted into a suitable format for use by Z39.50 client systems and returned to the client as a Z39.50 result set. An alternative approach would involve copying records from a ROADS database into another database that has a Z39.50 interface (28).

Metadata and Digital Preservation

The library and information community, and professionals in other disciplines, have other challenges to which metadata solutions can contribute. Publishers and other rights owners, for example, are increasingly giving consideration to using metadata to manage access to digital objects (29). This is one of the motives for publishers to develop and adopt a Digital Object Identifier (DOI). Similarly, the European Broadcasting Union (EBU) in association with the Society of Motion Picture and Television Engineers (SMPTE) have convened a Task Force to develop harmonised standards on the exchange of television programme material as bit streams—including metadata (30). However, there is one other challenge for the library and information community that brings together metadata issues related to resource discovery, rights management and administrative issues and places them in a more complex, long-term context. This challenge is digital preservation (31).

There is an increasing awareness that digital preservation will depend upon the creation, capture and storage of all relevant information (metadata) that is required to support a chosen preservation strategy, whether it be technology preservation, emulation or migration. This metadata should include technical data about file formats, software and hardware platforms, etc., but could also record information about authenticity and rights management issues (32). There are a variety of initiatives that have attempted to identify preservation metadata elements. For example, the recently published report of a working group constituted by the Research Libraries Group

(RLG) has specified metadata elements that could serve the preservation requirements of digital images (33).

A UK-funded project called Cedars (CURL Exemplars in Digital Archives) is beginning to address some of the strategic, methodological and practical issues relating to digital preservation. Cedars is funded by JISC under its eLib Programme and is managed by the Consortium of University Research Libraries—a group of research libraries in the British Isles whose mission is "to promote, maintain and improve library resources for research in universities." This project has recently produced a preliminary overview of preservation metadata issues that notes the importance of adopting or creating data models for digital archives, including their metadata systems (34). The National Library of Australia's PANDORA (Preserving and Accessing Networked DOcumentary Resources of Australia) project has, for example, developed a logical data model based on entity-relationship modelling which forms the basis of identifying the particular entities (and their associated metadata) that need to be supported by the PANDORA system (35). Cedars is likely to broadly adopt the approach embodied in the Reference Model for an Open Archival Information System (OAIS) being coordinated by the Consultative Committee for Space Data Systems (CCSDS).

The OAIS model was originally developed for digital information obtained from observations of terrestrial and space environments but should be applicable to archives. OAIS defines a high-level reference model for an archive, defined as "an organisation of people and systems, that has accepted the responsibility to preserve information and make it available for one or more designated communities" (36). The OAIS model has a 'taxonomy of archival information object classes' that includes:

Content Information:	This is the information that is the primary object of preservation. This contains the primary **Digital Object** and **Representation Information** needed to transform this object into meaningful information.
Preservation Description Information:	This would include any information necessary to adequately preserve the Content Information with which it is associated. It includes: **Reference Information**—(e.g., identifiers), **Context Information** (e.g., subject classifications), **Provenance Information** (e.g., copyright) **Fixity Information** (documenting authentication mechanisms).
Packaging Information:	The information that binds and relates the components of a package into an identifiable entity on a specific media.
Descriptive Information:	The information that allows the creation of **Access Aids**—to help locate, analyse, retrieve or order information from an OAIS.

The Cedars project will not just be adopting (or adapting) a high-level data model like OAIS. It will attempt to develop demonstrators that will implement selected aspects of digital preservation including those related to metadata. The precise nature of the metadata implementation has yet to be decided by the project but the Resource Description Framework (RDF) being developed under the auspices of the World Wide Web Consortium (W3C) is of potential interest—as it is also of interest to other

136

metadata initiatives, including Dublin Core. RDF provides a data model for describing resources and proposes an Extensible Markup Language (XML) based syntax based on this data model (37). The need to aggregate multiple sets of metadata was noted at the second Dublin Core workshop and was the principle that underlay the formulation of the Warwick Framework container architecture (38,39). Similarly, RDF aims to facilitate modular interoperability among different metadata element sets by creating what Eric Miller calls "an Infrastructure that will support the combination of distributed attribute registries" (40). The modular principle of RDF means that Cedars-defined preservation metadata elements could be aggregated with metadata types defined for other purposes, e.g., Dublin Core for simple resource discovery or structured data about terms and conditions. This type of interoperability is likely to be a useful aspect of preservation metadata systems.

References

1.   Dempsey, Lorcan and Rachel Heery with contributions from Martin Hamilton, Debra Hiom, Jon Knight, Traugott Koch, Marianne Peereboom, and Andy Powell. *Specification for resource description methods. Part 1, A review of metadata: a survey of current resource description formats*. DESIRE deliverable D3.2 (1). Bath: UKOLN, March 1997. <URL:http://www.ukoln.ac.uk/metadata/desire/overview/>

2.   Dempsey, Lorcan and Rachel Heery. Metadata: a current view of practice and issues. *Journal of Documentation* 54 (2), March 1998, pp. 145-172; here p. 155.

3.   Dublin Core metadata: <URL:http://purl.oclc.org/metadata/dublin_core/>

4.   Weibel, S., J. Kunze, C. Lagoze and M. Wolf. *Dublin Core metadata for resource discovery*. RFC 2413. September 1998. <URL:http://info.internet.isi.edu:80/in-notes/rfc/files/rfc2413.txt>

5.   Weibel, Stuart L. The evolving metadata architecture for the World Wide Web: bringing together the semantics, structure and syntax of resource description. In: *Proceedings of ISDL '97: International Symposium on Research, Development and Practice in Digital Libraries 1997, Tsukuba, Japan, 18-21 November 1997*. Tsukuba: University of Library and Information Science, 1997, pp. 16-22; here p. 18. <URL:http://www.dl.ulis.ac.jp/ISDL97/proceedings/weibe.html>

6.   *Ibid.*, p. 19.

7.   Day, Michael. *Mapping between metadata formats*. Bath: UKOLN, August 1996. <URL:http://www.ukoln.ac.uk/metadata/interoperability/>

8.   MODELS project. <URL:http://www.ukoln.ac.uk/dlis/models/>

9.   Dempsey, Lorcan and Stuart L. Weibel. The Warwick Metadata Workshop: A framework for the deployment of resource description. *D-Lib Magazine*, July/August 1996. <URL:http://www.dlib.org/dlib/july96/07weibel.html>

10.   Russell, Rosemary. UKOLN MODELS 4: evaluation of cross-domain resource discovery. *Discovering online resources across the humanities: a practical implementation of the Dublin Core*, edited by Paul Miller and Daniel Greenstein. Bath:

UKOLN on behalf of the Arts and Humanities Data Service, 1997, pp. 18-21; here p. 19. <URL:http://ahds.ac.uk/public/metadata/disc_04.html#ukoln>

11.   Arts and Humanities Data Service. <URL:http://www.ahds.ac.uk/>

12.   Miller, Paul and Daniel Greenstein, eds. *Discovering online resources across the humanities: a practical implementation of the Dublin Core.* Bath: UKOLN on behalf of the Arts and Humanities Data Service, October 1997. <URL:http://ahds.ac.uk/public/metadata/discovery.html>

13.   Giordano, Richard. The documentation of electronic texts using Text Encoding Initiative headers: An introduction. *Library Resources and Technical Services*, 38(4), October 1994, pp. 389-401.

14.   Giordano, Richard. The TEI header and the documentation of electronic texts. *Computers and the Humanities*, 29 (1), 1995, pp. 75-84.

15.   Dempsey, Lorcan, Rosemary Russell, and Robin Murray. The emergence of distributed library services: a European perspective. *Journal of the American Society for Information Science*, 49 (10), 1998, pp. 942-951; here p. 950.

16.   Hakala, Juha, Preben Hansen, Ole Husby, Traugott Koch, and Susanne Thorborg. *The Nordic Metadata Project: final report.* Helsinki: Helsinki University Library, July 1998. <URL:http://linnea.helsinki.fi/meta/nmfinal.htm>

17.   d2m : Dublin Core to MARC converter: <URL:http://www.bibsys.no/meta/d2m/>

18.   BIBLINK: Linking Publishers and National Bibliographic Services: <URL:http://hosted.ukoln.ac.uk/biblink/>

19.   Day, Michael, Rachel Heery, and Andy Powell. National bibliographic records in the digital information environment: metadata, links and standards. *Journal of Documentation*, Vol. 55(1), 199, PP. 16-32.

20.   DC-dot. <URL:http://www.ukoln.ac.uk/metadata/dcdot/>

21.   ROADS project. <URL:http://www.ilrt.bris.ac.uk/roads/>

22.   Knight, Jon P. and Martin Hamilton. *Overview of the ROADS software.* LUT CS-TR 1010. Loughborough: Loughborough University of Technology, Department of Computer Studies, 1995. <URL:http://www.roads.lut.ac.uk/Reports/arch/arch.html>

23.   Deutsch, P., R. Schoultz, P. Faltstrom, and C. Weider. *Architecture of the WHOIS++ service.* RFC 1835. August 1995. <URL:http://info.internet.isi.edu:80/in-notes/rfc/files/rfc1835.txt>

24.   Kirriemuir, John, Dan Brickley, Susan Welsh, Jon Knight, and Martin Hamilton. Cross-searching subject gateways: the query routing and forward knowledge approach. *D-Lib Magazine*, January 1998. <URL:http://www.dlib.org/dlib/january98/01kirriemuir.html>

25.   CrossROADS. <URL:http://roads.ukoln.ac.uk/crossroads/>

26.   ROADS Template Registry.
<URL:http://www.ukoln.ac.uk/metadata/roads/templates/>

27.   Day, Michael. *ROADS Cataloguing Guidelines*. Bath: UKOLN, January 1998. <URL:http://www.ukoln.ac.uk/metadata/roads/cataloguing/cataloguing-rules.html>

28.   Powell, Andy. *ROADS and Z39.50: Searching ROADS servers using Z39.50 clients*. Bath: UKOLN, June 1998.
<URL:http://www.ukoln.ac.uk/metadata/roads/interoperability/roads-z3950.html>

29.   Rust, Godfrey. Metadata: The right approach. An integrated model for descriptive and rights metadata in e-commerce. *D-Lib Magazine*, July/August 1998.
<URL:http://www.dlib.org/dlib/july98/rust/07rust.html>

30.   Bradshaw, David. *EBU-SMPTE Task Force on Metadata*. Digital workflow through production and documentation: A seminar organised by the Documentation Commission of FIAT/IFTA, BBC Conference Centre, London, 7-8 May 1998.

31.   Beagrie, Neil and Daniel Greenstein. *A Strategic Policy Framework for Creating and Preserving Digital Collections*. London: Arts and Humanities Data Service, 14 July 1998. <URL:http://ahds.ac.uk/manage/framework.htm>

32.   Day, Michael. *Issues and Approaches to Preservation Metadata*. Joint RLG and NPO Preservation Conference: Guidelines for Digital Imaging, University of Warwick, 28-30 September 1998. <URL:http://www.rlg.org/preserv/joint/day.html>

33.   RLG Working Group on Preservation Issues of Metadata, *Final report*. Mountain View, Calif.: Research Libraries Group, May 1998.
<URL:http://www.rlg.org/preserv/presmeta.html>

34.   Day, Michael. *Metadata for Preservation*. CEDARS Project Document AIW01. Bath: UKOLN, 8 August 1998.
<URL:http://www.ukoln.ac.uk/metadata/cedars/AIW01.html>

35.   National Library of Australia, *PANDORA Logical Data Model*, Version 2. Canberra: National Library of Australia, 10 November 1997.
<URL:http://www.nla.gov.au/pandora/ldmv2.html>

36.   Consultative Committee for Space Data Systems, *Reference Model for an Open Archival Information System (OAIS)*, ed. L. Reich and D. Sawyer. CCSDS 650.0-W-4.0. White Book, Issue 4, 17 September 1998. Latest version available from: <URL:http://ssdoo.gsfc.nasa.gov/nost/isoas/ref_model.html>

37.   World Wide Web Consortium, *Resource Description Framework (RDF) model and syntax specification*, eds. Ora Lassila and Ralph R. Swick. W3C Recommendation, 22 February 1999. <URL:http://www.w3.org/TR/REC-rdf-syntax/>

38.   Lagoze, Carl, Clifford A. Lynch, and Ron Daniel. *The Warwick Framework: a container architecture for aggregating sets of metadata*. Cornell Computer Science

Technical Report TR96-1593. Ithaca, NY: Cornell University, 1996. <URL:http://cs-tr.cs.cornell.edu:80/Dienst/UI/1.0/Display/ncstrl.cornell/TR96-1593/>

39.   Weibel, Stuart L. and Carl Lagoze. An element set to support resource discovery: the state of the Dublin Core, January 1997. *International Journal on Digital Libraries*, 1(2), 1997, pp. 176-186.

40.   Miller, Eric. An introduction to the Resource Description Framework. *D-Lib Magazine*, May 1998. <URL:http://www.dlib.org/dlib/may98/miller/05miller.html>

Acknowledgements

UKOLN is funded by the British Library Research and Innovation Centre (BLRIC), the Joint Information Systems Committee (JISC) of the UK higher education councils, as well as by project funding from several sources. UKOLN also receives support from the University of Bath, where it is based. The views expressed in this paper do not necessarily reflect those of UKOLN or its funding bodies.

The author would like to thank Lorcan Dempsey (UKOLN), Kelly Russell (Cedars Project Manager) and Rosemary Russell (UKOLN) for comments on an earlier draft of this paper.

Gazetteer and Collection-Level Metadata Developments

LINDA HILL, Research Specialist, Alexandria Digital Library, University of California, Santa Barbara <http://www.alexandria.ucsb.edu>

ABSTRACT

The Alexandria Digital Library (ADL) includes both collections and digital library services that focus on georeferenced information. Georeferencing means that a key attribute of the metadata for the collection objects (COs) is geographic location as represented spatially with latitude and longitude coordinates—that is, the spatial representation of the locations that the COs are about. Collection objects include maps, remote sensing images, aerial photographs, and other obviously geospatial information; they also extend to texts, art objects, music, etc. That is, the ADL approach is designed to represent, find, evaluate, and retrieve any information that can be georeferenced. Metadata development and implementation are major components of the ADL Project. This presentation will give an overview of the ADL system architecture and then focus on two metadata areas where we have made major contributions and where action within the biodiversity community is recommended: (1) development and implementation of a Gazetteer Content Standard and accompanying Thesaurus of Feature Types and (2) implementation of a Collection Metadata that allows us to serve diverse collections through description of inherent and contextual collection data for the purposes of client-middleware communication and user documentation. Our definition of gazetteers is that they are indexes of geographic names (i.e., place-names or feature names) that contain at least three attributes per entry: name, coordinate location, and category. With such a digital tool, links can be made between direct geospatial reference (i.e., coordinates) and indirect reference (i.e., geographic names), and types of places can be identified in a specified geographic location.

The Alexandria Digital Library (ADL) is a georeferenced digital library, one of the six Digital Library Initiatives funded by the NSF, DARPA, and NASA. The funding period has now ended, and ADL is in the process of becoming an operational component of the UCSB library system and the California Digital Library that will have its public presence at the end of 1998 or the beginning of 1999. Currently access to ADL is limited to the University of California campuses only. We have limited computer equipment and help staff and cannot open it up to everyone.

All kinds of information can be georeferenced with latitude and longitude coordinates. You might think primarily about maps, aerial photographs, and remote sensing images, but text, specimen collections, music, people, and gazetteer entries can also be georeferenced to a place that they are about.

A description of the ADL client interface will illustrate a user's view of ADL. First, the user is presented with a Map Window where a query area can be drawn to indicate that area of the world in which the user is interested. In the Search Window, the user is given a choice of collections that can be searched and search options such as Type of Item (e.g., aerial photograph), Format (e.g., online image), and Topical Text (for freetext searching). The search results are returned to the Workspace Window. Each item is briefly described and its footprint (area covered on the map) is shown in the Map Window. If a thumbnail image of the item is available, it is also shown. By highlighting listings in the Workspace Window or clicking on footprints in the Map Window, the user can selectively review interesting items and move the most interesting ones to user-created folders. Online data can be directly accessed and downloaded. The user can save the status of the Workspace and reload it at a later time.

The ADL system architecture supports the user interface. The system consists of three levels: the database level, the middleware level, and the client level. The middleware level—including access control, translation, DB connection, and logging—is the heart of the system. Multiple clients can be developed for it. On the other side, the middleware interfaces with the database level. There can be multiple collections, held locally or remotely, and the collections can have their own structures. The databases present query and retrieval views of the collection objects to the middleware. The middleware dynamically discovers which collections are available for searching and how they can be searched, and presents these to the user through the client. User-created queries are fanned out by the middleware to the queryable parameters of the collections through appropriate retrieval software. The results are merged and presented back to the user.

Another view of ADL structure is the metadata view. Here we start with a *data set* that represents its objects through full object metadata. ADL does not specify what the metadata at this level needs to be; it can be whatever is suitable for the collection objects. In practice, creating metadata for the data is often a labor-intensive step. Object level metadata is mapped to ADL in three ways: (1) to the middleware *search buckets* and some additional *scan* attributes; (2) to the *access report;* and (3) to the *full metadata report.*

The *search buckets* provide a few high-level search parameters designed to search across diverse collections. This is somewhat like the Dublin Core approach of identifying core elements for description but the ADL *search buckets* are designed for searching. The ADL *search buckets* are:

> Location (latitude and longitude coordinates)
> Date (date of coverage, date of publication)
> Type (controlled domain)
> Format (controlled domain)
> Topical—Freetext
> Topical—Assigned Text (derived from controlled vocabularies)

Originator (author, publisher, etc.)
Identifier (ISBN, scene ID, etc.)

Buckets with controlled domains have a limited set of values that are shown to the user for selection.

The *access report* provides the links to the actual data set if it is online, or to the point of contact if it is offline. It also provides information about any constraints for accessing or using the data and sometimes links to related information.

The *full metadata report* is a report containing attribute labels and values from the object-level metadata. ADL has created a style for these that provides a common look for the metadata from the various underlying collections.

Metadata Developments: Collection-Level Metadata

The key to accommodating multiple collections, and multiple types of collections, in this search environment is *collection-level metadata,* which describes the collections and how they can be searched. The collection-level metadata gives the title and the ID for the collection, the search buckets populated, and the controlled lists and controlled vocabularies associated with the collections. It also gives a collection description of two kinds:

Inherent data
Contextual description

Inherent-collection metadata can be obtained from the collection itself and includes such information as the number of items in the collection and the types and formats of items in the collections. This information can be visualized by geographic and temporal coverage to show to the user.

Contextual metadata is provided by the collection owner and includes such information as the purpose and description of the collection, its frequency of update, any constraints to its use, and contact information for the responsible person.

ADL uses collection metadata for two purposes: collection registration and user documentation. Collections are made known to the ADL middleware through an XML version of the collection metadata. The middleware dynamically discovers which collections are available for presentation to the user through this method. This metadata also tells the middleware which *search buckets* are active for any particular collection and what the controlled domains are for the associated buckets. All mappings that are necessary for accessing the collection are contained in this XML registration version. User documentation is an HTML version of the collection metadata. This is displayed to the user on request.

Since the variety of collections is wide—indeed it is difficult to agree on the definition "collection" in the first place—ADL developed and implemented collection metadata to describe and register whatever collections come along. It has been very successful and provides us with a way to accommodate many more collections in the future. We therefore recommend the collection metadata approach to the biodiversity community. It is the key to accessing a variety of collections, where a "collection" is whatever someone decides to call a collection. It is a way to capture both inherent and contextual metadata for registration and user documentation purposes.

Metadata Developments: Gazetteer Metadata

The next ADL metadata development I will present is the work we have done with gazetteers. The word "gazetteers" is not familiar to everyone. They can be described as dictionaries of named geographic places. ADL further defines gazetteers to require three minimum descriptive elements for each place: (1) a name; (2) a location in latitude and longitude coordinates; and (3) a type or category. One example is:

> Name: Goleta
> Type: populated place
> Location: -119.83,34.44 (decimal degrees for longitude and latitude)

The following example illustrates the value of such a gazetteer in a digital library. A user has a "where is" type question: "Where is Philadelphia?" The system returns a footprint for Philadelphia, Pennsylvania, and displays it on the map (this is a simplified example, ignoring for the moment that there is more than one Philadelphia in the world). Next the user asks, "What rivers are in the Philadelphia area?" The system knows the footprint of Philadelphia and it knows the footprints of entries in the gazetteer of the type "rivers." It can make a match of these footprints and return a list of the rivers "in" the Philadelphia area. Next the user might ask a question like, "What remote sensing images are there of the Philadelphia area?" This is a search of the catalog rather than of the gazetteer. The system can compare the footprint of Philadelphia to the footprints of items of the type "remote sensing images" in the catalog and return a list of those whose footprints overlap the Philadelphia area. This retrieval is possible not based on the images labeled with Philadelphia but because the match can be made on the basis of footprints. This use of footprints is known as *indirect* georeferencing.

In building ADL, we developed a 6-million-entry gazetteer by combining the two large U.S. federal gazetteers from the U.S. Geological Survey (USGS) and the National Imagery and Mapping Agency (NIMA). In the process, we found out firsthand the difficulties of combining gazetteer data from different sources. We found out that there is no shared concept of how gazetteer information is represented. We therefore developed a Gazetteer Content Standard (GCS) and a Feature Type Thesaurus (FTT) to provide type categories. We are in the processing of implementing it.

GCS provides for the representation of names and variant names for places and information about these names: the source or authority of the name, the language, etymology, pronunciation, dates when the name was/is used, and more. Each name is assigned one or more type categories. If the place has a feature code (e.g., an FIPS code), it can be included. The location of the place can be given by a point, bounding box, or polygonal coordinate description. Features can be related to one another—e.g., one place "IsPartOf" another. Data such as elevation or population can be given for a place, and links can be made to other sources of information, such as a city's homepage. Temporal ranges can be given for the names themselves, the footprints, the data, and the relationships. Each entry, and each part of each entry, can be attributed to a contributor and to a source.

There is no common set of feature types for gazetteers and making different categorization schemes work together is one of the most difficult parts of combining data from various sources into a new gazetteer. We have developed a thesaurus of feature types that we are applying to our gazetteers and that we hope will be adopted by others. It is based on the Z39.19 standard for hierarchical thesauri designed for information retrieval. It includes broad term/narrow term relationships, synonymous terms, and related terms.

Both the Gazetteer Content Standard and the Feature Type Thesaurus are available through my homepage: <http://www.alexandria.ucsb.edu/~lhill>.

We are currently in the process of converting a current version of the NIMA gazetteer to the new Content Standard using the terms from the Feature Type Thesaurus. We already have sets of bounding boxes for countries and U.S. counties loaded as well as a set of volcano sites. We have various other sets waiting for conversion, including the GNIS from USGS. We are looking for sets of gazetteer information that include polygon or bounding box footprints to load. We are working on extracting polygon footprints for places from digital map products.

Georeferencing is an identification key that can be applied to all types of information—not all information, but to all types of information including place names. Georeferencing is a "natural bridge" across information types because latitude and longitude referencing is universally understood. A spatially referenced gazetteer is a powerful component of a georeference system because it adds the dimension of indirect spatial referencing through the use of place names.

We therefore recommend to the biodiversity community that standard practices for gazetteer development and use be adopted so that geographical site descriptions developed by one subgroup of the community can be shared and used by other subgroups and with other information operations as well.

Metadata Challenges for Libraries

CARL LAGOZE, Digital Library Scientist, Cornell University

ABSTRACT

Metadata creation, in the form of cataloging, has been a fundamental task of traditional libraries. The movement from physical to digital artifacts brings some fundamental challenges to this metadata creation process. These challenges include new types of documents, few controls over the quality of content, an unprecedented increase in the quantity of content, and distributed management of content and services. In such an environment, traditional metadata methods are neither appropriate nor sufficient. In this short talk, I will briefly review these challenges and describe some work-in-progress for creating new metadata practices and standards.

I am going to make some observations about metadata and how metadata has worked in traditional library environments. Then I will look at some of the challenges that we face regarding doing metadata on the Internet. My apologies to the librarians here if I make observations that violate your beliefs about libraries. I want to clarify that I am not a librarian. I try to give accurate observations based on my experiences with libraries.

The Purpose of Metadata

Earlier in this meeting, metadata was defined as being structured data about data. In this talk, I am going to focus on metadata as something that imposes structure. In fact, I am going to present the view that, overall, the purpose of metadata is to impose some order in a disordered information universe.

What we generally end up with when we search is a lot of "stuff," as many people call it these days. We may call the "stuff" documents or digital objects, but most seem to be comfortable with calling it "stuff." So, we have a lot of stuff out there, and as we access that stuff and as we try to find that stuff and use that stuff, we are more comfortable thinking of it in ordered categories and approaching it from an ordered point of view, rather than as an amorphous glob of stuff. One of the major roles of metadata in libraries is to help us impose some order, to make us think that the stuff out there all has an author or creator (as we like to call it in the Dublin Core world) and a title and a subject. Even if that is a myth, it at least helps us to think about it that way.

Order-Making as a Library Function

Many people think that all libraries are big warehouses of books and maps and things like that. But in fact, one of the basic functions of libraries is order-making. One of the things libraries do best is impose this order, and they do it in two ways. They do this with spatial ordering through shelving rules (e.g., the Dewy Decimal system), and they do this with a sort of semantic, logical ordering through cataloging rules (e.g., AARC2, MARC). These orders allow us to use libraries in lots of ways. We can enjoy walking up to the shelves and serendipitously browsing down the shelves or running into things in sort of familiar clumpings or going through the card catalog.

I have a rather elementary hypothesis that will be of no surprise to anyone: The ease of order-making is inversely proportional to the level of chaos. In fact, one of the reasons that libraries have been so successful—and this is not to demean their level of success or how hard the work actually is—is that the environment in which librarians work has a relatively low level of chaos. But as we step away from the physical artifacts and move beyond the walls, we are opening that chaos and making the chaos boundless. This makes the job very difficult.

Traditional Metadata-Creation Environments

Let's briefly look at the traditional cataloging metadata-creation environment within which libraries have worked.

Characteristics of the Environment. The metadata-creation environment has a number of characteristics. First is the notion of the stability of a physical artifact: I know that I have something and that I can describe it and it stays there and it doesn't disappear. It is something that has very stable characteristics.

The second characteristic of a traditional cataloging metadata-creation environment is that it has clearly established roles. Usually I know who is an author, who is a publisher, who is a consumer of the information, and all these roles sort of stay where they are—they don't shift.

Another characteristic is that there is a relatively small number of content producers. For example, the Cornell Library does not collect the works of everybody. Instead, it collects the works of an established set of content producers with which it has established quality and trusting relationships. This is very important to the way traditional libraries work. They know whom to trust, and therefore you can trust the libraries—you can assume when you go into the Cornell Library that you will find material that is accurate and acceptable.

Lastly, there is this notion of a defined "control zone." What is inside the walls is part of the library. What is outside the walls is, more or less, *not* part of the library. Of course, the walls are somewhat permeable, considering things like interlibrary loans, but they at least exist.

Effects on the Resulting Metadata. Together, these characteristics mean that library cataloging metadata is extremely high-quality. This is despite the fact that libraries are dealing with complex information. If you have ever actually read ACRII, for example, you know that it is not exactly the kind of thing you can go through in one pass. It requires an extremely high investment of time and money. I think that the general rule of thumb is $60 to $65 per record in original cataloging. That is a lot of money when you consider the acquisition rate of a place like the Cornell Library. Of course, there are a lot shortcuts that go on. For example, there is copy cataloging, and some follow shortcut cataloging rules. But in the end, cataloging remains a very expensive process.

In addition, the metadata resulting from libraries is professionally produced. The people who work there are professionals. They go to school to learn to be catalogers, and they do good cataloging work.

Networked Information Is Different

Networked information is profoundly different. The kind of information that is appearing on the Web—the information space that we are creating now—exists in an extremely distinct environment.

Changing Relationships. One reason for this difference is that networked information changes and makes fluid the relationships among stakeholders. For example, Carl Lagoze is, at one point, an author. Then suddenly, he is a publisher. And just as suddenly, he is a user of information. He shifts back and forth. He does all these things, all over the place. In other words, we can't really define who these people are. In addition, there are all these peculiar information intermediaries, of the America Online genre.

So these things get very fluid. And because they are fluid, the roles of these stakeholders interact in extremely complex ways. We cross paths all the time, and we would have all sorts of ways of talking to each other that really don't fit into the molds that traditional libraries have used for acquisitions and cataloging and so on.

Changing Content. In addition, content itself has changed. Those nice, packaged, physical artifacts with which we used to deal in the library are getting very fuzzy right before our eyes. One reason for this is that the amount of content with which we are dealing has vastly increased. The number of objects created is soaring, and those objects are pouring onto the Web at a phenomenal rate.

In addition, these objects are increasingly ephemeral. Things appear, they disappear, they change, they migrate to other places. There is just no stability in the environment.

The content also is changing with regard to quality. Because of the greatly reduced barriers to publication, we have extremely variable quality. And it is hard to differentiate the quality. On the Web, the works of Nobel prize-winners, for example, can sit next to the works of the local first-grade class's writing assignment. It is frightening to consider the number of public-school papers that are being written based on information taken from Websites. When a student brings in a paper talking about the Holocaust, for example, it may be based on material from sites most of us would not consider authorities on the subject. This is the kind of thing that should give us all pause.

New Content Forms. Most interesting from my research-point of view is the whole notion of new content forms. I don't only mean images versus data versus this versus that—I mean the inter-mixing of these things in all sorts of odd ways, picking out piecemeal bits, putting them together, and calling them a document or a digital object or a piece of "stuff."

There also is the question of preservation: How do we preserve data, a component of which is a live-data feed from, for example, a meteorology satellite image? How do we solve the problems of preserving multi-media information? And what does it mean to preserve that data?

A Blurring of the Control Zones. We also have experienced a blurring of the control zones that used to be in place. This makes librarians really nervous. For example, they give access to X-network document, which they say is part of their library. Well that document has a link to another document, and that document goes here, there, there, and there, and finally the user arrives at, for example, a pornographic site. Who is responsible? Is the library responsible for providing a public service by allowing access to the original document? Are librarians responsible for cataloging the document? As you can see, the control zone gets very, very, very strange, due to distributed and ill-defined administration across individual objects and within individual objects.

Metadata for Networked Objects

As I said before, I like to think of objects as these packages of things that come from all over the place. But who is responsible for all the individual pieces? And without knowing that, how do we ensure the integrity of the pieces?

Let me lay out a couple of metadata goals for networked objects. The first is that there are so many ways that these digital objects are treated, accessed, searched, and administrated that we need to accommodate in a metadata framework the multiple roles and responsibilities of the multiple stakeholders. We want to allow them to act in independent ways. For example, if I am a library cataloger, I don't want to have to complete the slot of the metadata record that deals with terms and conditions. Instead, I want to hand that off to my lawyer or my legal team or whoever has expertise in that area and say, "That is your domain. You administer that." I will take care of the thing I want to do. This is what Clifford Lynch and Ron Daniel and I wrote about in something called the "Warwick Framework." The Resource Description Framework (RDF) also addresses this issue.

The other thing that we want very much to accommodate is layered solutions. It is very important to recognize that people want to operate across these multiple roles in layered ways. So that there are multiple forms of resource discovery, and there are multiple ways that we want to do resource discovery. Things like Dublin Core may be good for what we call basic, simple resource discovery, and there may be other, coexisting, resource-discovery metadata forms that are targeted for specific disciplines. I am an extremely strong supporter of the Dublin Core. But we have seen efforts like the Dublin Core find themselves on a slippery slope as they say, "We can do this also, and we can do that also."

Other Issues to Consider

Let me close with some issues we have identified, given those goals on metadata for networked objects.

What to Trust? First is the whole issue of quality and trust, which I brought up earlier: How do you know what metadata to trust? A lot of us make the assumption that the metadata is embedded in the object in sort of a traditional way—you have an

HMTL page, and the metadata is in it. But the way that we are thinking in the RDF and other, similar architectures is that metadata is somehow associated with the object through *external* means.

Which metadata do you know to trust at that point? There is an incredible amount of index "spamming" going on on the Web today. People load their HTML pages with all sorts of junk, hidden from the user, that makes their pages come up first in a search. As a result, as information becomes a consumer object and a consumer commodity, some people are led to do things that aren't always honest.

The Issue of Interoperability. Interoperability is another issue we must consider as we consider the issues of metadata. We must remember the dimensions both of semantic and of syntactic interoperability.

Simplicity or Complexity? There also is continuing tension among simplicity, complexity, and extensibility. This has been apparent in the Dublin Core community from the beginning. Some say that we have to make this simple so that everybody will use it. But at the same time, others are insisting that it must be able to express everything we want to express down, down, down, down, a long hierarchy.

I urge all of us to consider the costs of complexity and whether we really gain anything from it in terms of resource discovery. My favorite example comes from the information retrieval community. This community has had a metric for measuring the effectiveness of information retrieval. In fact, we can bring in our latest research and measure its effectiveness, using a very strict metric and very fine granularity numbers. And every single year, the metric is raised by, I believe, .005%. Considering the huge amount of money that is put into this research, one has to wonder: At what point does increasing the complexity of this level really improve what users get?

Tools and Practices. A question one has to ask is, are common people going to create metadata that is useful? I work on a project called the Ancestral that is a distributed digital library of computer-science technical reports. And I have found it very difficult to convince those award-winning computer-science researchers who are involved that it is important to spend five minutes creating decent metadata for their research reports. They just don't want to spend the time. So we have to ask ourselves, is it worthwhile to create these simple forms? Are people really going to use them?

Administration Issues. Lastly, how do we administer metadata? We must create tools for administering this "stuff" without overloading the architecture in some horrible way.

Special Presentation

Perspective on Information Management on the Internet

WAYNE MOORE, Senior Scientific Software Designer, Flow Cytometry Instrumentation and Software Development Group, Stanford University

ABSTRACT

We have recently developed an Internet-based system for acquiring, storing, retrieving, and working with complex flow cytometry data. This system, which incorporates radically different methods for serving Internet data, is applicable across a wide variety of scientific disciplines, ranging from genomics to astronomy. In addition, it offers rapid and more efficient access to published information and provides more efficient routes for sharing and combining information from disparate sources. This technology may be particularly useful for information storage and exchange in the biological and medical sciences and in other areas that similarly deal with very large distributed information collections that are difficult to serve with current approaches. Our motivation for this project derives from a necessity to maintain and serve data from Flow Cytometry (FACS) instruments, which are used worldwide in basic science and medicine. These instruments, perhaps best-known for their use in monitoring CD4T cell counts to evaluate HIV disease progression, are used to characterize and determine the functions of cells from organisms as different as drosophila and man. We currently maintain an archive of over 200GB of FACS data, collected mainly in basic science studies at Stanford over the last 15 years. We will use our new technology to organize and serve these newly acquired data, which will be collected locally at Stanford or elsewhere, stored at the MSIA Management Sciences Associates, Pittsburgh, PA, and made available via the Internet to FACS users and other interested parties. This system, which is built with readily available components, is extensible and broadly applicable. It offers innovative tools for serving the information located in genomics and other large databases, and for combining scientific information from these disparate sources. Thus, it provides a general model for facilitating the electronic interchange of scientific data and the publication of scientific findings. This work was supported by grants from the National Institutes of Health, LM04836 and CA42509. In this presentation, I will describe the technology we plan to use and discuss its advantages over traditional relational database approaches to serving scientific information. These advantages include global information service, fine-grained access control, federated servers that need not be located within a single organization, and compatible client software that is widely available and runs on "lightweight clients" (e.g., PCs and Macs). I will illustrate this discussion with examples from our laboratory's work in lymphocyte biology and flow cytometry and from a variety of other areas, including genetics, genomics, taxonomy, museum and scholarly collections, electronic publication, and scientific literature index services.

Earlier at this meeting, someone said that the nice thing about standards is that there are so many of them. Therefore, I'm sure it won't come as a shock to anybody that there actually is a standard for directories.

Directory Service

Directory Service fundamentally is a database. The standardization effort started in the late 1980s with the International Standards Organization (ISO) and a series of standards starting with X500. It is a very complete, painstaking definition of all the fields of the directory, and it is based on the ISO Open Systems Interconnect (OSI) protocols that are very heavyweight. There is a very large buy-in to use them, and they are not generally available on smaller PCs or for Macintosh-type clients.

In the early '90s, a proposal was made to the Internet Engineering Task Force for what was called Lightweight Directory Access Protocol (LDAP), and this year it was adopted as a proposed standard for use on the Internet. In fact, some of you may be familiar with Yellow Pages, which is based on LDAP. So it is really there, it exists, and it is out on the Web.

Strategic Advantages. What are the advantages of a Directory Service over a more traditional database? One of the main advantages is that it provides a global naming system. ISO moderates the top level in the name space and parcels it out into countries and other organizations, which can then define lower-level standards. From the beginning it has dealt with one of the issues we have discussed at this meeting: synonymy, or having multiple names for things. The designers knew in advance that they were not going to be able to give a unique name to every single thing in the world. Therefore, we could have multiple common names. We could, for example, have a person who has multiple roles in different organizations, and those different organizations can have different entries, and those different entries can reference one another.

It was also realized that we weren't going to get the entire world's database in any given service. So it is designed from the outset to be interoperable and federated. It has very flexible searching mechanisms, including a syntax-specific searching mechanism, so that different ways of matching can be used for different types of data that are entered into the database.

Another aspect was the very fine-grained access control. It was known that we couldn't make every piece of every directory available to everyone, so there are very good controls on who can see what data elements in the directories. These are the strategic advantages of Directory Service.

Tactical Advantages. One of the tactical advantages of using Directory Service over other databases is that Directory Service is based on well-defined Internet standards. As I say, it is out there now. The United States government is using it. Stanford is using it. There are publicly available LDAP servers, with e-mail addresses, telephone numbers, and so forth—411-, Big Foot-, and Yellow Pages-kinds of directories.

Directory Service is supported by several vendors—Novell, Netscape, Sun, and IBM are all big vendors. In addition, I believe Microsoft has announced that, in its next version, it is going to become part of the operating system. There are client support packages in the C language and the Java language, and the packages are widely (and freely) available for all the major PC units and Macintosh platforms.

Directory Service Entries

The Directory is defined in terms of entries we like to call "cards," because each entry is the electronic equivalent of a Rolodex card or a catalog card—it is a defined bit of storage on which we can scribble down a wide variety of information attributes about some object, some person, some database, or some document.

The entries follow the so-called object model. This essentially means that we define a hierarchy of objects. For example, the base standard defining a "person" has fields that describe the personal name, the given name, the surname, the common name, and contact information. Then that is inherited by the "organizational person," which gives that person's relationship to some organization, and in Netscape servers the "Inet Org Person," which gives the person's e-mail address, home directory, and Web page URL.

As I mentioned, every record has the potential to have individual-access control information on it, and every record is identified by a distinguished name. But a distinguished name need not be globally unique. The components of the distinguished name are themselves attributes in the records, so they can always be used in a search.

Finally, if that wasn't flexible enough, there is the so-called extensible-object class, which is allowed to have any attribute whatsoever. So, we can define these things in a way whereby we can start collecting the data before we define—or even identify—all the data we need. This is a very important ability in my field, which is basic research. In basic research, we often don't know, when we start a set of experiments, what all the relevant criteria are going to be.

Each entry has a name, and each entry has a syntax. The syntaxes are defined in what is called Abstract Notation 1 (ASN-1). The standard defines the case-exact

155

string and the case-insensitive string. The case-insensitive string is the case in which we use different matching rules depending on the syntax, so that the case-insensitive string can compare strings without considering the case. Distinguished names themselves are defined as syntax. Telephone numbers, for example, are syntax, where the matching rule matches numerals but ignores punctuation. In the Department of Genetics, we are interested in extending this to include DNA sequences. But the searching rules are very different, because we want to take single-point mutations or deletions or other sources of comparisons.

The Standard. The standard is defined in such a way that new syntaxes can be defined and new matching rules implemented in the server without breaking all the other levels of the protocol. An attribute can have one or more values. This makes it easy to have people with multiple telephone numbers or multiple addresses. Different common names and attributes can be defined as optional or required, so it also is very easy to define a record that has a large number of values that are mostly not present—but occasionally *are* present—with very little overhead in the database.

Names Defined. Names that identify the entries of the database are composed of attribute-equal value pairs. The syntax is defined as reading from right to left, and it is comma-separated. If we use any special characters like commas or equals, we can put quotes around the values so that we can include those in the directories. The standard itself defines three varieties of names: geographic names, which are named relative to geographic or governmental entities; organizational names, which are made with respect to organizations; and domain names, which essentially subsume the Internet domain-name service.

Flow Cytometry. This naming scheme can be extended to include other kinds of objects—for example, a data-collection section, which is when a person comes to the instrument and collects data from one or more samples. It is qualified by the Cytometer, which is a kind of instrument qualified by my unique identifier of the protocol and then by the organization or organizational unit. It is expressed in terms of a data collection with a particular protocol coordinate that identifies which sample in the protocol it is. In this case, we would expect that the intermediate levels are optional but define the standard so that, for example, a small organization could define all their protocols uniquely within the organization. We could put the responsibility on the user to give unique identifiers. Or if we have an intelligent instrument, the instrument itself could assign its own unique identifier or some combination of the above, and all of these forms could be put in the same directory or a federated directory.

Monoclonal antibodies are biotechnology tools that are very important in Flow Cytometry and several other fields. For example, I can take my distinguished name and further qualify it with a clone name to indicate some monoclonal antibody that I had produced. If this were a commercially produced antibody, we could also name it relative to the manufacturer.

On the other hand, when we are discovering genes, we frequently work with them for a long time before it becomes clear what they are and before everyone agrees on what they are. So, I have a second form of the name that we can use to uniquely name a gene, early-on in the discovery process, relative to a specific investigator, and with the assumption that when and if this does become a globally recognized gene, we then will change that for a reference to the new standard name.

Directory Searching

Searching in directories is somewhat different from searching classical databases. We can search by object scope, which means that we are looking for some specific object. In other words, we give the qualifier that we want and it should come back with one object. We can also search for all the elements that are in one level in a tree. For example, we can find all the samples in a particular protocol, or we can search for a subtree and find all samples taken by a particular investigator.

Limiting a Search. Search filters are defined in terms of the usual Boolean: ANDs, ORs, and NOTs. And, as I discussed, we can use various exact and approximate matching patterns to search. We can also put limits on the search. We can say, for example, "I am expecting to get about 100 results here, so if you are finding 5,000 results, stop and tell me that before we grind our way through all the entries." Or we could say, "Don't spend more than 10 minutes looking for this—if you do, then I need to say something more specific."

Referrals and Federation. As I said, the Directory was designed from the ground up to have referrals and federation. What this means is, if we start with our local server or some home server, it will return to us the results of everything it found that matched our search criteria. In addition, we can decorate those entries with referrals to other LDAP servers so that it provides a list of other servers that it thinks might have information that would fulfill our query. Then we can either tell it to automatically follow referrals or to put up a list of the sites to which it was referred and let me choose which ones to follow.

Attributes of Metadata. A measure of metadata quality that has been discussed at this meeting is the 20-year-rule: If somebody goes to the directory and finds these 20-year-old data, can that person who was not the primary investigator find out enough information about the data to make intelligent use of them? In regard to that concern, biotechnology, instrument technology, and computer technology have changed so fast that 20-year-old data really are not relevant anymore.

There are attributes or aspects of the metadata that we feel need to be there and need to be well-defined in order for assessors to make use of the data. These attributes include information about who did the data and on what instrument; references to what data-collection protocol was used; and information about what reagents and what antibodies were used. Again, we want to maintain a directory of the reagents that we use in our facility so that, instead of just having a common name for the reagent, we can actually put a distinguished name for the reagent in the metadata. That distinguished name would then refer back to the card that really documents that particular reagent. We feel this has a much wider applicability than just to Flow Cytometry or any other particular field.

The Future of Directory Service

I mentioned that Stanford has a directory now that is, in fact, using LDAP. I have also talked about using LDAP's attribute equal value pair names as standard nomenclature. For example, taxonomic nomenclature could be subsumed into an X500 scheme just by adopting a set of coding conventions, and then existing nomenclatures can be mapped directly into this scheme.

Reagents. I have talked a bit about reagents. One of the things that we have been discussing with the commercial producers of these reagents is producing directories of catalogues essentially on-line. So we would have our individual directory, which would list the reagents that we actually had in our freezer. But if we had some sort of experiment-planning tool we are using and we decide we want to stain for something for which we don't have a reagent, it could potentially go out and look in the vendor's catalog to decide whether some reagent exists or could be ordered to fulfill that requirement.

Accessibility of Primary Data. Another thing we would like to do using this directory structure is to make the primary data accessible to later users. Flow data is much like genetic-sequence data in that it is voluminous and very complicated. It is difficult to analyze in one pass, but unlike genetic data, it is not currently available or databased after it is published. So, by establishing standards for naming and retrieval of these data, we would like to advance Flow Cytometry to the level at which publications would reference the primary data, so that if somebody wants to come back and use their favorite visualization tool or analysis tool or compare the data with their own data, they could have access.

Tag Sites. Eventually if we start making entries for all the samples in our experiments and all the reagents that we use, these subtrees or subcatalogs essentially become equivalent to a notebook that is online and searchable.

We think there are a lot of applications for Directory Service beyond those we have mentioned. For example, I am talking with the Human Genome Project about what I call sequenced tag sites, which are useful in mapping the genome. We can see how there are many sorts of collections that could be organized, or at least cataloged, this way online.

For example, radiation mapping is a panel of clones that has an object class and a common name. One example might have the distinguished name of Panel G3. That would be The Next Generation (TNG) hybrid panel, which has a finer resolution than the older G3 panel. A card would represent a specific clone within that panel. There are, I believe, almost 200 in the G3 panel, and that is a pretty typical number. Then when we actually do the mapping, we find that the tag site is about a 300-based sequence, which is not polymorphic in the species and is present in only one copy. So it would be a useful location map, showing positional location along the chromosome. We might also have a multiple-valued attribute for every clone in which this tag site is present in that database. Raw data are used to calculate what is called a map distance, which is essentially the probability that two genes will associate together into certain different fragments.

Finally there is a tag-site card, which is defined in terms of a particular chromosome relative to a particular species. It includes the tag sequence itself, so that we can find it at a map location. For example, I want things that are near this location on Chromosome 12. Or I want things that actually have this sequence in it, and it has a reference back to a distinguished name and back to the radiation hybrid panel that was used to make the map.

Taxonomic Names. Another application about which I spoke is just subsuming existing biological nomenclatures in a way that can be parsed and manipulated correctly and automatically by machines. We can also have synonyms, and we can have references.

Role in the Literature. Finally, we think that this could also be used for literature searching and references. For example, further inheritance from the person could include attributes that are relevant, such as the professional name, the name that a person uses to site in the literature, professional specialties, professional affiliations, and so forth. This probably ought to be a journal article card that gives us a title of a particular issue or particular volume in some journal and gives us the distinguished names of the authors; the distinguished name of the paper that it references; and, potentially, a citation of another paper that references it and, for example, the abstract. Most of the so-called Dublin Core elements are already defined within the ISO standard in terms of titles and dates and creator date and the abstracts and descriptions and so on.

Session 6

The Metadata Challenge for Museums

Museum Informatics: Where We Have Been and Where We Need to Go

JULIAN HUMPHRIES, Associate Professor/Research, Department of Biological Sciences, University of New Orleans

ABSTRACT

Fragments of the museum community were early adopters of the technology associated with personal computers and databases. However, early growth was sporadic and very un-centralized and, as a consequence, there were many singular efforts that died quick deaths. Other institutions or groups worked together but frequently without significant communication with peers. During the early and mid-'90s, the heterogeneity in system and logical design of museum information systems resembled a course patchwork of database technology and sophistication. The National Science Foundation (NSF) became frustrated with the repeated building of new systems and started requiring more thoughtful design and cooperation for institutions that sought their funds. Elements of the community started working on collaborative projects, and a few individuals spearheaded efforts to build some community infrastructure. To date, these efforts have achieved a small measure of success, but large-scale integration of the museum community (and its data) awaits as of yet unseen levels of cooperation and will require a healthy infusion of technology and personnel into the typical museum operation.

Today I would like to address issues about the expectations of a directory service community—especially the issue of what those expectations ought to be from the viewpoint of the people who actually have to provide data and metadata about their collections. I am also going to be talking about who we are, what we do (and why what we do is important), the priorities of natural history museums from the viewpoint of content providers, and the nature of the problem for biological collection and the corresponding biodiversity data providers.

The Role of Natural History Collections

The traditional and primary role of natural history collections is as archivers and catalogers of specimens and proxies for specimens. The result is a curated collection of objects and data about those objects. The product that comes out of natural history collections is dynamic knowledge about those specimens in a lot of contexts—taxonomic, ecological, and functional descriptions of species, higher level taxa, and communities.

The people in museums who make these products are also frequently the same people who are responsible for the curation and cataloging of these collections. As a consequence, their role is twofold. First, they have the responsibility for seeing that the collections are well maintained and curated. But they also have the responsibility for taking the information from those objects and doing something with it in terms of publication.

Why Biodiversity Data are Important

The importance of biodiversity data is probably fairly obvious, but I want to make a few points about the role these three billion objects play in this scheme of discovery about the Earth, the history of the Earth, and what is going to happen to the Earth with time. Virtually most of what we know about the natural world in some way or another works its way back to the truth that is represented in natural history collections. So that original piece of information that someone got about a bird, fish, or insect—as well as where the specimen was collected—is the start of a long pathway of knowledge and dissemination of knowledge about our natural world.

It is also true that those same data, once used as an indication of the past, are also valuable for prediction about the future in terms of telling us about parts of the world with which we are unfamiliar, about things that we can predict, and about the location of taxa that we have not yet collected. The data also help measure the impact of particular human activities on the natural world, as well as the likely impact of a human activity on flora and fauna.

Aspects of a Museum Curator's Job

I am speaking from the viewpoint of a former curator (and I actually remain curator of a small collection). If you look at the things that are important to me as a curator, the first thing is conservation of the specimens under my charge. It has been interesting to hear others relate the value of data to its age as they discuss the 20-year-rule. In contrast, our data don't even start to get interesting until they are more than 20 years old, and the older they are, the better they are. We think, literally, in terms of centuries—centuries past and centuries future. We are interested in data and specimens from a century or more ago. And we are interested in having those specimens that are under our charge be just as useful 100 or 200 years down the road.

That scope of time puts a very heavy load on us curators in terms of determining what to do first when we begin working with a new specimen. For the most part, the first thing we have to determine is that that specimen is going to be there tomorrow in the same condition in which we found it today.

The next aspect of being a content-provider curator is to understand that the specimens are to be used. Therefore, there must be in place tracking mechanisms that track the transactions associated with a specimen. Increasing specimen usage, contacting the researchers (both internally and externally) who might make use of the collections' specimens, and satisfying the funding requirements of the parent organization or agency also are part of a curator's responsibilities (in fact, they comprise a part for which the curators are not necessarily trained). At different times, this one position might be a service function, a training function, or even a research function.

Because of all this responsibility, data and data management—despite their importance—almost always comes at the end of the curator's priority list. In addition, since data management was simply paper up until 15 years ago, the idea of devoting additional resources to data management meant something had to be taken away from the other responsibilities.

The Internet Impacts Curators

What has happened since the advent of the Internet has been just amazing and has signaled a truly revolutionary change for natural history collections. Before the Internet, paper itself was very, very important to us. We cared a lot about physical paper. We made labels out of it, we wrote our catalogs on it. It was something that we studied and investigated and used for research.

Then the digital age came upon us. Now we had to take the records that we had carefully curated and managed for a century or more and transfer them to computer technology. This raised many questions about how we manage our collections and what we were going to do with those data. These concerns became even more acute when microcomputers moved into the collections, and it became possible not only to digitize our data but also to actually put the data on machines that sat right next to the specimens themselves!

Originally what we saw was the creation of a large number of disparate and heterogeneous information systems that did not do a very good job of talking to each other. Remember, at the time there really was no organization that dealt with issues of standardization in our museums. In fact, one of the first efforts in that regard took place just 10 years ago, in 1988, at a workshop organized and funded by the Association of Systematic Collections. At that workshop, one of our charges was to deal with issues related to standardization of hardware and software, necessary primarily because the era of the PC was anything but a standard at that time. Intel was certainly the primary vendor, but there were other, competing operating systems. There also were many software choices, and these software choices varied dramatically in their capabilities and in their interchange with other software choices.

A number of workshops followed. For example, in 1993, I helped organize a workshop on standards and the exchange of data. And Berkeley personnel organized a workshop on interoperability of mechanical databases. And all the while we talked about federation, federation, federation.

During this time, the data management systems that were being created got increasingly sophisticated. We moved from a written set of applications to a more sophisticated set of applications. But within the community, we still lacked any kind of high-level effort that would make it possible for all of these databases to speak to each other. So, the challenge was—and remains—to determine what is necessary for all of these biological data sets and the data associated with them to be readily accessible and available, and for the information about these data sets to be readily accessible and available in all of the variety of clearing houses and search engines and directory services that exist today.

Curators Consider Collection-Level and Object-Level Metadata

Earlier a distinction was made between collection-level metadata and object-level metadata. Collection-level metadata might involve the creation of 50,000 to 100,000 record objects to capture the data about all the places where museum information is stored. However, when we are talking about object-level metadata, we are looking at a number at least five or six orders of magnitude larger!

There is no easy way to move from good descriptions of our collection data sets to good descriptions of our collection objects. So if we take the numbers discussed earlier in terms of the cost per record—up to $60 for each record—we realize that more detailed metadata-descriptor creation would cost tens of billions of dollars. This is not a likely investment in the near future. On the other hand, when we are talking about collection-level metadata, the cost falls to the millions of dollars. I believe that <u>this</u> is a feasible goal for our community, and I believe that it is one that—with the proper incentives and resources—is attainable.

Museum Metadata: Who Pays?

RAY LESTER, Head of Library & Information Services, Natural History Museum, London

ABSTRACT

Global networks offer great opportunities to deliver representations of Museum artifacts to schoolchild, scientist, and sightseer—wherever they and the artifacts of interest are located in the world. Such networks allow curatorial, research, library, archive, and art data held in geographically separate organizations to be brought together and delivered seamlessly to the customer. "Metadata" provides a lens on this data cornucopia, ensuring retrieval of just that subset of the totality of data that is needed by the user for the current task in hand. BUT . . . who pays for the metadata?

In this Paper I have tried to relate in as simple a fashion as possible key themes discussed in the last few days to the reality of work in London, UK. The Natural History Museum is a reasonably significant institution in global terms:

- 68,000,000 biological/mineralogical specimens
- 1,000,000 library volumes
- 10,000 current serials
- 500,000 art and other information artifacts
- 300 scientists
- 30 librarians

And, as has been commented here for other large species- and specimen-based collections, the data relating to identification, location, habitat and so on, which can be digitally captured from the collections, converted into information, and delivered via the Web, is potentially of value to people worldwide, both in the developed and developing countries. That information, and its underlying "rich data"—the word "data" used of course here to encompass text, image, moving image, voice, and multimedia combinations of such—can be discovered and made accessible to the customer via meta-information and meta-data.

The Museum wishes to provide such electronically mediated access to representations of its library, art and archive holdings, as well as to those of its specimen collections, especially in the senses that "our" metadata—by "our" I mean metadata created by people employed by The Natural History Museum—is likely to be contributed in the future to what I term here **Web Consortia.** (The Museum for instance is already committed to participate in Species 2000 and is a sponsoring partner of the UK's proposed National Biodiversity Network.) Also, in creating "our" metadata, we might wish to make use of—query, make "fair use" of, in an intellectual property sense?— metadata stored in the print volumes of the Museum's Library (such as the scientific journals, and the abstracting and indexing volumes). In those contexts, I thought that it might potentially be useful to ask in this forum, at this juncture:

Who pays for metadata?

It will not surprise you that I do not expect here an answer to the question, though it would be nice if my comments stimulated some discussion. The question itself is obviously rather fundamental, and it would need more time and energy than we all have at this point in the conference to do it justice. Cliff Lynch in some comments earlier today eloquently elaborated some of the facets that would need to be addressed in producing anything approaching a comprehensive answer to the question. So my prime intention in this Paper—using The Natural History Museum as an exemplar—is to try to explain why we believe in London that the question needs to be answered—and moreover, to be answered through an international cooperative effort of the types of stakeholders represented at this conference. Once, with our now many and various "metadiversity" networks, we move from research grants and lottery funds and politically inspired initiatives to doing things "for real," we will need to put in place global mechanisms for deciding who pays for the metadata (and metainformation) used in the networks. The participating stakeholders will positively need to do that, because we are operating in a non-market economy or, at least, in a mixed economy. I presume none of the stakeholders who work outside of the market sector would wish the distribution of metadiversity information wholly to be market driven.

The Natural History Museum has a vision of its data and information flowing "freely" around the Internet. That vision is fully compatible with the Museum's overall mission:

> "The Museum's mission is to maintain and develop its collections and use them to promote the discovery, understanding, responsible use and enjoyment of the natural world"

and with the mission statement of my own Museum Department:

> "Organising, preserving and communicating knowledge of the natural world."

The vision is to make all "our" natural world data, information, metadata and metainformation available directly or indirectly to customers via the World Wide Web. We wish our offerings to be seamlessly entwined with the offerings of other compatible institutions worldwide. The Director of the Museum—as all such Directors!—would like this to happen next week, including extending our offerings to include tacit taxonomic knowledge and perhaps even the odd bit of wisdom!

There is a phrase often used in computing circles—"managing expectations." I guess one has not done that very well. We have painted a vision of using the wondrous technology to deliver data and information at all levels of granularity, in all media, to customers located in other institutions, in other professional domains, in other funding sectors, and in other political jurisdictions. But we have not said sufficiently is, "This is going to cost a great deal of money, and there are a number of critical global policy decisions that will need to be made before the vision can be realised, including a determination of who pays."

Naturally, when one starts to disentangle the policy decisions that need to be made, one finds that the necessary frameworks are all there in the literature—albeit framed at other times and in other milieu. A good example is the taxonomy represented in this Table, taken from Taylor's 1986 seminal text *Value Adding Processes in Information Systems* (Taylor 1986):

Action	matching goals compromising bargaining choosing	= DECISION PROCESSES
Productive Knowledge	presenting options advantages disadvantages	= JUDGMENTAL PROCESSES
Informing Knowledge	separating evaluating validating comparing interpreting synthesizing	= ANALYZING PROCESSES
Information	grouping classifying relating formatting signaling displaying	= ORGANIZING PROCESSES

Data

To ensure a productive debate leading to a single, agreed-upon, global, taxonomically-based information architecture acceptable to all significant stakeholders (and there has to be one seamless over-arching architecture—which is, of course, not the same as saying that there needs to be one over-arching global information system), we need to find the time and energy to work through the details, using agreed frameworks such as Taylor's.

I am fond of using the phrase "The Middle" to denote all those building blocks within the overall information architecture that are outside the direct management and command of either the resource-holding institution—in this case the Natural History Museum—or of the organisation, if any, wherein the customer for such held resources resides. In the widest sense, value-adding processes have to occur if the "rich data" captured and sitting on computer servers within my own and other similar resource-holding institutions is to be transformed into information which can be used by the remote customer for the task in hand. That value-adding clearly can occur:

• within the Natural History Museum (or other resource-holding institution);
• within the customer's own organization;

- in "The Middle," overseen by an entity, or entities, quite separate from the Museum or the user and his/her parent organization.

I am calling these "middle" entities here Web Consortia.

The overall network architectural infrastructure—or "superstructure"—has to characterise and maintain each of a number of types of building blocks: the building blocks of a particular type will occur within the resource-holding institution, within the customer organisation, or in "The Middle." These building blocks can be characterised as:

- information technology hardware/software
- information systems standards/protocols
- metadata
- rules and regulations of system use
- value-adding intermediaries, where needed
- coordinating bodies

A building block that is not optimally available and maintained will hinder, and may even prevent, the communication of a server-based resource to the customer for that resource. When we come to do this "for real," we cannot have the server going down, the wrong Z39.50 profile being used, the species name being entered incorrectly, the user un-authenticated, the customer interface being clumsy and leading to the user giving up, or the coordinating-body Help Desk being closed. And all such elements and much, much, more need **management**.

In an important book published earlier this year (Weill & Broadbent 1998), Marianne Broadbent and Peter Weill reported on some detailed empirical research carried out over a number of years. The question addressed was, "How is it that some large, multinational enterprises succeed in leveraging IT, whilst others fail?" In other words, what are the secrets of getting freestanding companies, albeit part of the same corporate conglomerate (and remember as regards "The Middle" in my conception, we have not even got that potential sanction) to work together and use global IT networks to deliver real cost/benefit?

I asked Marianne Broadbent, shortly after this book was published, what she would advise for Web Consortia of the type discussed in this Conference. Her recommendations were:

- Must have commitment from stakeholders at the level of CEO/The Board
- Must relate to maxims in each stakeholder that are strong and about the core roles of each parent organisation
- Must focus on the "have to" rather than the "nice to have"
- Must be able to display demonstrable benefits
- Must be a long-term, sustainable process
- Someone must have a remit to command the whole information system

The key recommendation, it seems to me, is the last. Someone has to be in overall command where, as noted earlier, the market-place is not wished to be the ultimate arbiter of who supplies and gets what globally dispersed metadiversity data and information.

And I suggest that such will need to be the case even when we do, indeed, agree on a single species name to link together data and information held in dispersed and disparate information systems. In fact, one critical element of the commitment needed from the participating stakeholders in Web Consortia is indeed to use that agreed-upon single-species name internally as a pointer to the other species and related specimen data and information each stakeholder holds and wishes potentially to make available to external customers. Note in passing that it has to be that way around. The model has to be the generation by the rich data-holding institution of a Dublin Core—or a Darwin Core or whatever—record containing the agreed-upon species name.

This speaker is in theory—in theory!—commanding the resources needed to deliver to the outside world this necessary metadata and metainformation about the resources held in the vaults of the Natural History Museum. But this speaker is in no sense in command of the Web Consortia via which such data and information might eventually be delivered to external customers. Even within the Museum, one's theoretically commanding role has to take account of the views of our friends in the Museum Department of Exhibitions and Education, who are much exercised by matters of corporate identity, and by our other friends in the Department of Development and Marketing, who similarly are exercised by the need to raise income for the Museum over and above that which arrives courtesy of the UK Government's grant-in-aid. And then, in the centre of all this, we have the information and communication needs of the Museum scientists themselves to address.

There is such a momentum now within the Natural History Museum to give Web access to the Museum's cornucopia of resources ("increasing access" being also a favourite theme of the Blair government) that I have been able to propose to the Museum the creation by my Department of a full-fledged Business Plan with costed options designed to achieve this. (The Museum's Director likes business plans with costed options!) In preparing this Business Plan, the environmental assumptions we would make are:

1. There is indeed customer demand for Web-based information relating to Museum "rich data" and made accessible via perusal of "metadata" (and "metainformation").
2. In making such Museum information electronically available, the most important factors to get right are quality, presentation, and indexing.
3. The prime strategic decision for the Museum is the extent to which it will participate in future Web Consortia, and whether as secondary, or as lead, partner.

"Web Consortia" are conceived as trusted gateways to the "best" pockets of data/information/metadata/metainformation accessible in total via the World Wide Web. Such quality gateways will gradually replace the generic search services such as the present Yahoo and HotBot for purposeful enquirers who do not know where in the world the reliable information (and data) they need resides. Given the universal nature both of the underlying Web technology and of the Museum's topical focus ("the natural world"), it is felt that it is inevitable that there will emerge for the Museum's subject field a relatively small number of Web Consortia "brand leaders." These organisations, which could be located anywhere in the world, will become the preferred first ports-of-call when customers wish to access and use data/information/metadata/metainformation about the "natural world" via the Web but do not know where trustworthy elements of such digital representations can be found.

The proposed study that would lead to the proposed Business Plan with costed options can be summarised:

- *Test environmental assumptions*
- *Audit of present Museum capabilities*
    IT infrastructure
    Staff for resource creation and maintenance, market interaction, and management/administration
- *Customer market analysis*
    Science
    Policy
    Public
- *Competitor analysis*
    Providers of data/information/metadata/metainformation
    Web consortia
- *Prospective Museum competitive advantage*
- *Marginal resources required to fulfill target market needs*
- *Revenue implications*

In conclusion, it is now easy to see why the Natural History Museum must determine an answer to the question, "Who pays for the metadata?" Answering the question for any specific object stored within the Museum is not, however, easy. Copies of most objects can be delivered in a variety of digital—and other—forms, each of which will need its own metadata. Such metadata—especially if the Museum is going to consider charging for access to the underlying object surrogate—will need to go beyond descriptive metadata, and include "rights" (and instantiation and administrative) metadata. The Museum will also need to recognise the different arenas wherein the metadata will be needed and will be used, e.g., at the point of resource creation, when it is made available, when it is used. And the Museum will need finally to recognise that even when it does decide that needed metadata must be paid for by the Museum, or by the customer, deciding how the former should be costed (or priced) and the latter should be priced (or costed) brings in train a whole new set of challenges—given the underlying economics of information, with its non-depletability, its potential non-excludability, and its almost-always positive externalities. To show to you a slide by McGillivray of a wonderful image of a heron stored in our art collections did not "cost" me anything. Or did it?

References

Taylor, R. S. 1986. *Value-adding processes in information systems.* Ablex, Norwood, NJ.

Weill, P. and M. Broadbent. 1998. *Leveraging the NEW infrastructure.* Harvard Business School Press, Boston, MA.

Session 7

Working Groups

Reports from the Working Groups

RICHARD T. KASER, NFAIS Executive Director, Metadiversity Principal Investigator

At the end of the second day of the Metadiversity program, participants were formed into groups of four, and then these groups were combined into groups of eight, to list issues for further discussion. The recommendations from these small working groups were compiled and merged into five discussion topics.

1. **Leadership & Consensus Building**, including national vs. global issues, organizational framework (infrastructural issues), interconnection of efforts (across domains, disciplines, and organization types), and how to achieve support from individual organizations (including ones own organization) and related communities.

2. **Technology**, including how to establish priorities, how to assure distributed but interoperable systems, how to handle data archiving and assure long-term data access, and data security.

3. **Standards for Biodiversity Data**, including taxonomy (controlled vocabulary), thesauri, models, and tools. This group also touched on the larger issues of how to involve professional communities in developing interoperable systems.

4. **Funding & Economics**, including funding strategies, developing incentives and rewards, business models, test beds, and business plans.

5. **Users**, including identification of user groups, their requirements, standards, privacy issues, etc.

Participants in the symposium then registered to participate the following day in one of these discussions. There were four discussion groups in all. A single group considered both topics 4 and 5.

Facilitated Discussions

The four discussion groups were facilitated by: Anne Frondorf, Program Manager, National Biological Information Infrastructure; Bonnie Carroll, President, Information International Associates; Gail Hodge, Information International Associates; and Susan Warner, President, The LEAD Alliance, a consulting firm.

Each group reported its recommendations in a concluding plenary session of the symposium. Results are summarized below.

Recommendations

At the highest level, all of the reports and recommendations can be said to have focused on infrastructural concerns. The symposium program as a whole had stressed the range of agencies, data types, and systems already in existence. Many presentations had also emphasized the need for developing interoperable systems so that users of biodiversity information could have the capability of seamlessly crossing organizational and subject lines in order to obtain the information they need.

But what is the motivation for agencies to work together to create an interoperable system that exceeds the mission of their individual organization? How to inspire cooperation? And how to develop and win acceptance for standards that would achieve these ends?

The Call for Community. All of the Metadiversity working groups picked up on this theme. The Leadership and Consensus Building Group, for example, focused on how to get administrative officials (both in the government and at individual agencies and non-governmental organizations) to buy off on the need for cooperation. Another discussion group originally set up to discuss technological matters redefined its charter to discuss the culture of the scientific community and how to get working scientists to buy off on the concept that capturing data about data sets (metadata) is even important. The Standards group considered the issue of how to get organizations to develop and accept metadata standards for their individual projects. And finally, the Economics/Users group ended up proposing activities that would result in better coordination of efforts throughout the world. The overall outcome of these group discussions, therefore, appears to be that consensus building within the entire community of biodiversity-related agencies itself needs to be a high priority.

The Metadiversity symposium aimed to produce a call to action. By the end of the conference it was clear that the call that emerged from the discussions was a call for community. Before we can proceed to solve the grand challenge of biodiversity information management, those who must be a part of the solution must first recognize that they are part of the "biodiversity information community." Then they must accept that they need to work with each other to create a common solution. But how will this be achieved?

Consensus-Building at High Levels. The "Leadership" group focused in particular on the need to develop consensus across disciplines, across international boundaries, and across organizations.

Emphasizing that the system needs to built with consensus from the bottom up and not by imposition from the top down, the group recommended a four-part strategy:

- Define biodiversity communities
- Define the scope of the metadata framework
- Proactively communicate across communities
- Build cross-community linkages

To implement this strategy, the group felt it was critical to make a convincing case to leaders of the value of metadata. It suggested that one way of doing this was to develop a prototype system that would show the benefits and demonstrate the capabilities of a fully deployed biodiversity information management system. Specifically, the group proposed that CIESIN, with international endorsement (e.g., from IUBS), should be asked to select one or several queries/examples that would include a range of organisms and geographical coverage. The BIOECO working group of CENR would advise on the selection of examples.

Development of such a prototype would also depend on the prior definition of an information model, which would include all the various kinds of data necessary to support the full-fledged system—in other words, a scope description of the metadata framework for biodiversity information management.

The group proposed that NBII should be responsible for contracting with a third party to both define the framework and to obtain the sample content to demonstrate the viability and usefulness of the desired system. In order to secure grassroots support, NBII would distribute a draft of this plan for community input.

Proactive communication across communities was also considered imperative. Specific recommendations were:

1. Approach relevant umbrella groups to carry message to their memberships—for example, AIBS for professional societies, CENR for governmental agencies.
2. Encourage NSF to include metadata as part of the products it funds.
3. Encourage the development of a biodiversity informative consortium by communicating through professional societies (e.g., AIBS).

4. Encourage NBII and CANBII to establish a resource site, including tools and resources.

As part of this effort, it was also considered important to develop creative relationships with non-traditional partners—i.e., non-governmental organizations, including private industry, not only as funding sources but also as contributors to the development of system plans.

And finally, the group suggested that NFAIS sponsor a follow-up meeting to Metadiversity to continue the dialog that began here.

Consensus at the Grassroots Level. While the first group looked at building consensus at high levels, a second discussion group approached the subject by focusing on the need to have a buy-in from practitioners (scientists, researchers, and scholars) who produce and subsequently use (or could use) data related to biodiversity. This group first observed that the development of an integrated biodiversity information management system was more limited by cultural factors than by technological factors. Researchers currently have few incentives and little motivation to provide documentation for the data sets that they create. Such documentation, however, was considered necessary to support and encourage information reuse.

Cultural factors that were identified by the group included the academic reward system (which currently does not require the sharing of data), funding mechanisms (which do not currently require that data be submitted with the results), instrumentation functionalities (which do not automatically record data about the data being computed), and professional standards (which do not universally extend to data documentation).

As recommendations, this discussion group called for a combination of educational efforts aimed at the research community and for the development of incentives that would encourage researchers to create and capture data about their data sets. The group also suggested that colleges and universities should extend the current system of rewarding researchers for publication to also credit researchers who publish data sets. The group also recommended that funding agencies require grant recipients to submit data as part of the results, and that the manufacturers of laboratory instruments be persuaded to incorporate software that requires the capture of metadata about the tests being run.

To encourage the above developments, the group proposed the creation of an Information Technology Resource Center. The center, which could be sponsored by the NBII, a professional society, or even a journal publisher, would develop and promulgate technical requirements for the collection and reporting of data, define specific data that should be collected, and provide resources, demos, etc.

This group also discussed the need for a browser/search engine that "understands biology," i.e., a search interface that can handle the technical vocabulary and can be used to qualify resources. It specifically suggested that one R&D priority should be the development of the basic ontology to support a biodiversity knowledge base.

This group echoed the first discussion group by concluding that in order to achieve these goals it would be necessary (and desirable) to bring the various communities together who need to support such developments.

Involving Users. While the second discussion group was deliberating about cultural factors affecting the user community, a third group was specifically focused on discussing user needs. Noting that the user community is diverse—consisting of multiple user types and "market segments" that have differing but overlapping needs and metadata requirements and includes K-12 students as well as professional research scientists—this third group stressed that proactive means of assessing user needs and collecting feedback are very important.

In order to involve users, the group recommended the following steps be taken:

1. Create an international association of biodiversity data providers and user representatives.

2. Address the issues of economics/politics, regarding open international access to data/Metadata.

    Academic/scientific communities must develop a consensus position—perhaps facilitated by the National Academy of Science or National Research Council.

    This biodiversity data community should propose an holistic assessment of user needs, including both current and potential users.

3. Metadata must be extensible for future use based on need. It must be an evolutionary process. It must be proactive.

In addition, the group proposed that funding sponsors—as well as core members of such a group—be identified.

The group also proposed that another workshop or symposium be held to:

- identify gaps in information needed to support users;
- identify places user needs are being met and how they are being met;
- bring in domain expertise in user assessment (library and social science);
- identify populations of priority potential users; and
- include Information Industry representatives to assist with value-added assessment.

Economic Factors and Incentives. Given the size and scope of what could conceivably be defined as the "biodiversity community" (which in its ultimate sense could well include most government agencies and a whole range of industries), economic factors were perceived as an important area for discussion. Because the private sector needs to play a role, it cannot be assumed that all information that should be included in such a system can be provided for free. Thus the challenge in this area extends to considering intellectual property issues. A fourth discussion group took up this topic.

This group defined the problems as:

- Funding mechanisms differ for industry, academia, and government. There are three different business models involved: for-profit, cost recovery, and public domain.
- There is no funding for inter- and intra-sector collaboration.
- There is no funding for international liaison for metadata (e.g., IABIN).
- Often there is no direct funding for data management and metadata in government organizations or as a requirement of government grants.
- Bio-eco metadata communities cross many sectors, sometimes working at cross-purposes and competing for funding.
- Intellectual property rights issues affect funding approaches. This may create an increasing divide between information "haves" and "have-nots."
- There is little understanding of the user community and how users value information.

What needs to happen? The group envisioned the following ideal situation:

- There exists a sustainable, financially stable, transnational, and cross-sector group to coordinate the creation, support, and promotion of bio-eco metadata (such as the Global Biodiversity Information Facility—GBIF).
- There is resolution on a global scale of the intellectual property rights issue with respect to bio-eco metadata as well as the existence of a continuing mechanism for managing requirements for multiple property rights.
- Bio-eco metadata is universally available in holistic environments that integrate elements of business models of for-profit, cost recovery, and public domain sectors.

- Bio-eco metadata from within and across sectors is universally available in a coherent fashion.
- There are funded mandates to government agencies for metadata creation and management at the international, federal, state, local, and tribal levels

How to get there? The group recommended these "bold steps":

1. **International, cross-sector body**: Establish ongoing national funding for bio-eco metadata activities and interests within an international, cross-sector body such as GBIF.
2. **National dialog on intellectual property rights**: Fund a national dialog encompassing diverse views on international intellectual property rights as they relate to bio-eco metadata (e.g., through NFAIS facilitation).
3. **Development of an economic model**: Fund R&D study to develop an economic model for making bio-eco metadata universally available in holistic environments that integrate elements of business models of for-profit, cost-recovery, and public domain sectors (e.g., a Harvard Business School study funded by the Melon Foundation).
4. **Support for and promotion of existing successful activities**: Fund the enhancement and promotion of existing successful models of cross-sector collaboration for bio-eco metadata.
5. **Support for government agencies and government-funded activities**: Put in place funding and incentives for government agencies (at all levels) and for recipients of government funding to create, manage, and share bio-eco metadata.

All of this, again, implies the need to achieve a consensus among the leaders of many organizations. However, this same discussion group also stressed the need to recognize that in the end it is all about users and their need for information. Thus this group reaffirmed that we also need consensus building from the bottom up, including the close involvement of the user community in defining what a distributed biodiversity information management system needs to do.

Standards Development. Finally, the fifth discussion group considered the need for standards as a unifying element in the creation of an interoperable biodiversity information management system.

Their recommendations were:

1. Continue prototypes and test beds for interoperability based on existing and emerging metadata standards
2. BRD, NCEAS (and any other relevant stakeholder organizations within the BioEco community) should convene a working group to develop a

report/document and "tool kit" that will help our community to develop metadata standards.

- The document and tool kit would inform community members about resources available to help in establishing development and maintenance processes for metadata standards.
- The document should recognize that the biodiversity community is an assembly of smaller communities, and that these sub-communities have different information characteristics (e.g., diversity of data concepts and data distribution/partitioning) and culture. This means that particular standards development mechanisms might not be appropriate for all communities. The recommended best practices should reflect this heterogeneity.
- The document should include a time line describing milestones in standards development.
- The document should include recommendations about identifying, informing, and engaging stakeholders, such that the standards development process is open and representative of the community.
- The document should emphasize that every standards development effort must have an explicit scope, goal, and audience.
- The tool kit should make standards developers aware of the resources, particularly technical and human, that are available to facilitate the processes of standards development and adoption.

3. EPA (Bargmeyer), CAS (Blum), and TNC (Howie) will collaborate to enter a manageable number (~10) data elements into a data registry modeled on that of the EPA Environmental Data Registry.
4. Create a locator/registry of biodiversity organizations and/or data providers, perhaps similar to the Taxonomic Resources and Expertise Directory (TRED). This will help the community members become more aware of each other and will also help in identifying stakeholders in standards-development activities.
5. Continue work on shared vocabularies, including: create a registry of relevant vocabularies and thesauri, and do research into and develop prototypes of interoperability mechanisms for thesauri.
6. Tell BRD and NSF that an NCEAS-like center should be established to facilitate metadata and data synthesis. This center could then be used to host standards development and maintenance activities. At present, member organizations do not have the resources (staff time) to give standards development and maintenance the attention they require.

Summary of the Recommendations

In general what we saw being proposed was the creation of a centralized coordinating body, appropriately funded, to first identify and define the community and then conduct outreach, community-building, and support activities.

APPENDIX A

METADIVERSITY

A Call to Action:

Responding to the Grand Challenge for

Biodiversity Information Management through

Metadata

PROGRAM

Monday, Nov. 9	WELCOME TO NATURAL BRIDGE

Monday, Nov. 9 WELCOME TO NATURAL BRIDGE

3:00 p.m. Registration–Small Lobby

6:00 - 8:00 p.m. WELCOMING DINNER–JEFFERSON BALLROOM

Opening Remarks: A Global Call for Action

Dennis Fenn, Chief Biologist, Biological Resources Division,
U.S. Geological Survey

William Brown, Science Advisor to the Secretary,
Department of the Interior

Tuesday, Nov. 10 THE CHALLENGE OF BIODIVERSITY INFORMATION
MANAGEMENT

7:00 - 8:00 a.m. BREAKFAST–COLONIAL DINING ROOM

8:00 - 10:00 a.m. ALL PLENARY SESSIONS–WASHINGTON HALL

Session 1: The Nation's Call to Action

Moderator: Dick Kaser, NFAIS Executive Director

"CBD's Clearing-House Mechanism: Biodiversity Metadata
And Information"–Beatriz Torres, Program Officer, Secretariat,
Convention on Biological Diversity

"Implications for Informatics of the Report of the PCAST Committee on
Biodiversity and Ecosystems"–Geoffrey Bowker, Associate Professor,
University of Illinois

"The National Biological Information Infrastructure (NBII) Framework
Plan–A Road Map for Interoperable Sharing of Biodiversity Information"
–James L. Edwards, Deputy Assistant Director, Directorate for Biological
Sciences, National Science Foundation

"The Metadata Landscape: Conventions for Semantics, Syntax, and
Structure in the Internet Commons"–Stuart Weibel, Senior Research
Scientist, OCLC

10:00 - 10:30 a.m. REFRESHMENT BREAK

**10:30 - 12:30 p.m.   Session 2: The Challenge in Species Discovery
                        and Taxonomic Information**

Moderator: Maureen Kelly, Vice President for Planning, BIOSIS

Lead Presentation:

"Doing the Impossible: Creating a Stable Species Index and Operating a
Common Access System on the Internet"–Frank Bisby, Director, Centre
for Plant Diversity and Systematics, University of Reading, Species 2000

Speakers/Panelists:

"On Conventions, Standards and Systematic Practice: How Far Can
(or Should) We Go?"–Peter Stevens, Professor, Harvard University,
Taxonomic Databases Working Group

"Discover Life in America & the Database Needs of the All Taxa
Biodiversity Inventory (ATBI) of Great Smoke Mountains National Park"
–John Pickering, Associate Professor, University of Georgia,
All-Taxa Biodiversity Inventory

"Taxonomic Information Systems–Stability Through Diversity"
–Hugh Wilson, Professor, Texas A&M University,
American Society of Plant Taxonomists

"ITIS, The Integrated Taxonomic Information System"
–Bruce Collette, Senior Scientist, National Marine Fisheries Service,
Integrated Taxonomic Information System

12:30 - 2:00 p.m.   LUNCH–COLONIAL DINING ROOM

2:00 - 3:00 p.m.   Perspectives:

"A Pragmatic Approach to the Challenge of Metadata Management for
Genome Information"–Victor Markowitz, Senior Vice President,
Data Management Systems, Gene Logic, Inc.

3:00 - 3:30 p.m.   REFRESHMENT BREAK

3:30 - 5:30 p.m.   **Session 3: The Challenge in Earth Observation, Ecosystem Monitoring and Environmental Information**

Moderator: Richard Hallgren, Executive Director, American Meteorological Society

Lead Presentation:

"The Challenge in Earth Observation, Ecosystem Monitoring and Environmental Information"–Roberta Balstad Miller, Director, CIESIN

Speakers/Panelists:

"Locating Biodiversity Data Through the Global Change Master Directory"–Lola Olsen, Project Manager, NASA Global Change Master Directory

"The Global Information Locator Service"–Eliot Christian, Computer Specialist, U.S. Geological Survey

"The Committee on Earth Observation Satellites Working Group on Information Systems and Services"–Gerald Barton, Physical Scientist, NOAA

"Beyond Metadata: Scientific Information Management Approaches Supporting Ecosystem Monitoring and Assessment Activities" –Robert Shepanek, Jeffrey Frithsen, National Center for Environmental Assessment, U.S. EPA

"Environmental Metainformation in the Work Program of the European Environmental Agency"–Stefan Jensen, Project Leader, European Topic Centre/Catalogue of Data Sources, European Environment Agency

6:30 - 8:00 p.m.   **DINNER–JEFFERSON BALLROOM**

Wednesday, Nov. 11   META-ISSUES & ANSWERS

7:00 - 8:30 a.m.   **BREAKFAST–COLONIAL DINING ROOM**

8:30 - 10:00 a.m.   **Session 4: Building the Infrastructure**

Moderator: Bonnie Carroll, President, Information International Associates

"The Metadata Challenge for NBII"
—Anne Frondorf, Program Manager, National Biological Information Infrastructure, USGS

"The National Spatial Data Infrastructure: Coordinating Geographic Data Acquisition and Access"–John Moeller, Staff Director, Federal Geographic Data Committee, USGS

"Digital Libraries Research and Infrastructure"
–Stephen Griffin, Program Director, Division of Information and Intelligent Systems, National Science Foundation

10:00 - 10:30 a.m.   **REFRESHMENT BREAK**

10:30 - 12:30 p.m.   **Session 5: The Metadata Challenge for Libraries**

Moderator: Sally Sinn, Associate Director, Technical Services, National Agricultural Library

Lead Presentation:

"Building Digital Libraries for Metadiversity: Federation Across Disciplines"–Clifford Lynch, Director, Coalition for Networked Information

Speakers/Panelists:

"The Metadata Challenge for Libraries: A View from Europe"
–Michael Day, Research Officer, UKOLN

"Alexandria Digital Library: Gazetteer and Collection-Level Metadata Developments"–Linda Hill, Research Specialist, UC Santa Barbara

"Metadata Challenges for Libraries"–Carl Lagoze, Digital Library Scientist, Cornell University

12:30 - 2:30 p.m.   **PICNIC LUNCH AT THE SUMMER HOUSE
AND EXPEDITION TO NATURAL BRIDGE**

2:30 - 3:30 p.m.	**Perspectives:**

"Perspectives on Information Management on the Internet"
–Wayne A. Moore, Senior Scientific Software Designer,
Stanford University

3:30 - 4:00 p.m.	**REFRESHMENT BREAK**

4:00 - 6:00 p.m	**Session 6: The Metadata Challenge for Museums**

Moderator: James H. Beach, Assistant Director for Informatics,
University of Kansas Natural History Museum and Biodiversity
Research Center

Speakers:

"Museum Informatics: Where We Have Been and Where We Need to Go"
–Julian Humphries, Associate Professor, University of New Orleans

"Museum Metadata: Who Pays?"
–Ray Lester, Head of Library & Information Services, Natural History
Museum, London

6:00 - 8:00 p.m.	**COLLABORATIVE DINNER–JEFFERSON BALLROOM**

Thursday, Nov. 12	**ACCEPTING THE GRAND CHALLENGE**

7:00 - 8:00 a.m.	**BREAKFAST–COLONIAL DINING ROOM**

8:00 a.m. - Noon	**A Call For Collaborative Action**

Facilitated Parallel Working Groups

Facilitators:
    Bonnie Carroll, Information International Associates
    Anne Frondorf, USGS/BRD
    Gail Hodge, Information International Associates
    Susan Warner, The LEAD Alliance

Meeting Adjourned!

APPENDIX B

National Biological Information Infrastructure

Strategy for Biodiversity and Ecosystems Information

Framework Document

STRATEGY FOR
BIODIVERSITY AND ECOSYSTEMS INFORMATION
FRAMEWORK DOCUMENT

The basis of all efforts to effectively conserve biodiversity and natural ecosystems while supporting economic development lies in the ability of scientists, resource managers, policy and decision makers, and the concerned public to have the widest possible access to the existing body of knowledge on biodiversity and ecosystems resources and processes. While much biodiversity and ecosystem information currently exists (from a legacy of past research and inventories), and much more is collected on a daily basis, it is still not possible for all those who could benefit from having access to this information to locate, retrieve, integrate, and apply it in any consistent fashion. In many cases, public and private funds are unknowingly spent on re-collecting information that may actually already exist in some undocumented or unavailable fashion. Much existing biodiversity and ecosystems information cannot be widely used (and may be in danger of being permanently lost) because it is not yet converted into an electronic (computerized) format. In most cases, because of different formats, conventions, or technologies, it is difficult to truly integrate information from more than one source or system.

The Biodiversity and Ecosystems Panel of the President's Committee of Advisors on Science and Technology (PCAST) in its 1998 report, *Teaming with Life: Investing in Science to Understand and Use America's Living Capital*, has recommended that, "We need to elevate the national biological information infrastructure (NBII) to a new level of capability—a "next generation"—that can make maximal use of and fully and openly share on a global basis the information generated by research on biodiversity and ecosystems."

The strategy outlined below would build on and expand recent efforts to link together the various organizations and communities that are involved in the collection and application of biodiversity and ecosystems information in a collaborative effort to create a means through which this information can be more easily accessed and shared. Development of a national biological information infrastructure, including biodiversity and ecosystems information as a major emphasis, is part of the evolving National Information Infrastructure and also a biological resource complement to the National Spatial Data Infrastructure, which focuses on expanding access to and sharing of geospatial data and information.

Because the existing (and potential) producers and users of this broad array of information come from local, state, and federal government; from non-government organizations; from academia; and from the public; planning and development of a distributed information network must be a collaborative effort. The strategy identifies major goals and objectives that all of the interested participants can agree to and identify with, while allowing freedom for these various communities to contribute toward achieving this vision in ways that are most suited to their respective missions and responsibilities.

GOAL 1:   **OBTAIN THE BROADEST POSSIBLE PARTICIPATION OF BOTH PUBLIC AND PRIVATE SECTORS.**

Working together, all interested participants develop the national biological information infrastructure through which biodiversity and ecosystems data and information provided by many distributed sources can be readily accessed and shared.

Objectives:

1. Through outreach and education, enhance understanding by all existing and potential participants of the common vision and mutual benefits of a national biological information infrastructure.

2. Define the fundamental data and information components of a fully functional national biological information infrastructure, and formulate a long-term plan to ensure that these biodiversity and ecosystems data and information components are developed and maintained as an essential part thereof.

3. Encourage biodiversity and ecosystems data and information providers to incorporate their data and information into a national biological information infrastructure.

4. Coordinate development of a national biological information infrastructure with other related national and international data and information access and sharing networks, such as the National Spatial Data Infrastructure, the Global Change Data and Information System, and the Convention on Biological Diversity Clearinghouse Mechanism. Identify areas of mutual interest and opportunities for resource sharing and leveraging among these different initiatives.

5. Identify and promote policies and programs that will stimulate governmental and non-governmental entities to participate fully in the planning, development, and operation of a national biological information infrastructure.

GOAL 2:   **ENCOURAGING GREATER COORDINATION OF AND SUPPORT FOR R&D ON ADVANCED SYSTEMS AND TECHNOLOGIES**

Encourage greater coordination of and support for research and development in order to provide more advanced, efficient systems and technologies for collection, access, sharing and exchange, and application of biodiversity and ecosystems data and information.

Objectives:

1. Identify and promote research, development, and implementation of tools, technologies, and architectures that are needed to enable greater sharing and exchange of biodiversity and ecosystems data and information for a broad range of applications.

2. Provide a mechanism through which participants can define their respective interests and complementary roles in supporting research, development and implementation of new tools, technologies, and architectures for the biodiversity and ecosystems component of a national biological information infrastructure.

3. Promote specific activities that allow participants to work innovatively and cooperatively on tool and technology development by linking related and complementary development efforts, sharing resources, and leveraging existing investments.

4. Identify and work to remove any significant barriers (policy, regulatory, institutional) to pursuit of these innovative, cooperative opportunities.

GOAL 3: **PROMOTING THE USE OF COLLABORATIVELY DEVELOPED STANDARDS**

Promote collaborative development and implementation of data standards for collection, access, sharing and exchange, and application of biodiversity and ecosystems data.

Objectives:

1. Work in public-private partnerships to identify and prioritize data standards that will enable greater data access, sharing, and application of biodiversity and ecosystems data and information.

2. Promote development, adoption, and implementation of biodiversity and ecosystems data standards.

3. Encourage linkages among development and implementation of biodiversity and ecosystems data standards and comparable standards development activities in the Federal Geographic Data Committee, as well as with national (ANSI) and international (ISO) standards programs.

GOAL 4: **INCREASING FEDERAL R&D TO SUPPORT BIODIVERSITY AND ECOSYSTEMS INFORMATICS**

Promote greater use of existing federal research and development programs (including federal grants programs) to support advancements in the area of biodiversity and ecosystems informatics, as part of the development of an overall national biological information infrastructure.

Objectives:

1. Identify existing federal R&D programs that have the greatest potential to help support technology and infrastructure development for biodiversity and ecosystems data (e.g., Digital Libraries Initiative; NSF's Knowledge and Distributed Intelligence Initiative and Life in Earth's Environment Initiative; and R&D programs under auspices of NSTC's Committee on Computing, Information, and Communications).

2. Promote measures through which the offices/agencies responsible for each of these existing programs can increase the portion of funding resources directed toward biodiversity and ecosystems informatics.

GOAL 5: **COOPERATIVELY DEVELOP THE LONG-RANGE IMPLEMENTATION PLAN FOR THE NEXT GENERATION NBII**

Develop a long-range plan for design and implementation of the "next generation" national biological information infrastructure. This system should include several specialized regional nodes that would support information sciences research and development involving biodiversity and ecosystems data, as well as the automatic discovery, indexing, retrieval, integration, and archiving of biodiversity and ecosystems data and information.

Objectives:

1. Establish a national-level interagency and public-private task force to plan the development of the "next generation" biological information infrastructure. This task force would build on the recommendations for the National Biological Information Infrastructure (NBII) provided in the PCAST *Teaming with Life* report.

2. Identify the funding and coordination mechanisms for the information science research needed to fully realize the biodiversity and ecosystems components of the "next generation" biological information infrastructure.

3. Develop an out-year (FY 2001) cross-agency budget initiative to provide initial federal funding support for development of the biodiversity and ecosystems components of the "next generation" national biological information infrastructure. This cross-agency initiative would include a competition for funding to establish the initial set of regional research nodes, and would require development of a Request for Proposals, as well as planning for the funding mechanism.

Comments ~ We are soliciting input from all stakeholders; please send any comments or interest in getting involved in NBII development to:

Biodiversity and Ecosystems Informatics Work Group
c/o Bonnie C. Carroll
Information International Associates, Inc. (IIa)
P.O. Box 4219
Oak Ridge, TN   37831
E-mail: **bcarroll@infointl.com**
Tele: 423/481-0388
Fax.   423/481-0390

NBII Program Manager
c/o Anne Frondorf
USGS/Biological Resources Division
12201 Sunrise Valley Drive
Reston, VA 20192
E-mail: **anne_frondorf@usgs.gov**
Tele: 703/648-4205
Fax: 703/648-4224

APPENDIX C

Acknowledgements

NFAIS expresses thanks to:

"METADIVERSITY" ADVISORY BOARD

William Brown, Science Advisor to the Secretary of the Interior
Dennis Fenn, Chief Biologist, U.S. Geological Survey
Thomas Lovejoy, The World Bank
Robert MaGill, Director of Research, Missouri Botanical Gardens
Winston Tabb, Associate Librarian for Library Services, Library of Congress

"METADIVERSITY" PLANNING COMMITTEE

Barbara Bauldock, USGS
James Beach, University of Kansas
John Busby, World Conservation Data Center
Gladys Cotter, USGS
Marian Gloninger, NFAIS
Gail Hodge, USGS
Paul Kanciruk, California Academy of Sciences
Maureen Kelly, BIOSIS
David Lide, CRC Press for CODATA
Tom Moritz, California Academy of Science Library
Sally Sinn, National Agricultural Library
Frederick Spangler, Cambridge Scientific Abstracts
Steve Young, Environmental Protection Agency

"METADIVERSITY" MODERATORS AND FACILITATORS

James H. Beach, Assistant Director for Informatics, University of Kansas Natural
History Bonnie Carroll, President, Information International Associates
Anne Frondorf, USGS/BRD
Richard Hallgren, Executive Director, American Meteorological Society
Gail Hodge, Information International Associates
Maureen Kelly, Vice President for Planning, BIOSIS
Sally Sinn, Associate Director, Technical Services, National Agricultural Library
        Museum and Biodiversity Research Center
Susan Warner, The LEAD Alliance

GLOSSARY OF ACRONYMS

AAAS	American Association for the Advancement of Science
ADL	Alexandria Digital Library
AHDS	Arts and Humanities Data Service
ASC	Association of Systematics Collections
ASN-1	Abstract Notation 1
ATBI	All Taxa Biodiversity Inventory
BIN 21	Biodiversity Information Network
BioEco	The Biodiversity and Ecosystems Informatics Working Group
BLRIC	British Library Research and Innovation Centre
CBD	*Convention on Biological Diversity*
CCRS	Canadian Center for Remote Sensing
CCSDS	Consultative Committee for Space Data Systems
CDS	Catalogue of Data Sources
Cedars	CURL Exemplars in Digital Archives
CENR	Committee on Environment and Natural Resources
CEOS	Committee on Earth Observation Satellites
CHM	Clearing-House Mechanism
CIESIN	Consortium for International Earth Science Information Network
CIMI	Consortium for the Computer Interchange of Museum Information
CIP	Catalogue Interoperability Protocol
CNI	Coalition for Networked Information
COP	Conference of the Parties
DARPA	Defense Advancement Research Projects Agency

DESIRE	Development of a European Service for Information on Research and Education
DIF	Directory Interchange Format
DOI	Digital Object Idenfier
EAD	Encoded Archival Description
EBU	European Broadcasting Union
EEA	European Environment Agency
EEA-EIONET	European Environment Agency – Environmental Information and Observation Network
ENRM	Environment and Natural Resources Management
ETC/CDS	European Topic Centre on Catalogue of Data Sources
FACS	Fluorescence-Activated Cell Sorting
FGDC	Federal Geographic Data Committee
FTT	Feature Type Thesaurus
GBIF	Global Diversity Information Facility
GCMD	Global Change Master Directory
GCS	Gazetteer Content Standard
GEF	Global Environment Facility
GELOS	Global Environmental Information Locator Service
GIS	Geographic Information Systems
GSD	Global Species Database
G7-ENRM	Environmental and National Resources Management G-7 Global Information Society Initiative
GSMNP	Great Smoky Mountains National Park
IABIN	Inter-American Biodiversity Information Network
IAC	Informal Advisory Committee
IAFA	Internet Anonymous FTP Archive

IGOS	International Global Observation Strategy
ILDIS	International Legume Database and Information Service
INABIN	InterAmerican Biodiversity Information Network
IPNI	International Plant Names Index
ISO	International Standards Organisation
ITIS	Integrated Taxonomic Information System
JiGi	Java Interface for Georeferenced Information
JISC	Joint Information Systems Committee
LCNA	Library of Congress Name Authority
LDAP	Lightweight Directory Application Protocol
MITWG	Metainformation Topic Working Group
NABIN	North American Biodiversity Information Network
NASA	National Aeronautics and Space Administration
NBII	National Biological Information Infrastructure
NBII-2	National Biological Information Infrastructure, next generation
NFAIS	National Federation of Abstracting and Information Services
NGO	Non-Government Organization
NIMA	National Imagery and Mapping Agency
NIH	National Institutes of Health
NMFS	National Marine Fisheries Service
NOAA	National Oceanic and Atmospheric Administration
NRC	National Reference Centre
NODC	National Oceanographic Data Center
NSDI	National Spatial Data Infrastructure
NSF	National Science Foundation
NSTC	National Science and Technology Council

OAIS	Open Archival Information System
OAS	Organization of American States
OCLC	Online Computer Library Center
OECD	Organization for Economic Cooperation and Development
ORD	Office of Research and Development
PANDORA	Preserving and Accessing Networked DOcumentary Resources of Australia
PCAST	President's Committee of Advisers on Science and Technology
PDB	Protein Data Bank
RDF	Resource Description Framework
RLG	Research Libraries Group
ROADS	Resource Organisation and Discovery in Subject-Oriented Services
SBSTTA	Subsidiary Body on Scientific, Technical and Technological Advice
SMPTE	Society of Motion Picture and Television Engineers
SQL	Structured Query Language
TDWG	Taxonomic Databases Working Group
TEI	Text Encoding Initative
TFP	Thematic Focal Point
TSN	Taxonomic Serial Number
UKBD	United Kingdom Biodiversity Database
UNCED	United Nations Conference on the Environment and Development
UNEP	United Nations Environment Programme
USGS/BRD	United States Geological Survey Biological Resources Division
WGISS	Working Group on Information Systems and Services
W3C	World Wide Web Consortium

INDEX BY AUTHOR

INDEX BY ORGANIZATION